Y0-CRW-111

Northwest Vista College
Learning Resource Center
3535 North Ellison Drive
San Antonio, Texas 78251

EDUCATION IN THE JAPANESE LIFE-CYCLE

Implications for the United States

Lucien Ellington

The Edwin Mellen Press
Lewiston/Queenston/Lampeter

Library of Congress Cataloging-in-Publication Data

Ellington, Lucien.
    Education in the Japanese life-cycle : implications for the United
States / Lucien Ellington.
        p.   cm.
    Includes bibliographical references and index.
    ISBN 0-7734-9609-2
    1. Education--Japan. 2. Education--Social aspects--Japan.
3. Education--United States. 4. Education--Social aspects--United
States. I. Title.
LA1312.E45 1992
370'.952.--dc20   92-27797
                                                      CIP

A CIP catalog record for this book
is available from the British Library.

The Edwin Mellen Press   The Edwin Mellen Press
        Box 450   Box 67
   Lewiston, New York   Queenston, Ontario
        USA 14092   CANADA L0S 1L0

            The Edwin Mellen Press, Ltd.
               Lampeter, Dyfed, Wales
            UNITED KINGDOM SA48 7DY

        Printed in the United States of America

I dedicate this book to my wife, Betsy, and son, Bobby. They are my major sources of inspiration.

Contents

List of Tables

Table

Preface

This book is a description of teaching and learning in Japan. As is the case in every society, education in Japan occurs both in formal and informal settings and in a wide range of institutions.

Even though Japanese education has its flaws, Japan's great post-war success is in large part a result of the fact that the Japanese truly place a high value on lifetime learning. It is my wish that this book will contribute both to the current dialogue in the United States about our own education process and to a better understanding by Americans of an extremely important Asian society.

Since this work contains a number of Japanese words, a glossary is included to assist readers. All Japanese names are listed in traditional style with family name coming before an individual's given name.

Acknowledgements

This book would have never been possible without the help of many people in Japan and the United States. The Japanese who assisted me in my work are too numerous to possibly mention. However, I am particularly indebted to Professor Uozumi Tadahisa of Aichi University of Education. Professor Uozumi arranged interviews and school visits for me and spent much time correcting my misimpressions about teaching and learning in Japan.

I would also like to thank Professor Daniel Metraux of Mary Baldwin College who read the entire manuscript and made invaluable comments. Thanks are also extended to Robert August for his excellent suggestions pertaining to Chapter One and Linda Gehron for her assistance in word processing and copy editing. Sincere acknowlegements are also due to The University of Tennessee at Chattanooga. Without my institution's financial and moral support I would not have been able to write this book. Finally, the Southeastern Association for Japan Research deserves sincere thanks since a grant from that organization funded one of my research trips to Japan.

Chapter One

Japanese Education: A Cultural and Historical Context

Introduction

The 1964 Tōkyō Olympics are remembered by many as much more than just games. It was during that year that international visitors took note that something exceptional was occurring in Japan. Japan in 1945 lay in ashes because of the devastating effects of World War II. Just nineteen years later, foreigners visiting for the games saw not only the efficiency with which the Olympics were conducted, but the gleaming new buildings and the emerging array of goods and services available as well. Perhaps, most notably, people from other countries noticed the upbeat and determined spirit of the Japanese people. Many non-Japanese first sensed in 1964 the phenomenon later to be known as the "economic miracle."

As time passed the quantity and quality of Japanese goods became more apparent to the peoples of other countries. Interest mounted in many countries, including the United States, in learning more about both Japan's economic accomplishments and the nation's social institutions.

By the early 1980s many Americans were particularly interested in Japan's schools.   While Japanese students attained impressive achievements on international science and mathematics tests, American young people did not fare nearly as well.

In 1983 when President Reagan and Prime Minister Nakāsone met, a result was an agreement to establish a cooperative study of education in each other's country. Since both countries were interested in educational reform, it was thought that both the United States and Japan might benefit from such work. By 1987 the U.S. Department of Education released the publication <u>Japanese Education Today</u> amidst growing American media and scholarly interest in Japan's schools. In the 1990s the attention continues.[1]

Although there has been some distorted information disseminated about Japanese schools in the U.S., several books available here on Japan's elementary and secondary schools are quite good. Yet there is also a need for works on Japanese education that examine teaching and learning not only in elementary and secondary schools but throughout the entire life course as well.[2] Numerous examples exist in Japan of the great effort at learning that people make far past childhood and adolescence. The following three cases are representative of such efforts.

International and Japanese tests indicate that Japan is among world leaders in literacy rates. Except for certain handicapped youngsters, almost all Japanese students achieve functional literacy by the end of the ninth grade. Evidence of the ability of virtually all Japanese adults to read is reinforced to the foreigner who visits Japanese cities. There are enormous numbers of book stores present and a large amount of people who are reading on subways and trains.[3]

Statistics on reading confirm this impression. In any given year Japanese publishers come out with approximately 35,000 new titles. This figure is about equal to the number of new books published annually in the United States, which has twice Japan's population. Approximately 93 percent of Japanese read newspapers regularly. Per capita newspaper sales in Japan are higher than any

---

[1]Cynthia Hearn Dorfman, ed., <u>Japanese Education Today</u> (Washington, D.C.: Government Printing Office, 1987), iii.

[2]The late American educational historian, Lawrence Cremin, in the preface to <u>American Education: The Colonial Experience 1607-1783</u> (Harper and Row, 1970), defined education as "The deliberate, systematic, and sustained effort to transmit or evoke knowledge, attitudes, values, skills, and sensibilities." Cremin's definition of education is particularly appropriate for this study since the book is a broad examination of Japanese education.

[3]For an extensive discussion of the achievement of mass literacy in schools see Benjamin Duke, <u>The Japanese School: Lessons for Industrial America</u> (Praeger, 1986), 51-79.

other country in the world except Sweden. Even though students are among these readers, a sizable number of people hanging out in book stores and reading on subways are adults.[4]

One recent summer evening in an auto supply plant in Togo Town, a suburb near the city of Nagoya, this writer sat in on a weekly Chinese language class where seven middle-aged men dutifully read passages in Chinese for a young woman who served as their teacher. The men had studied the language for two years in class with the aid of radio and cassettes. They went on a field trip to China. This class is only one example of a varied and widespread education and training process occurring throughout Japanese industry. Although the company mentioned has no business interests in China, a pragmatic reason is one important motivating force for the students. The company hoped to establish a market in the next ten years in the Peoples' Republic of China.

By contrast, "The College for the Aged" is one of many teaching and learning situations in Japan with no obvious practical ramifications. All enrollees are over 60 years of age in this program that is administered by Nagoya's Lifelong Learning Center. These senior citizens, who have no career aspirations, study everything from geography to Japanese literature with a refreshing eagerness. [5]

Much learning in Japan occurs outside of conventional precollegiate and higher educational institutions. In order to understand education in Japan, it is essential to consider both formal and informal educational institutions. It is also important to understand education at various times in the life cycles of Japanese. The major objective of this book is to provide readers with a knowledge of the variety of educational experiences Japanese encounter as infants and small children, adolescents, adults and old people.

A secondary objective of this book is to provide readers with a means to compare Japanese educational institutions and pedagogy with those of the United States. However, while discussion questions of a comparative nature are provided for readers at the end of each chapter, the large majority of information in the book focuses upon the Japanese experience.

---

[4]Robert C. Christopher, The Japanese Mind (Fawcett Columbine, 1983), 194-196.

[5]Descriptions of the Chinese class and "College for the Aged" based on the author's fieldwork in June 1990.

Learning and Cultural Values

The educational environments any society constructs reflect dominant cultural values and influential historical events. The remainder of this chapter is designed to give those readers with limited knowledge of Japan a better context to understand contemporary education in that country. Two values in particular, the group orientation of Japanese and the hierarchical nature of Japanese society, are examined in detail. Groupism and hierarchy are far from the only normative beliefs shaping education in Japan. Yet the two values affect virtually every Japanese endeavor. A correct sense of Japanese beliefs about the group and the importance of hierarchy are sound points of reference to later examine education in its various guises in Japan.

The Group in Japanese Life

During the 1970s and 1980s, a normally placid Japan was shocked by a rash of bank robberies, murders, and other terrorist acts conducted by a Marxist organization of radical young university graduates and former university students known as the Red Army, or Sekigun. Although Sekigun members rejected commonly shared Japanese beliefs of capitalism and liberal democracy on ideological grounds, there was more to the story. Sekigun bore a close organizational resemblance to a typical Japanese business corporation. Just as in the world of Japanese business, Sekigun depended upon the existence of smoothly functioning internal groups to attain its objectives.

First, the Sekigun group captain announced a possible new assignment such as a bank robbery. Then the group held a free and open discussion and decided by consensus what information was to be gathered first. In a potential robbery, for example, several possible sights were targeted and careful preliminary research conducted on each to determine how easily a site might be attacked and if a safe getaway was possible. The group then discussed preliminary research results and selected a sight by consensus. Then the group planned other operational details. Individual Sekigun members performed specific tasks such as shoplifting the necessary equipment. Last-minute group planning discussions were conducted. After group rehearsals the mission was carried out.

One expert on Sekigun concluded that, although the young terrorists ostensibly rejected dominant Japanese corporate and political values, members were quite conventional in their group orientation. The organizational behavior of Sekigun members bore a striking resemblance to that of well-trained employees of government or business. Anyone familiar with Japan is aware of the propensity of the Japanese toward group rather than individual orientations. Although Japanese business people or tourists who seem to dress alike and travel in groups are now a familiar site all over the world, extreme examples such as Sekigun graphically illustrate the dominance of group thinking in the lives of most Japanese.[6]

Bernard Krishner, former <u>Newsweek</u> Japan bureau chief who spent twenty years in the country, perhaps best summed up the influence of the group in Japanese culture by remarking in a recent interview that, "In most other countries, you would say a French journalist, for example, was more similar to an American journalist than to another Frenchman. But in Japan the culture is so strong that a Japanese Communist, for example, is not so different from a Japanese businessmen, or even from a member of the United Red Army. They have the same relationships within the organization...."[7]

In any society, dominant values represent ideals, and exceptions are frequent. Individualism does exist to some extent in Japan. The Japanese are not robots, and examples exist throughout Japan's history of political leaders, warriors, and writers who were famous because of their individual deeds.

Still, even today, most Japanese from earliest childhood and through the adult years are influenced by larger group purposes and goals. Japanese learn in families, schools, work places, and clubs to identify so much with the group that ideally they become one with it. Each member learns it is best to be rid of ego and to dedicate the total self to the group's success. As a result, the group and all its members will triumph. Some linguists even advance the somewhat controversial argument that spoken Japanese serves to deaccentuate individuality.

---

[6]Patricia Steinhoff, "Hijackers, Bombers, and Bank Robbers: Managerial Style in the Japanese Red Army," <u>The Journal of Asian Studies</u> 48, no. 4 (November 1989): 724-740.

[7]Bernard Krishner, <u>Japan As We Lived It: Can East and West Ever Meet</u>? (Tōkyō: Yohan Publications Inc., 1989), 164.

Words such as I, you, he, and she, that emphasize individual identity, are often dropped in Japanese conversation.

✳ In business, introductions to Japanese who work for large companies often illustrate the high priority an employee places upon his work group. Japanese often identify themselves by group affiliation rather than functional specialty. When a Japanese is introduced to another Japanese or to a foreigner, he or she is likely to say, "I am Mr./Ms. Yamato and I work for Toyota," rather than name an occupation such as engineer, accountant, or secretary for which he or she might have been trained.

Decision-making in any Japanese institution is much more likely to be a group rather than individual action. The literature on Japanese business management is full of references to the "Nemawashi," or "root binding" process. Originators of ideas cautiously discern feelings of other group members by circulating written memos. By Western standards the process is time consuming. To Japanese, Nemawashi ensures that everyone either has a chance to modify a possible course of action or at least have their feelings toward the plan known by writing responses. In the typical Japanese organization, once consensus is reached about an idea or option, quick action often occurs through smooth group cooperation.

The positive and negative effects of such a high degree of group orientation upon both individual Japanese and institutions are manifest. Perhaps the most publicized examples are to be found in the many descriptions of large Japanese business and government institutions. In addition to the much-heralded Nemawashi process, the atmosphere among employees of such organizations evokes images of work place as family. Although the "Japanese company as family" notion is an idealization, it influences behavior. Actual work place practice in Japan comes closer to realization of the family image than is often true in the typical, rather depersonalized, American organization.

In fact, for many contemporary Japanese, particularly males, the work place has replaced the traditional extended family of earlier times as the primary group. When employees enter many Japanese organizations, they are treated as much like new family members as workers. Companies often conduct emotional induction ceremonies for workers. Top executives make motivational speeches about reciprocal lifetime commitments.

In many Japanese companies and government ministries, the group ethos is physically apparent to the observer. There are few individual offices, but rather one large room where white collar workers are all together side by side in their desks. In Japanese schools the teachers' room is arranged in a similar manner.

The sacrifice and teamwork inspired by the Japanese group orientation is a major reason why many Japanese products are of such superior quality and Japanese governmental institutions such as police and schools are so successful. However, subordination of individual to group interests also negatively affects the lives of many Japanese and, from time to time, peoples of other nations as well.

The often overwhelming pressure placed upon an individual to conform to group goals is best illustrated by one of the oldest Japanese proverbs, "The nail that sticks up gets pounded down." Often Japanese employees are expected by their companies to dress alike and stay at work the same amount of time. Employees of some companies, government agencies, and even schools, take vacations together. The tremendously inhibiting effect groupism and pressures to conform have on individual creativity and initiative has been a much-discussed concern in Japan for many years.

Individual abdication to group pressures also produced some of the most nasty incidents in modern Japanese history. Minorities such as Koreans living in Japan and burakumin who are considered out-groups have been subjected to a wide range of prejudice and discrimination by other Japanese throughout the twentieth century. The senseless killing of millions of innocent Chinese and the mistreatment of prisoners of war by the Japanese during World War II resulted in large part because these unfortunates were considered to be less than human. They were not members of the Japanese group. Even today, although Japanese possess substantial intellectual knowledge about foreigners, many individual Japanese are still quite uncomfortable with people from other nations. Foreigners are not part of any identifiable Japanese group. Individual Japanese can even be quite cold to other Japanese who are not class, work or club mates![8]

---

[8]Burakumin, Japan's largest minority group, although they have the same racial, cultural, and national origins as other Japanese, were historically discriminated against and are still subject to de facto prejudice and discrimination. Discrimination against burakumin is thought to have originated because burakumin participated in occupations such as butchery that violated religious teachings. Koreans, who constitute Japan's largest ethnic minority and many of whom have lived

8

Still, groupism, for better or worse, is an integral part of Japanese culture. Learning processes are not only affected by a group orientation but often designed to inculcate or reinforce a sense of group loyalty in children and adults.

Hierarchy and Status

When Japanese police prevented an attack on the Prime Minister's residence by Sekigun, they seized the group's organizational chart in a raid on Sekigun headquarters. The chart illustrated the influence of another important Japanese value upon this group of young people who professed egalitarian ideals. All Sekigun members were organized into separate squads for attacks. The squads that drew the most dangerous and critical assignments consisted of graduates of Japan's most famous universities. Hierarchy and status are much more important influences upon human behavior in Japan than in Western societies.[9]

Many Japanese place great emphasis upon both an individual's place within the hierarchy of the group and upon the status of a particular group when compared to other groups that perform similar functions. This seems contradictory to the team spirit that is so characteristic of Japanese life. Yet hierarchy and status issues often determine how individuals and groups of Japanese react to various situations.

A strong emphasis upon rank and status dates back to feudal Japan. It is still an important determinant of individual conduct in the home, school, and work place. In the home, one's older sister or brother is addressed by the Japanese words for older sister or older brother rather than by a first name. The latter form of greeting is not considered to be as respectful. Within most Japanese school groups the hierarchical designations of sempai (seniors), kōhai (juniors), and doryo (equals), rival economic class as an indicator of individual status. In a typical high school or university club, whether the activity is baseball or flower arrangements, third-year students are treated as superiors, or sempai, by the new

---

in Japan for two or three generations, are legally still aliens. Kōdansha Encyclopedia of Japan (Tōkyō: Kōdansha, Ltd., 1983), vol. 1, 216-217, and vol. 4, 291-292.

[9]Steinhoff, "Hijackers, Bombers, and Bank Robbers: Managerial Style in the Japanese Red Army," 736.

members, or <u>kōhai</u>. Years later when former members meet again as adults, the <u>kōhai</u> still treat <u>sempai</u> in a deferential manner.

In the Japanese work place, individual educational attainment levels divide employees into separate, if unofficial, groups. Within each of these groups, however, those individuals who entered the company or ministry first are usually deferred to by their younger colleagues. Although in Japanese organizations, merit as well as seniority determines individual status, seniority is usually the more important factor. Generally juniors are paid less than seniors and not promoted over their older colleagues. Even if a younger employee is more competent than a senior colleague, the senior receives the more prestigious job title.

As alluded to earlier, the Japanese language is employed frequently in the home, the school, and the work place to enforce status designations. <u>Sempai</u> use the somewhat condescending suffix added to a name, "<u>kun</u>," when addressing their younger associates. <u>Kōhai</u> are expected to use the much more polite suffix "<u>san</u>" when addressing their senior colleagues. The practice of exchanging personal business cards is much more common in Japan than in other countries. A major reason for business card exchange is to quickly inform two strangers of each other's respective status.

What is true within organizations or groups in Japan is also true in the case of groups that perform similar functions. The corporation, school, professional baseball team, or tea ceremony club has an unofficial but well-known place within its respective group hierarchy. Although other factors are important, often the age of an organization is a major determinant of prestige. For example, seven of the more prestigious universities in Japan are the institutions that constituted the original prewar imperial universities. Among this group, Tōdai, or Tōkyō University, is the most prestigious university in all of Japan in part because it is the oldest institution of higher learning.

Status considerations also serve to regulate the behavior of individuals and organizations in Japan. The famed group spirit and team play works so well for the Japanese in part because every individual knows his or her place within the organization and usually behaves accordingly. Prestigious companies and government ministries hire graduates from a very few top-ranked universities. Middle-level companies recruit their employees from middle-level universities.

Japanese derive some advantages from the great attention they pay to hierarchy and status. High-status corporations and government ministries are assured a steady influx of new highly qualified employees. Some observers of the Japanese work place argue that the apparent absence of relatively extensive amounts of backbiting and office politics in Japanese firms is largely because everyone knows his or her place and is aware that with the accumulation of experience and seniority, the appropriate rewards will come. Yet in Japan, the rigidity with which status and hierarchy are applied as indicators of individual or group talent has a dark side as well.

Individuals must constantly watch their behavior to avoid offending others. This is particularly true of younger members of an organization. Japanese seniors in leadership positions must often take responsibility for misdeeds committed by someone below. Even if the leader is not technically responsible, assuming blame is a symbolic gesture to cleanse the shame brought upon the group by the junior's incompetency.

The rigid application of hierarchical and status classifications to groups and individuals makes Japan a society ill-designed for late bloomers. If a student does not enter a prestigious high school, there is little chance of later entrance into a top university. If a student then enters a middle- or low-level university, no matter how well he or she performs, entire future career avenues are closed forever.

Traditionally, women have been assigned inferior status relative to men in Japan in education and in the work place. Despite some changes, it is still incredibly difficult, even for women graduates of prestigious universities, to obtain managerial or professional positions in high-ranked institutions. Often the women who do obtain high-ranking positions are unmarried and are treated as men by their colleagues.

One reason that many observers consider Japanese universities to be mediocre by world standards is the spirit of academic inquiry is distorted because younger professors often find it impossible to criticize an older colleague's work.

Rigid in-group and out-group stereotypes present in Japan cause problems for outsiders. Foreigners, Japanese who receive any form of education other than graduate studies abroad, and, in some cases, Japanese business employees and their families who have lived long periods outside Japan often have status problems in Japanese society. Such negative stereotyping causes both friction within Japanese society and with the rest of the world.

Regardless of the positive or negative ramifications, group dominance and extreme attention to status are values that most Japanese learn in formal and informal situations throughout life. Why did these values emerge in Japan's past? How have they interacted with other cultural, philosophical, and political forces to help build the formal and informal environments in which modern Japanese learn?

The Development of Groupism and Hierarchy

Throughout the centuries, the very nature of life in the Japanese archipelago encouraged the development of social organizations where individual interests were subordinated to the greater needs of the group. Over time, Japanese came to believe that ascribed roles in social groups were important in providing focus and direction for an individual's life.

Although Japan is a temperate and quite beautiful mountainous country, it has never been, by world standards, a particularly easy place to live. Central Honshū, which for centuries has contained the largest concentration of people in Japan, and most major cities including Tōkyō and Ōsaka, is one of the world's worst earthquake areas. Tōkyō was destroyed by earthquakes and accompanying fires in 1657, 1703, and 1923. As if earthquakes were not bad enough, Japan has an annual average of six to seven typhoons, which can often be devastating to both humans and property. Faced with natural disasters throughout history, Japanese people were forced constantly to work together to survive.

Also, with the exception of the sea, Japan has less natural resources than any other major nation on earth. The Japanese lack vitally important commodities such as iron ore, petroleum, lead, zinc, copper, and timber. The energy situation is particularly critical. Japan must depend upon foreign countries for over 99 percent of its oil and over 80 percent of its total energy requirements. The Japanese are not even able to feed themselves without foreign assistance. Since the beginning of the twentieth century, Japan has imported 30 to 35 percent of its total food supply in order to supply the needs of the approximately 122 million people who live in the archipelago.

Japan's lack of self-sufficiency is due largely to the lack of yet another critical natural resource, living space. Although Japan is larger in land area than countries such as Italy and Great Britain, when the amounts of usable land in the three nations are compared, Japan is in practical terms much smaller than it appears on a map.

Because the Japanese islands are extremely mountainous and contain few plains, almost the entire population lives on only about one-sixth of the total land space. Even though Belgium and the Netherlands have higher ratios of people to total land area than Japan, in terms of habitable land, Japan is much more crowded than either country. Because of lack of living space, small and expensive houses, two-hour commutes to work, and little privacy are inescapable facts of life for most Japanese.

Japanese, beginning with group-oriented wet rice paddy cultivation around 300 B.C., adopted cooperative strategies in order to cope with the problems of living in an often inhospitable land. Because Japan was a relatively homogeneous society, it was much easier for group cooperation to develop than in many other countries.

In early Japanese history, the East China Sea and the Korean Straits kept people relatively isolated from the Asian mainland. Later the Tokūgawa Government's seclusion policy limited, from 1640 until 1853, contact Japanese could have with foreigners to a few Chinese and Dutch traders. Throughout this time, the group orientation of the society grew without the influx of major ethnic groups or other outside interference. A Japanese variant of feudalism was institutionalized by the Tokūgawa Period. Samurai, peasants, artisans, and merchants were the four distinct groups that emerged. Each was subject to different laws based upon its relative status in the larger society.

Ironically, China, the foreign country that most influenced Japan before the latter half of the nineteenth century, was the source of an ethical system, Confucianism, that reinforced and strengthened Japanese values of groupism. Confucianism also provided an intellectual and philosophical rationale for the pervasive attention to individual and group status that developed in Japan.

The writings of the Chinese philosopher Confucius (551-479 B.C.) were by the sixth and seventh centuries an integral part of Japanese intellectual thought. By 604 A.D., Prince Shōtoku, credited with writing the first constitution for a

Japanese Government, included several Confucian moral admonitions in the document. Also by 704, the government established a college primarily devoted to Confucian studies. Confucianism was not a religion, but rather a moral/ethical system that stressed practical advice for societal cooperation and good government.

Early Confucianism recognized and approved of the existence of separate classes and stressed interclass harmony for the betterment of society. Filial piety, much emphasized in Confucianism, formed a philosophical basis for daily life. Various family members were, according to age or gender, assigned specific status and roles. In the larger society, Confucian admonitions that moral people followed form and ritual and exhibited appropriate respect for superiors reinforced the growing Japanese adherence to status and hierarchy as an important form of social organization.[10]

The cooperation and harmony that Confucianism called for between all members of society also contributed to the growth of the Japanese preference for shaping individuals to be group oriented in their attitudes and behaviors. For example, in The Analects Confucius warned those looking to be moral to not mind failing to get recognition, but rather to be too busy doing things that entitle people to recognition.[11]

Confucianism, along with other philosophical and religious systems such as Buddhism, and other physical and ethnic characteristics of Japan also influenced the development of many other contemporary Japanese values. Emphasis on harmony, the conceptualization of learning as a moral activity, hard work, and a distrust of excessively verbal people became a part of the Japanese value system. The following brief description of the evolution of formal Japanese educational institutions illustrates how the overarching values of groupism and

---

[10]Even though China and Japan shared Confucianism, there were important differences between each nation's version of the teachings. Many of the differences are a matter of dispute among Confucian scholars. While Chinese Confucianism placed an emphasis upon the need for ethical government, Japanese Confucianism stressed the importance of loyalty and devotion of people toward government. The latter emphasis could partially explain the hierarchism that has always been present in Japanese society.

[11]The Analects of Confucius, trans. Arthur Waley (Random House, 1938), 105.

hierarchy, other dominant cultural beliefs, and Japan's response to external events, combined to shape the nation's contemporary educational institutions.[12]

Education in Classical and Medieval Japan

Although there was no widespread systemization of education in the Classical Japan of the Nāra (710-794 A.D.) and Heian Periods (794-1185), and the Medieval Japan of the Kāmākura (1185-1333) and Murōmachi Periods (1333-1600), important events occurred and trends were established that still have profound contemporary influences.

Early on, China played a paramount role in the development of Japanese learning, and surviving Chinese records reveal that representatives of that nation's government visited Japan as early as 57 A.D. The Japanese saw themselves as culturally inferior compared to the advanced Chinese civilization and were eager to learn from China.

The introduction of Chinese writing early in the fifth century made formal education possible for the first time for Japanese, who, heretofore, had no written language. Before the tenth century, education consisted primarily of the study of Confucian and other Chinese classics and was communicated through written Chinese. Education was also almost entirely for the aristocracy. In addition to the Daigaku-Ryō, which was intended for the court nobility in Heian (present day Kyōto) branch schools, or kokugaku, provided training for provincial aristocracy. By the ninth century, aristocratic families established private schools for members of their class and there was at least one school open to commoners. However, formal learning remained largely an endeavor of the aristocracy and court in the Japanese capital city.

By the ninth century, what constituted formal learning expanded to include more subject matter than simply the study of written Chinese classics. During that century, with the development of written syllabaries, or kana, the Japanese developed a national written language. The rise of kana led to both a decline in the exclusive focus upon Chinese learning, and the growth of native Japanese poetry and prose. The latter development is best epitomized by the most famous

---

[12]The description of historical aspects of value development in Japan excerpted from Lucien Ellington, Japan: Tradition and Change (Longman, 1990), 42 95.

of all Heian literature, Lady Murasaki's novel <u>The Tale of Genji</u>. By the 1100s, as various warring families attempted to seize power from a declining court in Kyōto, literacy spread, albeit slowly, to individuals and groups previously excluded from formal learning processes.

From the late 1100s through the beginning of the seventeenth century, Japan was rocked by numerous wars between powerful families who desired control of the nation. Although these centuries were characterized by political decentralization, figurehead emperors, and, at times, virtual anarchy, educational developments occurred.

In 1192, the head of one powerful family, Mināmoto Yorĩtomo, forced the emperor to confer upon him the title of chief general or <u>shōgun</u>. As de facto ruler of Japan, Yorĩtomo established a military government in Kāmākura, a seaside city near present-day Tōkyō. Yorĩtomo exerted his power throughout Japan by utilizing a cadre of loyal warrior-administrators, later to be known as <u>samurai</u>. Mināmoto Yorĩtomo, the <u>samurai</u>, and the Hōjō family who, in 1199, wrested power from the Mināmotos, were quite influenced by Buddhism. In particular, Zen, a relatively new Buddhist sect imported from China, was popular with the aristocracy. Zen Buddhist monks in the great Kāmākura monasteries and temples traveled to China. The Buddhist clergy and government officials engaged again in an active intercourse with China after over two hundred years of little contact.

The resumption of interactions brought both Chinese products and ideas to Japan. There was a renewed interest in Confucian scholarship among educated Japanese. New styles of Chinese art also became popular in Japan. In various parts of Japan, Buddhist temples became centers of Chinese learning. In the temples, acolytes, as well as other children, particularly those of <u>samurai</u> families, received instruction in basic literacy.

In addition to some instruction in Chinese and Japanese languages, the arts, and basic techniques of war, many <u>samurai</u> by the late 1100s were inculcated with a general code of ethics. This code came to be known as "<u>bushidō</u>," or "the way of the warrior." As in medieval Europe, <u>samurai</u> were taught to be heroic and to value family honor, but absolute loyalty to superiors and individual self-discipline were also considered particularly vital characteristics for young members of this class. The latter two values represented a synthesis of Confucian and Buddhist thought. Although today, loyalty to superiors and individual self-discipline are largely divorced from their origins, they still constitute integral parts of the moral education of young people in contemporary Japan.

Although Japan had long been influenced by China and other parts of Asia, the nation's first contact with the West occurred in 1543 when Portuguese traders landed off southern Kyūshū. Japanese became exposed at that time and during the following decades to foreign ideas such as Christianity and, more importantly, technology. The Japanese showed immediate adeptness at learning Western technology. For example, Japanese became interested in European guns immediately after they were introduced to Japan. In less than twenty-five years after they first learned about guns, the Japanese were manufacturing excellent rifles.

By the end of the medieval period, the Japanese were not only exhibiting competence in learning Western technology. The dominant values that are still influential today were already integral parts of aristocratic culture. Also some diffusion, both geographically and between socioeconomic classes, of formal opportunities for learning had occurred. However, not until the Tokūgawa Period did large numbers of Japanese become literate, inculcate similar values, and learn the practical arts, as the first widespread national diffusion of Japanese educational institutions occurred.[13]

Education in Tokūgawa Japan

The constant strife between opposing families and the anarchy and decentralization characteristic of medieval Japan came to an end in 1600 when the head of one powerful family, Tokūgawa Iēyāsu, defeated his opponents in the Battle of Sekigahara and unified the nation. Tokūgawa, who a few years before assumed the hereditary title shōgun, became de facto ruler of Japan. The Tokūgawas ruled a Japan which from the mid 1600s until the 1850s was virtually isolated from the rest of the world because of government policies they initiated.

When Japan was forced by the American Navy during 1853 and 1854 to resume relations with foreign powers and later went on to become a prominent political and economic actor on the world stage, many Westerners came to accept

---

[13]Ellington, Japan: Tradition and Change, 43-62.

a largely untrue myth about Japanese history. Many foreigners came to believe that Japan was an undeveloped primitive nation before the latter nineteenth century. It is true that Japan, because of Tokūgawa fears of foreign political and ideological domination, fell behind the West scientifically and technologically during the years it was isolated from the world. However, the Tokūgawa Period was also a time of rich economic and cultural progress. Much of this progress rested upon the existence of a collection of, by the latter Tokūgawa years, approximately 17,000 educational institutions.[14]

By the early 1700s Japan already possessed, in many ways, a sophisticated economy and culture. Millions of people lived in large urban centers such as Tōkyō, Kyōto, Ōsaka, and 250 smaller cities. They engaged in wholesaling, retailing, banking, visiting department stores, and reading books. Shortly before the eighteenth century, a publishing industry developed and books were often published in editions of more than ten thousand copies to satisfy the large number of literate city dwellers. People learned in schools the prerequisite skills to enjoy such a pleasure as reading.

Tokūgawa education was largely a reflection of a political system that rested upon rather rigid class divisions. Although the samurai were at the top of Tokūgawa society, they only constituted approximately seven percent of Japan's population. By the latter Tokūgawa years, in the 260 feudal domains in which Japan was divided, there were over two hundred fief schools, created primarily for samurai education. Male samurai attendance was compulsory in many domains. Students were in school from childhood through late adolescence.

Even though great variation in the curricula, organization, and size of fief schools existed, there were also commonalties. The basic philosophical underpinning of the fief school was clearly a Confucian one. Knowledge produced virtue. Because of their class, the samurai were destined to become government bureaucrats. They were obligated to increase their virtue through formal schooling. Later, according to Confucian beliefs, samurai would be virtuous and ethical administrators and serve as positive examples for the larger society.

---

[14]Herbert Passin, "Japan," in Education and Political Development, ed. James S. Coleman (Princeton University Press, 1965), 274.

The samurai, and in some cases commoners who attended their schools, usually spent mornings with the study of the Confucian classics and the Chinese language. Lower-ranking samurai who were Confucian scholars served as teachers. In the afternoons, students engaged in learning military skills, fencing, martial arts, and other physical activities. Authorities and educators did not consider important the question of the relevance of the Chinese classics to a student's practical affairs in later life. Academic study was for a moral purpose. Virtue was developed in large part by the cultivation of a resilient spirit. The more difficult and agonizing a subject, the greater was its worth in character development. The study of literary Chinese and Confucian classics certainly could be described as "difficult" and "agonizing!"

Fief schools proved successful in improving education for the samurai in comparison to alternatives that existed in the beginning of the Tokūgawa years. Earlier, what education samurai received was in homes or in temples. By the end of the Tokūgawa Period, the majority of samurai, thanks in part to their experiences in fief schools, were fully literate and relatively sophisticated urban bureaucrats.

Commoners, including primarily merchant children and youngsters from relatively affluent peasant families, usually received a more practical basic education at institutions called terākoya, or temple schools. Terākoya was a somewhat misleading name since the evidence indicates that large numbers of these schools were in private homes rather than terā or Buddhist temples. By the late Tokūgawa years ,one survey revealed that only 20 percent of terākoya teachers were Buddhist priests. By then the aims of terākoya were almost entirely secular.

Terākoya, established by village heads and private individuals, numbered over 14,000 by the end of the Tokūgawa Period. Although quite diverse, terākoya tended to serve between 30 and 60 pupils per school, usually under the supervision of a single teacher. The boys, and in the case of the children of rich urban merchants, girls who attended terākoya, received four or five years of practical instruction. The majority of content focused upon reading and writing the Japanese language. In addition, terākoya children studied arithmetic and, in some schools, vocational subjects such as accounting. Moral education, consisting of instruction in etiquette with Confucian overtones, was also an important subject in every terākoya.

Even though lessons in Confucian morals were part of the terākoya experience, unlike that of the fief school, the terākoya curriculum was designed to meet the everyday needs of future merchants and village headmen. School primers used for terākoya reading lessons in the 1800s with such titles as Bumper Crops, Country Reader, Merchant's Reader, and Wholesale Reader were indicative of the practicality of the commoner schools.

Unlike the case in fief schools, anyone who so chose could become a terākoya teacher. During the early Tokūgawa years, the shōgunate and daimyō paid little attention to commoner teachers, or to the education of commoners in general, but later some terākoya in and near Edo were awarded financial support by the shōgunate. In some cases, other domains followed the example of the shōgunate. Tokūgawa authorities even came to encourage the establishment of gogaku, or local schools, to provide leading commoners a kind of secondary education after terākoya. However, gogaku were not nearly as pervasive as terākoya.

Although the large majority of terākoya only provided at best a primary education for students, in many cases this was a foundation for the children of commoners to receive more advanced training. Also, the extensive number of people who read books during the Tokūgawa years was largely due to the existence of terākoya.

The most advanced and, in many ways, innovative education during the Tokūgawa years took place in the approximately 1,500 higher academies, or shijuku, that existed by the end of the period. Shijuku, originally established as institutes of higher education for the samurai, dated back to the founding in 1630 of the Shōheikō in Edo. At first the Shōheikō and other shijuku that followed were known as centers of Confucian orthodoxy. As time passed though, shijuku became extremely heterogeneous as to curriculum, teachers, and students.

Because they were private, shijuku were free of government control and most came to admit commoners. Ranging in size from 20 to 30 to thousands of students, each shijuku was established by a distinguished teacher. Shijuku curricula was as varied as shijuku size. The most important academies offered specialized studies in Confucianism, including unorthodox, officially unsanctioned brands of the philosophy. Medicine, Western studies, navigation, military studies, and engineering were taught in some shijuku as well.

It was in some shijuku that the principle of advancement by merit instead of class, a value not supported by the rigid, class-conscious Tokūgawas, first took root in Japan. In such shijuku, students were awarded certificates and other honors on the basis of achievement. The concept of meritocracy never gained official acceptance during the Tokūgawa Period. However, the eventual creation of an educational system based in part upon advancement by merit was made much easier by the earlier precedent established in the shijuku of the Tokūgawa years.

The Tokūgawa Legacy: Achievement and Values

The best literacy estimates suggest that by the end of the Tokūgawa Period 40 percent of Japanese males and 15 percent of females could read and write at some level. These literacy rates meant that, at the time, Japan, based on this most fundamental educational standard, was comparable to Western European countries and the United States instead of the rest of Asia. Practically, the most important legacy of Tokūgawa education lies in this statistic.

But the overarching values that influence Japanese today, groupism and hierarchy, were also strengthened through educational practices of the Tokūgawa years. The fief schools and, to a lesser extent, the shijuku and terākoya, were strongly influenced by Confucianism. Confucianists celebrated both of the above values. Groupism and hierarchy were not only dominant values in the schools but also constituted an integral part of official Tokūgawa ideology.

Other Confucian ideas influenced the young in Tokūgawa Period educational institutions. Teachers were highly respected and students were expected to passively absorb knowledge. Learning was considered a virtue. In an individual student, effort, as opposed to brilliance or creativity, was considered the superior trait. These values would survive later periods of Japanese history.

However, a value not associated with Confucianism, advancement based upon merit, also was introduced in the shijuku of the Tokūgawa years. This principle would become institutionalized as a result of late nineteenth century public policy. Other late nineteenth century initiatives such as government encouragement of ardent study of scientific and technical subjects are also rooted in the private Tokūgawa academies.

When examined through modern eyes, Tokūgawa education certainly had a host of problems. There was no national school system. Access to formal education was still based largely upon class, gender, and geographical location. Yet much of the Tokūgawa educational legacy, particularly the inculcation of the values just described, is still present in Japanese education.[15]

Education in Mēiji and Prewar Japan

Although the two and one-half centuries of Tokūgawa rule formally ended early in 1868 when anti-government forces took over the shōgun's palace, Japan actually entered a new era fifteen years earlier in July 1853 when the U.S. Navy sailed into Edo bay. In the years between this event and the end of Tokūgawa rule, Japan was forced, in the face of the threat of Western military power, to both open its doors for trade and, more ominously, to make other political concessions to American and, later, European powers.

The new government was composed of a small band of mostly younger samurai who had disposed of the Tokūgawas. The new leaders created an autocracy in the name of the young emperor, who named his reign Mēiji or "enlightened rule." Domestic political change took place during a time of continual international problems for Japan. The Mēiji leaders were forced by the Western powers to sign a set of treaties in which foreign powers operated under their own judicial system on Japanese soil. The treaties also prevented the Japanese from charging tariffs on products Western merchants wished to sell in Japan.

Such a situation was unacceptable to the Japanese. During the rest of the century, Japan embarked upon a whirlwind modernization campaign. Its goals were to build an economy and military strong enough that the country could be on an equal footing with the Western powers. If this goal was achieved, Japan would

---

[15]Descriptions of Tokūgawa education drawn from Edward Beauchamp and Richard Rubinger, Education in Japan: A Source Book (Garland Publishing, Inc., 1989), 139: Ronald P. Dore, Education in Tokūgawa Japan (University of California Press, 1965); and Herbert Passin, Society and Education in Japan (Teachers College Press, Columbia University, and East Asian Institute, Columbia University, 1965).

escape the semi-colonial status of the 1860s and regain its own destiny. From the very beginning of their tenure, Japan's new power brokers realized that education was a key to modernization.

The tone for the radical societal leap in learning characteristic of the Meiji years was set in the Charter Oath issued in 1868 in the emperor's name. The document contained the injunction that knowledge should be sought from all over the world. As early as the 1700s, the Tokūgawas had eased seclusion policies in order that some Western military and scientific knowledge could be introduced to Japan. By the early 1870s an intensive national effort to learn was in place.

The policy was two pronged. Thousands of young Japanese were sent to the industrialized countries to learn everything from banking to constitutional law. Americans, English, French, and Germans were paid lucrative salaries to come to Japan to impart knowledge.

In addition to the export and import of human beings, the Meiji Government set about to construct a national educational system. The September 1872 Fundamental Code of Education that established the groundwork for the national system was similar in design to the highly centralized French system. Devotees of Western, rather than Confucian, learning dominated thinking in both the new government and its ministry of education, the Mombushō. Early Meiji educational and political leaders aspired to create a cadre of young men quite competent in Western science and technology and a basic educational system for the entire population.[16]

In the 1870s, twenty thousand elementary schools were established throughout Japan. In addition, some middle schools, which were roughly equivalent to high schools, normal schools for teacher training, and an imperial university in Tōkyō were also created. The new government's reach, however, exceeded its grasp. Because of budget restraints and significant popular resistance to quick Westernization, many Japanese were still educated in Tokūgawa-style schools throughout the 1870s. Still, the trend toward standardization and central control was well under way by the end of the decade.

If France provided the administrative model for education, it was to the Americans that the Japanese turned for guidance in classroom content and

---

[16]Kenneth Pyle, The Making of Modern Japan (Washington, D.C.: Heath, 1978), 70-71.

pedagogy, particularly for elementary schools. David Murray, a Rutgers mathematics professor, served as the first national superintendent of schools and colleges. Marion Scott, a former San Franciso elementary principal, played a large role in the development of Japan's first teacher training institute. In higher education the Japanese adopted the German model of a few state-supported elite universities. Foreigners were placed in key positions in Tōkyō Imperial University as well as throughout other Japanese educational institutions.

While the 1870s were marked by a massive infusion of Western learning, by the 1880s policy makers developed a concern that another important goal of Japanese education, the creation of a loyal citizenry, was being hindered by too much Westernization. The central government assumed more power over education during these years by such policies as the 1881 law abolishing local textbook selection in favor of government-approved books. Conservatives also called for greater emphasis on moral education built upon Confucian principles and other traditional Japanese values such as subordination of individual to state interests.

The trends of greater state authority over education and a stronger emphasis upon traditional Japanese values in schooling culminated with the issuance, one year after the adoption of a new Japanese Constitution, of the 1890 Imperial Rescript on Education. The document, which constituted the moral foundation for education until after World War II, relied heavily upon Confucian ethics and group-oriented values.

The Rescript made filial piety, harmony, and absolute loyalty to the imperial throne, described as "coeval with heaven and earth," the major part of the basic education of every Japanese child. Copies of the document were distributed to every school in Japan and the Rescript was read on national holidays as part of school ceremonies in which students also bowed to photographs of the emperor. By the last decade of the nineteenth century, the Japanese Government managed to combine a new Western curriculum with an older moral underpinning designed to produce a citizenry subservient to the larger interests of the new empire.

This synthesis of the old and new that formed the basis of an educational system that would last until the end of World War II was the brainchild of Mori Arinori (1847-1889). Mori, the first Minister of Education in the new cabinet government system, was, although an advocate of Western learning, a political conservative. He believed schools existed for service to the nation rather than the students. It was this perspective that most manifested itself in the series of 1886 laws creating a system that served as a sorting mechanism designed to create a meritocracy. In this meritocracy it was intended that the most talented young men in Japan would rise to important leadership positions.

By the turn of the century, the vast majority of both boys and girls received six years of compulsory education at the elementary level and then two more years of upper elementary schooling. After these common experiences, sorting based on gender and competition occurred. Because of their sex, girls were shut off from competing for the elite tracks. Females who went on for further schooling attended a variety of schools that evolved during the latter nineteenth and early twentieth centuries. These institutions included vocational schools, female high schools, and a small number of private colleges and normal schools for the more ambitious young women. Helping occupations such as elementary teaching and nursing were the best jobs that females could aspire to in prewar Japan.

Boys who continued education after the elementary years were presented with more options. Youth schools, which developed in the early part of the twentieth century, were the least elite institutions. Youth schools were not even officially part of the secondary education system. Students attended these schools part-time until about the age of seventeen and received some vocational and military training as well as basic education.

Two different types of middle schools, followed by university for a precious few students, constituted the elite educational paths. The system Mori Arinori devised provided for the creation and financing by each of Japan's prefectures of one ordinary middle school. Entrance to the two-year and, later, three-year ordinary middle schools was determined by competitive examination. After negotiating a difficult Western and traditional curriculum, those students who hoped to later attend university competed, again by examination, for entrance into at first, five and later, seven, national higher middle schools. The examination for the three-year higher middle schools was the critical test, as students who gained admission were virtually guaranteed later entrance into imperial universities.

Competition was ferocious for entrance into the elite higher schools. By the early twentieth century, 80 percent of ordinary middle school graduates did not qualify for higher schools, although these graduates represented the top 10 percent of the nation's young men. The graduates who failed higher school tests could, however, attend a variety of vocational, normal, and technical schools, some of which led to careers in business management and professions such as law or pharmacy.

Although private secondary schools and universities developed throughout the prewar period, it was the public middle and higher schools and universities that provided the very best career opportunities for Japanese males. It was to the original seven and later nine imperial universities, and, first and foremost, Tōkyō Imperial University, that the most prestigious government and private employers looked for new recruits. Despite major exceptions, private universities were inferior options relative to public institutions.

The Legacy of Mēiji and Prewar Education

Much of both the structure and values orientations of the educational institutions just described are still present in contemporary Japanese schools. Although prewar middle and higher schools, emperor worship, and militaristic values are no longer present today, the high prestige that public universities enjoy still is a dominant force in Japanese education. "Shiken jigoku" or "examination hell" was a part of the lives of some young Japanese long before World War II. Today the examination system not only remains, but, because so many young people aspire to university, is more important then ever before. Top-tier public universities enjoy high status because, just as in 1886, contemporary Japanese power brokers and much of the public believe an important function of education is to identify the most talented youth in the country. These youth through their examination performances win the right to attend elite universities and later assume leadership positions in society.

The development of Mēiji and Japanese pre-World War II educational institutions also strengthened the historic influence of the values of groupism and adherence to basic Confucian tenets upon young Japanese.   Also, if Japan was comparable in many respects to Western nations in educational achievement at the end of the Tokūgawa years, this was even more true on the eve of World War II. By 1941, elementary education was universal in Japan, and most youth were staying in school on a part-time basis until about age seventeen.

While gender discrimination and anti-democratic values were pervasive in prewar Japanese education, it should be noted that for males, equality of opportunity was present in the system before the Second World War. In 1868, primarily samurai received the benefits of higher education. By as early as 1890 the number of commoners relative to samurai in ordinary middle schools was over 50 percent. By the turn of the century most graduates of imperial universities were also of commoner stock. The egalitarian nature of the Japanese educational system, created during the Mēiji and prewar years, was greatly expanded by the American Occupation following World War II.[17]

The American Occupation

In August 1945 Japan was a totally defeated and devastated nation. Over 4,000 schools were destroyed as a result of U.S. bombing and many other school buildings damaged. More significantly, because of defeat, a large majority of Japanese considered the authoritarian and militaristic aspects of their educational system to be morally bankrupt. The U.S. Occupation authorities also felt these normative elements of Japanese education to have been a major cause of Japan's military aggression. General Douglas MacArthur, who as head of Occupation forces in Japan, enjoyed virtually absolute power in reshaping the country, considered educational reform to be the critical key to a major U.S. goal, the democratization of Japan.

By the end of 1945 American authorities had already issued directives purging teachers who overtly supported the militarists. The Americans also suspended school moral education because of the authoritarian content. Occupation officials requested that a high-level American educational mission be sent to Japan to examine the system and recommend further reform.

---

[17]Descriptions of prewar Japanese education drawn from Dore, Education in Tokūgawa Japan; Passin, Society and Education in Japan; Beauchamp and Rubinger, Education in Japan: A Source Book; and Thomas Rohlen, Japan's High Schools (University of California Press, 1983).

The 27-member mission, headed by former New York State Commissioner of Education and University of Illinois President Elect, Dr. George Stoddard, consisted primarily of school administrators and education professors. Mission members represented the mainstream of U.S. "progressive" educational thought. The members of the mission were also ignorant of Japan. Within a month the mission "studied" the situation and issued a report, which the Japanese considered to be MacArthur's wishes even though they were told to treat the document as a set of suggestions.

The visiting educators recommended a virtual re-creation of public schools along American lines. The report called for democratization and decentralization of the system. The Mombushō was to be an advisory and research organization stripped of centralized power. Local control was to be guaranteed through the democratic election of school boards. An American 6-3-3-4 system should be adopted with nine years of compulsory and free education.

The American educators also recommended that social studies replace the old moral education, history and geography courses to ensure that the young learned democratic citizenship. Other recommendations included a greater emphasis on physical, vocational, and adult education; equal educational opportunities for both sexes; the establishment of American-style comprehensive high schools; the abolition of normal schools and the integration of teacher education into universities; and the replacement of the Japanese language, which was viewed as too inscrutable, with Roman script.

The American mission recommendations, the 1947 Japanese Constitution, and Occupation-era educational laws did result in fundamental changes in Japan's schools. Many of these still shape today's formal educational system. For example, the 6-3-3-4 grade sequence, education for democratic citizenship in the form of social studies, legalized equality of educational opportunity regardless of sex, and nine-year compulsory education, all of which date back to the Occupation, are now institutionalized components of contemporary Japanese education.

However, Japanese historical and cultural forces were too different from American culture to allow the complete reconstruction of an educational system that would be a simple copy of a foreign one. Some suggestions such as the abolition of the Japanese language got nowhere from the beginning in Japan.

28

Other proposed changes such as the attempt to weaken the Mombushō by the creation of strong democratically elected school boards and the initiation of American style multi-track comprehensive high schools, never took firm root.[18]

While the authoritarian spirit epitomized by the 1890 Imperial Rescript on Education apparently died with the Occupation, other traditional values, as well as structural aspects of Japanese education that date back to the Mēiji era, coexist today with democratic values and other American-inspired reforms.

The dominance of the group, Confucianism, hierarchy, and the role of formal educational institutions as sorting devices remain important keys in understanding how, what, when, and, even, where the Japanese learn. In one sense the rest of this book is a very specific portrait of how these traditional Japanese values, along with newer but important forces in Japanese life such as democracy and a desire for individualism, shape the concrete learning environments of contemporary Japanese.

---

[18]Descriptions of education during the Occupation drawn from Rohlen, Japan's High Schools; and Beauchamp and Rubinger, Education in Japan: A Source Book.

Questions for Comparison

The primary objective of this book is to provide readers with a comprehensive overview of Japanese education. However, learning about Japan might stimulate the desire in some readers to engage in systematic, reflective thinking about the American educational system. Therefore, a series of questions of a comparative nature are provided at the end of each chapter.

1. Groupism and hierarchy are dominant values that shaped Japanese culture and schools. What are dominant values that exerted similar powerful influences over American culture and schools?

2. Japanese education was clearly influenced by foreign cultures at various times in the nation's history. What foreign cultures influenced American education? How does that influence continue to be a part of our educational system today?

3. When did public education become institutionalized in all parts of the United States? What are major differences in the organization and administration of American and Japanese public education?

4. Confucianism was a major philosophical influence in Japanese education. What philosophical doctrines or religious theologies exerted similar influences in American education?

5. The American Occupation resulted in some changes in Japanese education, but several attempts by the Americans to change Japan failed, primarily because of the difference in our two cultures. Based on what you now know about Japanese education, are there any aspects of education in Japan that, because of cultural differences, stand very little chance of being applicable to the American situation?

Additional Reading

Readers who are interested in a survey of Japanese history but have limited time should examine the late Edwin Reischauer's book, Japan: The Story of A Nation, revised edition, New York: Knopf, 1981. Although the book is over twenty years old, the best single history of Japanese education from Tokūgawa times through the Occupation is Herbert Passin, Society and Education in Japan, revised edition, Tōkyō: Kōdansha Press, 1983. Edward Beauchamp and Richard Rubinger, Education in Japan: A Source Book, Garland Publishing, Inc., 1989, is an excellent general reference. The late educational historian, Lawrence Cremin, won a Pulitzer Prize for his monumental works on American education. The entire three volume set, beginning with American Education: The Colonial Experience 1607-1783, is available through Harper and Row Publishing Company. Readers who desire to examine a shorter work on American educational history should see John Pulliam, History of Education in America, fifth edition, New York: Merrill, 1991.

Those who would like to explore the relationships between dominant values and historical and contemporary culture in Japan might examine a second book by Reischauer, The Japanese Today: Change and Continuity, revised edition, Belknap Press, 1988, or Peter Tasker, The Japanese: A Major Exploration of Modern Japan, New York: E.P. Dutton, 1987. Habits of the Heart: Individualism and Commitment in American Life by Robert Bellah, Richard Madsen, William M. Sullivan, Ann Swidler, and Steven M. Tipton is an insightful analysis of the role of values in American life. Habits of the Heart was published by Harper and Row in 1985.

Chapter Two

Learning in the Preschool Years

Introduction

It is around ten in the morning when the foreign visitor arrives at the Japanese kindergarten, or yochien. In one sense, noisy disorder is an accurate description of the scene in the dirt playground encompassed on three sides by a "U" shaped classroom building. About half of the school's 271 three-, four-, and five-year-olds are outside engaging in morning exercise while being supervised by seven teachers.

Some of the children are engaging in side straddle hops and other physical exertions. Many youngsters are running all over the playground. There is an incredible noise level. At the edge of the playground is a large water trough with four faucets. Several little boys and girls, naked to the waist in the summer weather, are throwing water all over each other and yelling merrily.

Continual shouts of children make it almost impossible to hear. A couple of teachers are leading the exercises while the other instructors are chatting with each other or answering questions from individual children. The six female teachers and their one male colleague all have pleasant expressions on their faces and don't look at all disturbed by the uproar.

When the children notice the visitor there is a great hue and cry. Several youngsters immediately surround the outsider and simultaneously yell questions, tug at his clothes, and in the case of at least two children, deliver blows to his legs as they continue to shout. After a moment, one of the teachers walks over and in a gentle voice suggests to the children that it is impolite to hit the foreigner. One child stops but another youngster continues to deliver "love blows."

At 10:00 a.m. recorded music begins over a loud speaker. Immediately afterward there is an announcement that it is time to return to the classrooms. While several youngsters pick up flags and others congregate around the flag bearers and walk toward the rooms, at least 10 percent of the children continue playing. The teachers wander around to little groups still on the playground and seem to try gently to convince them to go into the classroom buildings. Most, but not all, of the children comply.

In the classrooms, children engage in musical chairs, group art work, and a game where one child is in a circle of other children who sing and walk around the youngster. Outside there are still a few children playing at the water trough. The teacher in the classroom nearest the trough makes no effort to retrieve the four or five children. A couple of kids in the classroom who aren't very interested in the game that is being played wander back outside to the water trough.

During both the exercise period and the classroom activities, seeming disorder is the rule rather than the exception. Children in no classrooms are counting, practicing beginning writing, or engaging in any other activity that could be clearly categorized as academic.[1] Given the reputation older Japanese students and adults have for deference to authority and orderliness, the prevailing behavior by the children in this kindergarten seems exactly opposite to what is expected of Japanese later in life.

However, what was observed in this kindergarten is quite typical of the Japanese preschool experience. One of the great paradoxes in Japanese education is that preschool children, both at home and in kindergarten or nursery school, are allowed great latitude in behavior compared to that of young children in many nations. Yet out of this seeming disorder the seeds are sewn that produce adolescents and adults who function competently in one of the most structured societies on earth.

Although this great difference in the behavior of young Japanese children when compared to what occurs later in life may seem strange to an outsider, there

---

[1] Opening case study based upon author's observation of Taiyō Yochien in Aichi Prefecture on June 14, 1990.

is a cultural logic present. It is based upon several prevailing perceptions about young children that are present in Japanese society.

Culture, Family and the Child

All societies nurture and treasure their young, but infants and children are particularly valued in Japan. Traditionally in Japan a strong belief has existed that children are inherently good. Some scholars argue that this notion can be traced to the writing of the Chinese Confucian Mencius who contended that all evil in human beings is the result of events that corrupt the originally good nature of the child. This Japanese belief is in stark contrast to the Western and Western Christian notion of Original Sin, and subsequently, of rebellious young spirits that must be broken.[2]

The belief that children are inherently pure is still strong in contemporary Japan. Anthropologists cite numerous examples of how much children are valued in Japanese society. In Japan there are an impressive number of ceremonies that surround infancy and young childhood. Celebrations occur during the mother's pregnancy, at the time the infant is named, when it is first taken to a shrine, and when it is weaned. There is a special ceremony for the infant's first birthday and national children's holidays that celebrate seven-, five-, and three-year-olds.[3]

In contemporary Japan the nuclear family is the dominant vehicle through which young children are nurtured. However, a communal spirit regarding the care of young children that dates back to earlier times still exists in Japanese society. The following examples found in Shizumi, a small city two hours southwest of Tōkyō, are typical contemporary manifestations of that spirit.

The Shizumi Municipal Government offers a systematic set of programs for mothers of small children. Free pregnancy information is provided for all expectant mothers. Children until the age of three receive free physical and mental examinations from the child welfare office. Regardless of whether welfare

---

[2] For an extended discussion of this topic see chapters on children and culture by Yamamūra Yoshiaki and Kōjima Hideo in Child Development and Education in Japan, eds., Harold Stevenson, Āzuma Hiroshi, and Hakuta Kēnji (W. H. Freeman and Company, 1986).

[3] Joy Hendry, Becoming Japanese: The World of the Pre-School Child (University of Hawaii Press, 1986), 39.

office employees are acquainted with the family, it is common for an examiner to admonish mothers for doing too much for children or to advise the parent that young children should have more neighborhood playmates. The municipal government also conducts a variety of classes for mothers with titles such as "Classes for Mothers of Three-Year-Olds," and "Home Education Class for Mothers of Kindergarten Children." Most of these classes are held once a month for a year and feature guest lectures by school teachers and other child care experts.

In Shizumi, private groups and individuals are also quite active in assisting in the nurturance of small children. A local supermarket publishes free newsletters for housewives with information on various aspects of child rearing. Newsletter topics include how to sensitize young children to musical sounds, how to make them fond of animals and plants, what the normal state of intellectual development for four- and five-year-olds would be expected to be, and how to teach very young children to put away their things. The anthropologist who conducted research in Shizumi was impressed with "...the sense of communal nurturance pervading the feeling that being mother and child is not a private matter but involves the community's responsibility and guidance."[4]

Besides the celebration of children and the retention of some collective responsibility for child nurturance, another aspect of Japanese culture is important in the socialization of young children. Japanese culture places more value on the role of motherhood than other industrialized societies where adult women have more varied lifestyles and roles. Attitudes in Japan toward the role of women are changing. However, a strong belief on the part of both the general population and women still exists that no job is more suitable for a woman than mothering. There is also an equally strong societal belief that the mother is, by far, the best care giver for children.

In a recent survey of women, 76 percent of respondents said their first responsibility was to their children. This strong attachment to motherhood is present even among well-educated women, the segment of the population that would be expected to hold significantly different opinions compared to their less-educated peers. In a recent Japanese national public opinion poll, 72 percent of

---

[4] Takie Sugiyama Lebra, Japanese Women: Constraint and Fulfillment (University of Hawaii Press, 1984), 211-213.

university graduates expressed the sentiment that women should cease working after they have children.[5]

Motherhood in any culture is a role that takes place in the context of the family. Japanese families, while being subjected recently to significant changes, still retain traditional cultural characteristics, particularly with regard to child-rearing.

Japanese marriages are still as much based upon traditional beliefs that household members have a primary duty to the ancestors of the family to provide descendants as upon the Western notion of marriage for love. Despite a growing acceptance of love marriages in Japan, personal affection between husband and wife is considered by many to be less important than making a family. A married couple without children is rare in Japan. Most families have their first child fairly soon after marriage.

Within the Japanese family, fathers have less responsibility for raising children than is usually true in many societies. Japanese males work on average the longest hours of employees in any modern industrialized nation. On week nights many male employees of large corporations or government ministries socialize with colleagues. The latter practice, along with often long commutes, means many men don't get home until the late evening. Many Japanese, particularly male salaried employees of large companies, work on Saturdays until noon. It is also quite common for many male employees to spend Saturday afternoons playing golf or engaging in other social events with their work mates.

The hectic work schedule and lack of a sense of responsibility by many Japanese men for child rearing leaves the mother as the primary care giver to children. Fathers are, with the exception of Sundays, so noticeably absent from the family that a few years ago a children's book about fathers with the very revealing title, Nichi yōbi no Tomōdachi, or in English, My Sunday Friend,

---

5 Fūjita Mariko, "It's All Mother's Fault: Child Care and the Socialization of Working Mothers in Japan," The Journal of Japanese Studies 15, no. 1 (Winter 1989): 67-92. Also, Merry White, The Japanese Educational Challenge: A Commitment to Children (The Free Press, 1987), 34.

36

became popular . Researchers of the Japanese family characterize the role of the father within the family as "high-status guest," and "superficial authority figure."[6]

Since World War II there has also been an organizational shift in families from an extended arrangement with several generations under one roof to nuclear families containing only parents and children. This change seems to have further weakened the father's role as parent. Historically in Japan, within the self-employed worker's extended family, the business was handed down from father to son. Therefore, an educational and economic relationship existed between the father and at least one of the children. Today, for every one extended Japanese family there are three nuclear ones. Most Japanese fathers are also no longer self-employed. Changes in the structure of the family and employment mean many Japanese fathers spend less time with the family than in the past.[7]

Even though approximately half of Japanese mothers now work outside the home, many of the jobs women perform are part-time. Even many working mothers still have significant time for child rearing. Also, when the labor force participation rates for Japanese women in the prime child-bearing years (25-34) are compared to those of American women in the same age category, almost 20 percent less (54%) Japanese women work outside the home than their American counterparts (73%). The first and most important daily "teacher" of an infant and very young child in Japan is still much more likely to be the mother than is the case in other industrialized societies. What is the nature of the relationship between the Japanese mother and her young child? What are the most important first lessons most young Japanese learn?[8]

First Experiences of Young Japanese Children

Fundamental differences exist between perceptions of Japanese mothers about their relationship to newborn infants and perceptions of mothers in many

---

[6] Morioka Kiyomi, "Privatization of Family Life in Japan," Child Development and Education in Japan, 63-74; and White, The Japanese Educational Challenge: A Commitment to Children, 108.

[7] Morioka, "Privatization of Family Life in Japan," 70.

[8] Lucien Ellington et al., The Japanese Economy: Teaching Strategies (Joint Council on Economic Education, 1990), 34-36.

other industrialized countries. In Western cultures, mothers view a newborn child as dependent. The Western mother's task is to assist the child to become a separate self. In Japan a mother is more likely to see a gap between herself and her baby at birth. The Japanese mother believes she must try to bridge this gap by forming a bond with the child.

The Japanese view manifests itself in the everyday ways mothers treat infants. Comparative studies indicate that Japanese mothers and babies have greater bodily contact at all times in the day than mothers and infants in the United States. Japanese mothers call this relationship "hada to hada no fureai," or "skin-to-skin contact," and consider it a very desirable situation. Babies in Western countries are often put in a separate room. In Japan most mothers sleep with their infants, carry them on their bodies rather than in a stroller, and bathe with them. Japanese mothers, through such large amounts of physical contact and by careful observation, learn to anticipate and then meet the baby's needs.[9]

The same studies also suggest that the close mother-child physical proximity has important effects upon communication. Great mother-child physical contact stimulates the growth of nonverbal communication skills. There is less of a need for as much verbal interaction between Japanese mothers and babies as their counterparts in other industrialized societies. Other factors could be at work also. Verbal ability has never been particularly highly regarded in Japanese society, and from infancy onward most Japanese are taught to be relatively guarded in verbal interactions with others.

Another major goal of Japanese mothers in early bonding experiences is to create in infants what the Japanese call a feeling of "amae." Although difficult to define in Western terms, amae is a person's desire to be passively loved or the expression of the wish to be dependent and to be taken care of unconditionally. The Japanese mother encourages amae by physical closeness and by fulfilling the infant's and young child's desires over a longer period of time than is the case in

---

[9] See studies reported by William Caudill and Helen Weinstein in "Maternal Care and Infant Behavior in Japan and America," Psychiatry 32, no. 1 (1969): 12-43; and Lebra, Japanese Women, 177.

38

many other cultures. For example, Japanese mothers allow young children to breast-feed and co-bathe for much longer than Western mothers.[10]

Just how paramount mother-child amae is in determining the later mind set of adult Japanese toward interpersonal relations is somewhat controversial. However, there is little doubt that in group interactions Japanese adults often expect to unconditionally take advantage of the help of close others. In return, Japanese are ready to provide unconditional help when needed. One Japanese anthropologist perhaps best defined the important role of amae in adult relations when she stated, "The person who knows how to amaeru has an easier time in Japan than one who does not."[11] Amae, or dependency, is the basic glue that makes groupism work in Japan, and is one of the first important lessons most Japanese infants and young children learn from mothers.

Japanese mothers also differ from their Western counterparts in their reactions to child misbehavior and their employment of control strategies. It is a common Japanese belief that because young children are incapable of reason punishment is impractical. This belief, along with the desire to build harmonious relationships with children, often causes mothers to be very tolerant of loud rambunctious behavior by young children.

In studies where Japanese and Western mothers were presented with hypothetical scenarios of child misbehavior, researchers found that Japanese mothers were much more likely to give into a child's demand than create a disharmonious situation. While over 50 percent of American mothers upon encountering misbehavior invoked their parental authority, the same response was true of only 20 percent of Japanese mothers.

If misbehavior becomes too intolerable for the Japanese mother, she often tries to persuade the child to change its behavior. If this doesn't work she may gently attempt to invoke guilt feelings by such statements as, "How do you think I will feel if you don't eat the vegetables I cooked for you." Such repeated actions by Japanese mothers early on inculcates in young children the desirability of

---

[10] Doi Takako, The Anatomy of Dependence (Tōkyō: Kōdansha, 1973), 7; and Lebra, Japanese Women, 176-177.

[11] Takie Sugiyama Lebra, Patterns of Japanese Behavior (University of Hawaii Press, 1976), 55.

harmony. Children also develop feelings of guilt if they are disappointing significant others.[12]

The importance Japanese culture places on motherhood influences mothers' behavior patterns in other ways. Japanese mothers are judged by other adults on the basis of how they treat their children in public. While a Western mother might appear ridiculous to bystanders if she begs and pleads with a three-year-old, Japanese don't have the same negative reaction to such behavior. In contrast most Japanese view a mother who is authoritarian in public with a misbehaving child as lacking the appropriate human feelings.[13]

It is important to bear in mind how much most Japanese women focus upon the task of mothering. Many Japanese still believe that if a woman strives for a career or an active social life with a spouse, she is not engaging in proper motherly behavior. Most Japanese women are still expected by the larger culture to center their whole lives on child nurturance. Surveys reveal, when given a list of various activity alternatives, over 70 percent of Japanese mothers agreed with this expectation. They chose their children to be their <u>ikigai</u> or major reason for living.[14]

As the infant becomes a young child, the mother continues to be its major teacher. Before they enter preschool, young children are likely to learn from their mothers appropriate social behavior, rudimentary academic skills, and the importance of process.

Young Japanese children learn group and hierarchy and status lessons in the home and neighborhood. Most Japanese draw sharp distinctions between "insiders" who are members of one's group and "outsiders," or everyone else. Japanese adults help the child differentiate quite early, to a greater extent than in the West, between the family and other people. The child learns special behavior toward both family members and the home space itself.[15]

---

[12] Robert Hess et al., "Family Influences on School Readiness and Achievement in Japan and the United States: An Overview of a Longitudinal Study," in Stevenson, <u>Child Development and Education in Japan</u>, 155-156.

[13] Hendry, <u>Becoming Japanese: The World of the Pre-School Child</u>, 105.

[14] Lebra, <u>Japanese Women</u>, 162.

[15] Hendry, <u>Becoming Japanese: The World of the Pre-School Child</u>, 50.

40

Very young Japanese children learn the somewhat formal greetings for older and younger siblings and for father and grandparents. In the home, preschoolers learn rites of cleanliness such as removing shoes at the entrance of a house. Most Japanese consider the use of appropriate greetings with others and the removal of shoes before entering homes and certain other buildings to be essential social behavior.

Many mothers also give preschoolers academic as well as etiquette lessons. Most urban mothers teach young children to read and write the two Japanese phonetic alphabets, to count to one hundred, and to work arithmetic problems involving numbers of less than ten before they enter kindergarten. Japanese mothers are often found on busy streets or in the subway asking preschool children such questions as "What is that color?," "How much change do you get if you buy six tangerines at 100 yen each with a 1000 yen bill?," and "How do you read that ad?"[16]

How mothers teach young children is important in understanding Japanese education. Teaching and learning in Japan is often characterized by frequent use of repetition and attention to process. Mothers stress to their children the importance of practice, concentration, and attention to detail in learning a task. In particular, most mothers are likely to emphasize to young children to concentrate and to focus upon one task at a time. These behaviors are so treasured in Japan that mothers encourage their children, even when they are engaging in recreational activities such as watching television, to do nothing else but that one act.[17]

Such behavior is extremely consistent with what the larger culture considers proper values for older Japanese. In Japan other people often assess the character of children and adults as much by the way something is done as by the particular outcome of a given task. In teaching their children social behavior, tasks, and values, mothers continually reinforce the importance of process.

---

[16] Lebra, Japanese Women, 199.

[17] White, The Japanese Educational Challenge: A Commitment to Children, 97.

Formal Preschools: An Introduction

Even though Japanese mothers are probably the most important teachers of children, there are both affective and cognitive lessons that are better learned outside the home. Traditionally, in Japan young children were introduced to the wider world through such mediums as the extended family and the neighborhood. In contemporary Japan the rise of the nuclear family and increased urbanization and mobility have caused traditional socialization agents to decline. Their place has been taken by preschools.

Although introduced to Japan over a century ago, yochien, or kindergartens, and hoikuen, or nursery schools, were still marginal in the care and socialization of most children as late as the 1960s. Today both kinds of preschools are institutionalized. Over 96 percent of Japanese children attend either a yochien or hoikuen for at least one year before beginning first grade.[18]

Yochien, the oldest and somewhat more prestigious of the major kinds of preschools in Japan, serve three-, four-, and five-year olds. Hoikuen also serve children of these ages, but take children of working mothers from the ages of six months through two years as well. Sixty percent of yochien are private. About the same percentage of hoikuen are public. As of the late 1980s, approximately two-thirds of Japanese preschool children attended yochien, while one-third attended hoikuen.[19] Yochien attendees are likely to be, with major exceptions, the children of mothers who are full-time, middle- and upper-class housewives. Hoikuen attendees are more likely to come from middle- and lower-class families which contain mothers who work outside the home.

Even though the curricula of these two types of preschools are extremely similar, important differences exist in organization and funding. Nationally, yochien are ultimately responsible to Mombushō. Hoikuen are under the jurisdiction of Koseishō, or the Ministry of Health and Welfare. Eighty percent of hoikuen funds are covered by national subsidies. The remaining amount is

---

[18] Joseph Tobin, David Wu, and Dana Davidson, Preschool in Three Cultures (Yale University Press, 1989), 216.

[19] For further statistical information on preschools see Education in Japan 1989: A Graphic Presentation, 11th ed. (Tōkyō: Ministry of Education, Science, and Culture, 1989). For more information on social class and preschool see Hendry, Becoming Japanese: The World of the Pre-School Child, 61; and Tobin, Wu, and Davidson, Preschool in Three Cultures, 48.

42

derived from local funds and a sliding-scale tuition formula that is based upon the economic resources of the individual family.

Yochien receive much less national government funding. They depend largely upon flat-rate tuition that is charged to families. Generally however, Japanese preschools are inexpensive compared to other Western countries such as the United States.[20] Although public and private preschools are administered by local governments and private individuals, both public and private licensed schools are subject to inspection by officials from one of the two national ministries.

A major reason costs are low in both types of institutions is that teachers, who tend to be female graduates of two-year colleges, are paid relatively low salaries when compared to Japanese elementary and secondary instructors. Also, although hoikuen teachers tend to work somewhat longer than their yochien counterparts, most preschool teachers are unmarried and remain in the classroom for only four to six years. While some preschool teachers return to the classroom later, marriage or the birth of the first child usually means the end of a preschool teacher's career. Preschool teachers who continue to work after marriage are often viewed with misgivings by parents who feel a mother, because of concern for her own children, cannot give complete attention to her students.[21]

Although the large majority of preschool faculty are female, preschool directors are usually men who are untrained in preschool education. For example, some private preschools are Buddhist and the directors are often priests. Also, older unmarried women sometimes move from social work or public school teaching to preschool directorships. A few preschool directors were formerly preschool teachers who advanced through the ranks. Typically, however, the highest position a preschool teacher attains is that of assistant director or head teacher. According to parental surveys, desirable traits of preschool teachers include affection and warmth toward children, tolerance, and lively childlike mannerisms. The latter characteristic is often not difficult for a preschool teacher to exhibit, since on the average, educators at this level are twenty-five years old.

---

[20] Tobin, Wu, and Davidson, Preschool in Three Cultures, 46-47 and 216-217.

[21] Ibid., 68-70.

Goals of Preschools

The <u>Yochien</u> visit described in the introduction of this chapter provides important clues to understanding dominant beliefs most Japanese share about preschool education. The sense of playfulness that pervaded the kindergarten and the lack of highly structured activities and extensive supervision of the children by their teachers was by adult design. Most Japanese think it is imperative that preschool educators establish a free and open environment for youngsters. When such an atmosphere is created, children can better learn proper human relations skills through interacting with each other. Adults keep interference to a minimum.

Learning human relations skills is the primary goal established by most preschools. The majority of Japanese parents and virtually all preschool teachers believe that for young children, learning affective and social skills is more important than gaining academic knowledge.

There are Japanese preschools that feature academic goals and curricula. However, these types of institutions, all private, only account for approximately 5 percent of Japanese preschools. The parents who do want academics in preschool are often the most vocal in their feelings and are frequently the subjects of newspaper and television stories. As a result, many people have been led to believe that all Japanese preschools stress academics. However, most Japanese agree with the often-heard statement of preschool teachers that they are attempting to produce a "<u>kodomo rashii kodomo</u>," or "childlike child."[22] The national government preschool curricula are clear reflections of the views of the majority of Japanese people. The nationally prescribed curricula of both government ministries responsible for preschool education emphasize social skills much more than is true of preschool curricula in Western societies. Although mothers often teach their children beginning writing at home, learning <u>hiragana</u> and <u>katakana</u> are part of the first-grade but not the kindergarten curriculum.[23]

Instead, one finds such expressions in the Mombushō kindergarten standards as "love and trust of people," "safety and happiness," and "instruction

---

[22] Ibid., 30-32.

[23] Ibid., 56-58.

through play."[24] It is expected that a Japanese child will first learn to love and be loved at home. Later in the preschool experience, according to the Mombushō written preschool curriculum, the child should learn to enjoy ties to peers and to deal effectively with a broader set of human relationships than what is found in his or her home experiences.

The great majority of preschool educators, when asked in surveys what is the most important work they do with their students, give answers congruent with the goals of the national government preschool curricula. Preschool teachers cite as their major tasks the development of such characteristics in children as empathy, gentleness, social consciousness, kindness, cooperativeness, enthusiasm, liveliness, perseverance, and obedience.

Preschool educators consider obedience, or sūnao in Japanese, to be particularly important for children to learn. Sūnao is perhaps more accurately translated as compliance to the desires of others rather than blind obedience to an authority figure such as a teacher. Preschool teachers consider the nurturance of sūnao in children especially important because flexibility about the needs of others is a key to development of good group skills.

While some Japanese disagree on the goals of preschool education, in general parents and teachers concur as to what young children should be taught. Japanese women usually cooperate willingly with the expectations and requests of preschool educators.

Mothers frequently take part in school activities and are expected to attend outings, talks, and luncheons sponsored by the school. Preschool educators also expect mothers to spend considerable time preparing the o-bentō or box lunch many Japanese children take to school each day. It is common for preschools to send a renraku chō, or daily record book, home each day with records of a child's mood, health, and eating and elimination habits. The daily activities of the preschool are a central concern of the often isolated non-working Japanese mother and, as much as possible, for the working mother as well. Most Japanese

---

[24] Education in Japan 1989: A Graphic Presentation, 58.

preschool instructors teach the curriculum with the solid support of a cadre of active and compliant mothers.[25]

Daily Life in the Preschool

There is slight variance in activities and schedules in Japanese preschools. Hoikuen allow more time for naps than yochien since the former institutions accept younger children. Still, the similarities among Japanese preschools far exceed the differences. The following depiction of a day in the life of Aichi Tāiyō Yochien, a private preschool near Nagoya, is quite similar to what occurs on a daily basis in most Japanese preschools.

Children are brought to Tāiyō by their parents around 8:30 a.m. During the first hour at school the children play outside on pretty days and in a large assembly hall in bad weather. Teachers watch over the children's play, but seldom organize or closely supervise it. Beginning around 9:15 a.m., teachers lead children who wish to participate in various exercises. Often, however, groups of youngsters mill about and pay no attention to what is occurring. At 9:50 a.m., recorded music is played over two large loud speakers, which is a signal for children to put away toys and prepare to enter individual classrooms.

Music is a major part of the life of virtually all Japanese preschools. All preschool teachers play piano. Every school has a piano or organ and a phonograph machine that are used daily. Recorded music is used constantly to signal children to begin or end an activity. Each day children sing songs and play small pianos, drums, and tambourines.[26]

Around 10:00 a.m. most, but not all, of the children enter their classrooms and spend some time taking off their shoes and putting away their matching blue hats and book bags. Shoe removal is as major an activity for young children in preschool as it is for them at home. The same is true for the daily ritual of putting away belongings in the classroom. Every child has his or her own space for their belongings. The four or five children who did not enter classrooms with the other students eventually tire of playing and wander in fifteen or twenty minutes after

---

[25] Tobin, Wu, and Davidson, Preschool in Three Cultures, 238.

[26] Ibid., 56.

the others. In one classroom a laggard is admonished by fellow students but, significantly, not by the teacher.

From about 10:15 a.m. until 11:30 a.m., teachers lead students through such classroom activities as group songs, a Japanese version of musical chairs, and art projects. The classes at Tāiyō, as is the case in most Japanese preschools, are subdivided into small groups of five to six children. The groups work on painting murals or play together in various games.

At 11:30 a.m. classroom cleanup occurs and one group from each classroom is responsible for walking to the kitchen and bringing food back to the room for the other children. After the teacher and students eat lunch together in the classroom, in some classes teachers read students stories. The three-year olds, who are the youngest children in Tāiyō, take naps after lunch. Around 1:30 p.m. most children in the school return to the playground for supervised games that last until around 3:00 p.m. Then music is played on the speakers to signal the children that they are to return to their classrooms to gather their things. Mothers arrive to pick the children up about 3:15 p.m. As the school day ends, mothers and children leave to the sounds of recorded music.

In addition to the normal routine, Tāiyō children participate in periodic special activities that focus upon the seasons and various national holidays. Once a year, usually in summer, Tāiyō hosts a parents' festival. Children spend several weeks creating art, learning songs, and preparing skits for the festival. Recently Tāiyō's annual festival was quite special since it marked the school's tenth anniversary. Approximately 2,000 people attended the festivities.

Virtually all preschool activities are accompanied by steady and loud noise! The amount of noise in Japanese preschools so impressed one researcher who has spent extensive time in such settings that in describing it she wrote, "The noise and chaos level of Japanese nursery schools was perhaps the most astounding aspect of my observations. Almost one-half of the dictation in my tape recorder of teacher activities were obscured by spontaneous background noise."[27]

---

[27] Catherine Lewis, "Children's Social Development in Japan," Child Development and Education in Japan, 196.

Working Together Through Fighting?

Japanese preschool educators hold a benign to positive view of noise. They think it a sign that children are learning to get along with each other and work out their problems. Not only noise, but disagreements and fights as well, often occur between children during the preschool day. As a rule, teachers only interfere if a child is in physical danger. Many preschool educators view fighting, particularly in the case of boys, as natural, and even positive. In the words of one preschool teacher "...it's good for them to have the experience while they are young of what it feels like to be in a fight."[28]

Typically a teacher who sees a fight, rather than personally intervene, will encourage other children, particularly girls, to act as peacemakers. While in many other cultures preschool educators react negatively when fighting occurs, Japanese see such incidents as good learning opportunities. Preschool educators often view fights as a chance for children to experience a range of emotions. Children through fighting learn strategies for resolving their own disagreements and the conflicts of others.[29]

The following additional comments by two Japanese preschool educators are good concrete examples of the dominant Japanese attitude toward children's scuffles.

> When I see kids fighting, I tell them to go where there isn't concrete under them or where there are mats. Of course, if they're both completely out of control, I stop it. Fighting means recognizing others exist. Fighting is being equal in a sense.

> If children can solve fights on their own without people being hurt, I let them do it themselves and ignore it. Kids start out rooting for the weak kid if the teacher stays out of it. If I can, I let them solve it.[30]

---

[28] Tobin, Wu, and Davidson, Preschool in Three Cultures, 33.

[29] Ibid.

[30] Catherine Lewis, "Cooperation and Control in Japanese Nursery Schools," Comparative Education Review 28, no. 1 (February 1984): 78.

Japanese preschool educators also have different reactions than their counterparts in other cultures regarding the question of what is the best size for a preschool class. Japanese preschool classes usually contain about thirty students. This is twice as large as typical kindergarten classes in the United States and other industrialized countries. When researchers informed a representative group of Japanese preschool teachers that the average American kindergarten class contained twelve to fifteen students, although they expressed some envy, the Japanese educators also asserted that such small classes would not be good for young Japanese.

Their reasons tell us much about both cultural differences in the role of preschools in nurturing young children and of the special commitment of the Japanese preschool to teaching group skills. Japanese preschool teachers believe if their classes consisted of only twelve to fifteen students, they would be tempted to develop a mother-like role with each child. Japanese preschool educators believe that to develop a mother-like relationship with a student is to fail as a teacher. The preschool teacher's role in Japan is to assist children to become independent and well-functioning group members. It is not to serve as a surrogate mother for individual students. Large classes allow Japanese preschool teachers to fulfill exactly this role.[31]

Appropriate Group Behavior and Individual Responsibility

When Japanese preschool teachers encourage play, tolerate noise and fighting, call upon children to settle disputes, and divide their classes into small groups they are working toward a larger goal. Japanese preschool teachers believe all these initiatives are part of an effort to teach young children that true individuality can only be realized by learning to get along well with one's peers. Young children learn in preschool that their own happiness lies in becoming a good group member.

Rather than forcing children to participate in group activities such as exercise or games, preschool teachers present these events as enjoyable experiences that youngsters don't want to miss. One of the first lessons children learn in Japanese preschool is that most of the fun is for those who cooperate in

---

[31] Tobin, Wu, and Davidson, Preschool in Three Cultures, 30-40.

group activities. The child who refuses to come in for class is simply ignored by the teacher and the other students. What might be interpreted in another culture as loose discipline toward an uncooperative child actually comes to be viewed by most Japanese children as a form of punishment. They are ignored and left behind by the larger group.

The Japanese child is constantly reminded in preschool of his or her group affiliation. In a particular class everyone wears a special yellow or red cap for field trips. Children also wear assorted pins, name tags, or other paraphernalia to identify their particular class membership. Every class is assigned a name that will usually be that of a color, a flower, or an animal.[32]

Songs, activities, and stories also reinforce the values of group cooperation in children. Even the Japanese version of the Anglo-American story, the "Three Little Pigs", illustrates to children the importance of unity and group cooperation. In the Japanese tale the three pigs cooperate to kill the wolf!

In addition to encouraging children to settle disputes, Japanese kindergarten and nursery teachers also exercise minimal control in other ways. Children are often responsible for calling class together and overseeing class projects. Within preschool classes, one or two children on a daily basis are designated to serve as tobans, or leaders. The toban's authority might include deciding which of the class groups shall be dismissed first, giving children permission to leave the classroom, and even finding children who were missing at lunch or assembly time.[33]

Some international preschool experts contend that Japanese preschool teachers use of children to perform control tasks often carried out in other countries by teachers has several interesting effects. Since Japanese teachers delegate authority to groups of children or an individual youngster, they can assume a benevolent rather than authoritarian role. Therefore, preschool students don't view the teacher as primarily an authority figure. As a result, Japanese preschool teachers' suggestions for various group activities and student cooperation are not as likely to be resisted by Japanese children as in cultures where teachers have strong authority roles.

---

[32] Ibid., 40.

[33] Lewis, "Cooperation and Control in Japanese Nursery Schools," 80.

A different dynamic comes into play when Japanese children are given authority and fail. If a <u>toban</u> does not realize it is time for lunch and is hit by hungry class members, peer criticism, while not as devastating to the child as that of an adult, may be more effective in inducement of behavior change. To a young child, peer criticism may seem to be more a natural consequence of one's acts since other group members have reacted rather than a more distant adult.[34]

The Preschool Years: A Summation

In every society young children, through the acquisition of information and personal experience, learn an impressive amount before elementary school. However, a major difference between Japan and other cultures is that because of the relative homogeneity of Japanese society, the home and preschool messages children receive are likely to be mutually reinforcing.

By the time they enter first grade, Japanese children have learned the importance of having someone to depend upon and the higher status afforded by membership in inside groups. Because mothers take their role as teachers so seriously, most Japanese children learn basic rudiments of literacy and numeracy in the home.

In the preschool years, children learn to transfer their need to be dependent to the larger peer group. The group becomes, through the efforts of their teachers, a major source of pleasure for youngsters. Children also learn, through the responsibility that teachers give them, that group membership has its obligations as well as its benefits. These values are reinforced in the elementary school. At the same time, elementary children in Japan will receive one of the best basic academic educations in the world.

---

[34] Ibid., 84.

Questions for Comparison

1. Much of this chapter focused upon dominant Japanese cultural beliefs about the care of young children and roles of mothers. What are dominant American cultural beliefs about young children and mothers? How are American beliefs different and similar to those held by Japanese?

2. In Japan a large majority of young children now attend preschool. Is this also true in the United States? What are other similarities and differences in the demographics of preschools in Japan and the United States?

3. What kind of backgrounds are characteristic of American preschool teachers? While Japanese preschool teachers tend to leave the classroom after only a few years, is the same true of American preschool teachers?

4. American kindergarten curricula tend to be more academic than is the case in Japanese preschools. What is the nature of academic instruction in American kindergartens? What values do American kindergarten teachers stress with students?

5. What are typical ways American mothers and teachers deal with the misbehavior of young children? What underlying values influence American "control strategies?"

Additional Reading

Readers who are interested in a cross-cultural comparison of American, Chinese, and Japanese kindergartens should read Joseph Tobin, David Wu, and Dana Davidson, Preschool in Three Cultures, New Haven: Yale University Press, 1989. Some of the latest and most extensive research on young Japanese children, Japanese mothers, and socialization may be found in the Winter 1989 (vol. 15, no. 1) issue of The Journal of Japanese Studies. The entire issue is devoted to the world of the preschool child.

Those readers who, for comparative purposes, would like to learn more about a wide range of issues in the socialization of young American children and American preschools should examine Carol Seefeldt, Continuing Issues in Early Childhood Education, Columbus: Merrill, 1990.

Chapter Three

Learning in the Elementary School Years

Introduction: Among Children

Early one hot summer morning, 40 third-graders are hard at work in the classroom. The students attend Mitāka Elementary School, located in an upper-middle-class town by the same name about forty-five minutes from Tōkyō. The youngsters are just beginning a geography lesson. Two large maps of the town are on display in the front of the classroom. Each map contains blank spaces beside what appear to be major avenues and other points of interest. In response to the teacher's signal about one-half the class congregate around the maps. The children then begin to attach stickers containing names of major streets and other important places such as subway stations, the town hall, and Mitāka Elementary School on the map.

While two groups of children are working with the wall display maps, the remaining students are on the floor studying two color commercial maps of Mitāka and making entries in their social studies notebooks. Although student attention is high during the 45-minute lesson, there is low but continual noise present. Children ask the teacher questions, move back and forth between the groups and their desks, and occasionally stop work to stare at the two adult visitors in the back of the class.

54

After the lesson ends, the teacher informs us that the week before the class took a field trip in Mitāka. Upon returning, the students constructed the two large maps in the front of the room and the paste-on, place name stickers.

Although it is also summer, the weather is much cooler on the shore of Matsūshima Bay in Northern Honshū. Matsūshima Bay and the small, but very beautiful, verdant islands within it constitute one of the most popular tourist attractions in this region of Japan. A group of first-graders are among the many visitors who are walking along the shore of the bay. The children are, more or less, in single file as they trundle behind their teacher and two mothers who are serving as chaperones. Although children of both sexes wear identical blue jump suits, the boys have on blue baseball caps while the girls wear yellow ones. The children first visit a Shinto shrine and a Buddhist temple. Then they hike across a foot bridge to a small and uninhabited island that is a nature preserve. The group then stops in an open field for a picnic. The children arrange themselves in one large circle to eat. After eating their box lunches, the youngsters romp merrily around the field as the accompanying adults look on.

The atmosphere is quite pleasant on the smiling young woman's enclosed back porch in a suburb of the small city of Tsu in the heart of Japan's rice country. As she talks, twenty children, whose ages range from six to nine, sit on the floor around her. The woman, who spent a year in Great Britain when she was a university student, is now the wife of a university professor. She is the sole teacher and proprietor of a private English language juku school. Children attend twice a week to learn conversational English. They study primarily for enrichment purposes since English is not in the elementary school curriculum. Later in life their university entrance examinations will most likely measure written but not conversational skills.

The group and the enthusiastic young teacher sing several English songs to the accompaniment of recorded music. The children then play a game where the teacher shows pictures of objects such as cars, houses, and trees. Children shout the English names for each picture.

Each of the three above cases are quite common examples of the educational processes contemporary Japanese elementary children experience.[1]

---

[1] Opening case studies based on author's school visits in Mitāka City and Aichi Prefecture in 1987 and observations in Matsūshima and Aichi Prefecture in 1990.

Just as in preschools, the general atmosphere in which elementary children learn constitutes a different reality than what many in the West imagine to be the case. "Kind" and "nurturing" rather than "competitive" or "grueling" are generally the adjectives that come to the minds of those observers who have spent time in Japanese elementary schools. Yet, while the warm general climate of preschool is maintained throughout the elementary years, teachers and mothers have other quite specific intentions as they interact with children. Adults are preparing elementary children for the much harsher educational waters they must traverse before reaching adulthood. The remainder of this chapter is both a description of the elementary years and an examination of that preparation process.

The Administrative Structure of Elementary Schools

Japan, as is true with other affluent industrialized societies, has virtually all eligible youngsters (99.9%), enrolled in elementary schools. Since attendance in grades one through nine is compulsory in Japan, the same school participation level is true for older youngsters as well. For virtually all elementary students, education is in a public school. In the most recent year for which statistics are available, almost 99 percent of students in grades one through six attended local public elementary schools.

Although municipal and prefectural governments are responsible for aspects of elementary school administration, Japan has a national educational system. The Tōkyō-based Ministry of Education, Science, and Culture, or in Japanese, Mombushō, is the government ministry chiefly responsible for all levels of formal education in the country.

The Mombushō, unlike the relatively weak Department of Education in the decentralized American educational system, has broad authority over elementary education. Mombushō officials write the national curriculum, in large part determine teacher salaries, and impose various educational standards on schools. Mombushō also specifies lists of textbooks that prefectural and municipal boards of education may choose from to use in schools. Mombushō provides significant national subsidies for compulsory education schools, which include all public elementary and junior high schools. Private schools are licensed and provided some subsidies by Mombushō.

Mombushō is also, despite some slight local variation, responsible for the school calendar for elementary and secondary schools and universities. The Japanese school year begins on April 1 and ends on March 31 of the following year. Kindergartens, elementary, lower secondary schools, and most upper secondary schools adopt a three-term school year: from April to July, September to December, and January to March. The Japanese school year contains 240 days and students attend school half days on Saturday. However, the Mombushō plans to eventually abolish Saturday school attendance for both elementary and secondary students before the end of the 1990s, without reducing the number of class hours students are required to take. As of fall 1992, all Japanese students began taking one Saturday a month off from school as a first step in this goal.

Even though Mombushō's power over elementary schools is quite broad, other levels of government have roles to play. Japan's forty-seven prefectures, roughly analogous to American states or British counties, have some administrative responsibility for compulsory education schools including the establishment of special schools for the severely mentally or physically handicapped. Actual administration of both public elementary and junior high schools is primarily a function of local or municipal government. Municipal boards of education, appointed for four-year terms by the mayor with the consent of the municipal assembly, name the municipal superintendent and appoint and dismiss teachers subject to the approval of prefectural authorities. Along with other local officials, boards of education are responsible for provision of about 30 percent of elementary school funds.

On average, prefectural governments contribute about 36 percent of funds for elementary schools. The national government funds over 30 percent of elementary school costs, including one-half of teacher salaries in compulsory education schools. Since shortly after World War II, in an attempt to ensure equity in educational finance, the national government has also provided subsidies to poor areas for use in compulsory schools. As a result, studies indicate that elementary school expenditures are now only 1.6 times higher per pupil in prefectures with the highest elementary educational expenditures when they are compared with prefectures who spend the lowest amounts for education.[2]

---

[2] Sugihara Seishirō, "Educational Expenditure in Japan and the United States," East West Education II (Spring 1990): 32.

National, prefectural, and local governments are all involved in the certification and appointment of elementary school teachers. Although Mombushō proscribes most of the requirements for elementary school teacher licensing, certificates are granted by prefectural boards of education. Regular certificates are valid in all prefectures and for life. However, after obtaining certification, the prospective elementary (and junior high) teacher must apply with municipal governments. Appointment to a teaching position is largely determined by the results of an examination administered by municipal boards of education. Formal appointment to a teaching position is then made by prefectural boards of education, based on recommendations of municipal authorities.

Elementary schooling and all compulsory education in Japan is a collective endeavor dominated by a centralized national ministry but administered by regional and local authorities. The local elementary school is the most basic and important grassroots link in the enterprise. What are the common patterns of relationships between the "average" Japanese elementary school and the children and parents that it serves?

Elementary Education: The School as "Family" Ethos

It is early April and the first day of the new Japanese school year in a typical elementary school. Well-dressed adults including mothers, fathers, and grandparents arrive with their children. The entire school meets in an assembly where the first-graders are welcomed. Since they are the most senior students, the sixth-graders assist the newcomers. The school principal makes a welcoming speech that is a combination of uplifting remarks and introductions of teachers and staff.

After the assembly, first-graders are escorted to the classrooms with the help of older children to meet teachers. Teachers welcome the youngsters, call roll, and go over classroom routines. School is then dismissed. This entire process has been described by more than one foreign observer as similar to being welcomed into a new family.[3] Japanese society is considered by most foreigners to be extremely homogeneous. This stereotype is somewhat of an oversimplification of reality. Political, class, and even geographic divisions

---

[3] White, The Japanese Educational Challenge: A Commitment to Children, 111.

certainly exist in Japan. In fact, deep divisions exist within the enterprise of education. For example, Mombushō, which is dominated by conservatives, and the declining but still powerful politically leftist teachers' union, are often bitter foes.

Still, as might be gathered from earlier portions of this book, there is a higher level of agreement by Japanese than in most societies on the importance of education to both individual and national success. This agreement makes the elementary school as "new family" metaphor an accurate overall summation of the prevailing ethos in Japanese schools.

In the ideal family setting, parents take into account every aspect of the welfare of children. Ample evidence exists that Japanese elementary school teachers have a holistic concern for their charges. Schools often set boundaries for children's movements within a neighborhood. School officials recommend nightly curfews in newsletters that are distributed to parents. Every year, during the first few weeks of school, teachers visit the homes of each of their pupils in an attempt to better understand each family environment. Even during summer vacation schools continue to look after the welfare of their "family" members. In the summer, schools provide extensive sets of rules and recommendations to families concerning student behavior, daily study, and play schedules.

Concern for development of children's character is also a part of the formal curriculum in all compulsory education schools. Elementary and junior high teachers spend one class hour a week on moral education. In moral education teachers rely heavily upon a Mombushō curriculum guide. In elementary school, six topics are studied in moral education including the importance of order and cooperation, endurance and hard work, justice and fairness, the individual's place in various groups, harmony with nature, and the need for development of a rational and scientific attitude toward human life.[4]

The elementary school's effort to cultivate moral and character development as well as cognitive learning typically receives substantial support from the Parents-Teacher Association (PTA). All mothers are expected to attend PTA meetings. PTAs typically function as forums for the school to explain policies to parents and cultivate parental assistance for various projects. Virtually

---

[4] Japanese Education Today, 51-52.

all elementary and junior high PTAs publish six to nine newsletters a year which are edited by mothers. The newsletters cover such topics as proper activities for children after school, cultivation of good parent-child relations, and stages of child development.

However, mothers contribute far more to the education of Japanese elementary children than simply attending PTA meetings and contributing to newsletters. The role of the mother in the entire Japanese elementary schooling process is so extensive it deserves special attention.

"Kyōiku Mamas"

Recently, one foreign journalist in describing the role of housewives in Japan reported that "...It is a commonplace statement in Japan that the nation's hardworking housewives are its secret weapon...the backbone of the nation that enables its men to perform their economic miracle and the insurance that the next generation of Japanese will behave in the same hardworking way."[5] The larger society expects Japanese mothers to perform a continual and highly visible role in every aspect of the education of children. The mother plays so pervasive a role in education that the Japanese media employs a somewhat satirical but much used expression, "kyōiku mama," or "education mama," to describe her role in the educational enterprise.

Perhaps the typical mother's intense interest in her children's education is best symbolized by a home study desk for youngsters that was recently a hot item in Japanese department stores. The desk space is surrounded on three sides so the child won't be distracted from study. In addition to shelves at the front of the desk there is a dashboard-like set of lights, an electric pencil sharpener, a built-in calculator, and a button. The button is connected to a bell which is placed in the kitchen so that the child can ring for mother for homework help or for a snack.[6]

Most Japanese fathers perform a minimal role in the education of children. Although schools occasionally attempt to involve fathers, the efforts usually fail. One such attempt described by an anthropologist engaged in participant-observer

---

[5] Deborah Fallows, "Japanese Women," National Geographic 177, no. 4 (April 1990): 52-53.

[6] White, The Japanese Educational Challenge: A Commitment to Children, 145.

60

research on Japanese parents is a good example of both the physical and mental absence of many fathers in the education of young children. The case study is also illustrative of the high level of attention mothers pay to schooling.

The researcher joined parents of third-graders at the monthly parent class observation day sponsored by a school. Although school officials in an attempt to attract more fathers named this particular parental visit "Father's Class Observation Day," more mothers than fathers actually attended.

In a class of forty students, thirty-one parents were present including twenty-three mothers who were "deputies of fathers." As the children worked math problems, mothers stepped forward to examine their child's performance. Fathers all stood in the back of the room and looked bored. When teachers and parents exchanged ideas after class, the researcher detected clear differences in the typical questions of fathers when compared to mothers.

While fathers would tend to ask general questions such as "What is the standard level of sexual development for third-graders?," or "What can be done to develop the child's individuality?," mothers asked more specific questions. For example, mothers asked questions about homework such as "What will happen if my child does not finish a project scheduled for completion on a certain day?" It was obvious who was in charge of the child's day-to-day study progress.[7]

Several of the women attending the observation expressed ambivalence about having husbands involved in the education of their children. The women felt they were much more familiar with the policies of the elementary school and could do a better job than the husband. The anthropologist's conclusion that mothers of elementary school children were "agents of the school..." is supported by much corroborative research.[8]

Elementary Schools: Teachers and Administrators

If Japanese mothers are unofficial agents of the school family, teachers are of course the official agents. Who are the people who teach in Japanese

---

[7] Lebra, Japanese Women: Constraint and Fulfillment, 199-200.

[8] Ibid., 193.

elementary schools? What are their backgrounds and training? How are they regarded by other Japanese? What are their work lives like?

Although many professional jobs are not truly open to women in Japan, such is not the case with elementary teaching. According to recent Mombushō statistics, 55 percent of Japan's elementary teachers are women.

Until relatively recently in most countries, elementary teaching was not an occupation in which a four-year university degree was required for entry. In Japan it is still possible to become a teacher after completion of a two-year junior college program. However, elementary teachers with university degrees are paid higher salaries than their junior college-educated counterparts. The most recent government statistics indicate that 70 percent of Japan's elementary teachers now have bachelor's degrees, a significant increase compared to past decades.[9]

The university training that prospective elementary teachers receive in Japan is similar in most respects to programs that exist in other industrialized countries. Teacher education students receive courses in subject matter, pedagogy, and psychology, and engage in a two- to four-week student teaching experience. The latter segment of the program receives wide criticism from many Japanese educators as being too short.

Prospective elementary teachers are quite competent academically when compared with other Japanese university students. On average, elementary education majors score at the 50th percentile or better on standardized tests that university students take.[10] While the academic ability levels of elementary teachers in some countries, including the United States, have declined in recent years, this is not true in Japan.

The relative lack of opportunities for high-level positions for women in Japanese business and government makes teaching an attractive profession for talented females. However, many competent young women as well as men in Japan are attracted to teaching because of the profession's relatively high status, highly competitive salaries, and employment security.

Teaching in Japan and throughout much of East Asia, partially because of Confucianism's influence, has long been a high-status profession. The Japanese

---

[9] Education in Japan 1989: A Graphic Presentation, 79.

[10] Interviews with faculty of Ōsaka University of Education, Ōsaka Japan, June 1987.

word for teacher, <u>sensei</u>, is not only descriptive of that profession but is also used as an expression of respect for teachers, doctors, artists, lawyers, and other learned people. The majority of Japanese teachers come from middle-class homes where teaching is viewed as a quite prestigious career.

Economic factors also loom very large in the minds of many young Japanese who decide to enter the teaching profession. Even though Japanese elementary teachers earn slightly less than their senior high school counterparts, their salaries compare quite favorably with engineers, pharmacists, and other university-educated professionals. Although beginning teachers with bachelor's degrees earn somewhat modest initial salaries, a teacher's wages climb impressively with years of experience. Based on current exchange rates, a first-year Japanese elementary teacher with a bachelor's degree will earn somewhere between $12,000 and $14,000 annually. An elementary teacher with thirty years experience will earn $42,0000 or approximately three times as much as the amount of the beginning teacher.[11]

Employment security is another important economic consideration. Unless convicted of a serious crime, once Japanese teachers are employed they are guaranteed a position for life. However, teachers are subject to periodic transfers within a local school district.

Both the non-economic and economic appeal of teaching in Japan has two important results. Japan has a very stable teaching force. Recent Mombushō statistics indicate the average elementary teacher has seventeen years experience. One-third of the nation's elementary teachers have been in the classroom twenty years or longer.

Japan also does not lack a continual supply of prospective teachers. There are almost five times as many applicants nationally for elementary and secondary teaching positions as there are available jobs. Well over 80 percent of Japanese universities offer teacher training programs. Almost one-third of all Japanese university graduates have teaching credentials.[12] The high status of teaching and

---

[11] Japanese salaries from <u>Education in Japan 1989: A Graphic Presentation</u>, 84-85. Conversion rate calculated on 130 yen to one dollar.

[12] <u>Japanese Education Today</u>, 15-16.

the stiff competition to enter the profession means Japanese children work with highly qualified and seasoned professionals.

What are the attitudes of Japanese elementary teachers toward their work? What is a typical teacher's day like? Although there are obviously exceptions, the larger society and most teachers view the profession as a special calling with vital responsibilities. In addition to summer work and home visits, teachers are expected to do other work that goes far beyond instructing children in school subjects.

When the police arrest a child it is not uncommon for the youngster's teacher rather than parents to be called to the police station. If juvenile delinquency shows an abnormal increase during the summer vacation period in a community or city, teachers from local schools are called into the police station in order to confer with authorities.[13] The special nature of the teacher's work in a Japanese elementary school is perhaps best depicted by an examination of an actual day in the life of one teacher.

Shīmizu-sensei

Shimizu-sensei is a 32-year-old sixth-grade teacher with ten years experience who lives in a Tōkyō suburb. Although he only teaches about fifteen hours a week, Shimizu's other work activities make for a full day that extends from 7:30 a.m. until nearly 6:00 p.m. each evening.

When he arrives at school about 7:30 a.m., Shīmizu first works on lesson preparations. He then attends, along with all the school's teachers and students, a short daily morning convocation. The all-school meeting is usually followed by teachers' meetings from 8:15 until about 8:35 and then a short homeroom meeting supervised by teachers. Shīmizu teaches his class of forty students math and then Japanese language. Shīmizu knows the youngsters quite well since this is his third year with the same students. Japanese elementary teachers usually have the same children for at least two years. A short recess follows the two morning classes and Shīmizu, along with other teachers, supervises the children.

After recess Shīmizu has no scheduled class. Sometimes he sits in the back of the room while his students are in other classes to observe their work. On other days Shīmizu might grade papers or read during his free period. On the particular day being

---

[13] Sugīhara, "Educational Expenditure in Japan and the United States," 49.

described here, however, Shīmizu works in the teachers' room on a report he must give on the progress of the entire sixth grade at the upcoming weekly faculty meeting.

Shīmizu then eats lunch with his students. Lunch, as in most Japanese schools, is served by alternating small groups of students and is eaten in the classroom. After lunch, Shīmizu supervises recess and then teaches social studies, music, and science classes. After a final half-hour for a class meeting, the school day is over, but Shīmizu must stay for the two-hour weekly faculty meeting. He arrives home at 6:00 p.m. with papers to correct and lesson plans to prepare.

Although Shīmizu has problems, including pressure from parents who want more discipline and tougher assignments, he feels lucky to be an elementary teacher. Japanese secondary teachers must contend with tough pressure from parents because of the stress of entrance examinations. Japanese elementary teachers like Shīmizu can focus more on student learning rather than on examination preparation. Shīmizu, unlike secondary teachers he knows, can sometimes take Sundays completely off to be with his family or pursue hobbies such as fishing and watercolor painting. As is the case with most Japanese elementary teachers, despite occasional stress, Shīmizu-sensei seems to enjoy his job.[14]

Teachers such as Shīmizu, despite the fact they are part of a highly centralized educational system, still interact most frequently with local educational administrators. Local boards of education employ a school superintendent who is typically a low-profile business manager. Local districts also retain the services of a small subject area supervisory staff that conducts inservice programs for teachers and performs other tasks related to their content specialties. In Japanese elementary and secondary schools the principal and head teacher are the two administrators who work the most with teachers. Of these two administrators, teachers spend much more time with the head teacher than with the principal.

Although the principal is the school's head, with the exception of the weekly address and other ceremonial events, he is an external representative of the school. Principals are much more likely to be meeting with PTA representatives, the police, and other local government agencies and assorted groups than supervising daily internal school business. The principalship in Japan is often the

---

[14] Case study adapted from White, The Japanese Educational Challenge, 87-90.

final reward for a good career. Ninety-eight percent of Japanese elementary principals are men and most are over the age of 55. Principals are all former teachers and most also served as head teachers. Principals are compensated quite well for their services. Annual salaries for principals in Japan range from $57,000 to $70,000.

The head teacher is the most important administrator in the elementary teacher's work life. Head teachers, who are almost all men, average between fifty and fifty-five years of age. They play a large part in directing daily school life while still teaching about three hours a week. Although the position is a desirable job for those educators who aspire to the principalship, it can also be the final reward for an outstanding teacher's long and faithful service. Most Japanese elementary schools, unlike the situation in the schools of several other foreign countries including the U.S., have no other administrators or nonteaching staff such as counselors who hold administrative rank. Teachers perform counseling and administrative functions as part of their daily duties.[15]

Elementary Schools: Subjects and Pedagogy

Mombushō is responsible for formulating the national curriculum or "course of study" for all elementary and lower and upper secondary schools. The following table depicts the present elementary school course of study, formulated in 1977 and implemented in April 1980, as well as recent revisions. Although Japanese educators place special emphasis upon certain subjects, for the most part the subjects taught in Japanese elementary schools are similar to what may be found in the schools of other nations.

In 1989 a revision of the course of study was completed and was later implemented in April 1992. Revisions include the abolishment of science and social studies in first and second grades and the replacement of these courses with a unified science-social studies course entitled "living studies." Homemaking will also be deleted from grades one through four beginning in 1992. The numbers by

---

[15] Japanese Education Today, 25. Calculation of Japanese administrator salaries based upon author interview with Professor Uōzumi Tadāhisa, Aichi University of Education, June 12, 1990.

Table 1

**Prescribed Subjects and Number of
School Hours in Elementary School**

Subjects	I	II	III	IV	V	VI
			Grade			
Japanese Language	272 (306)	280 (315)	280	280	210	210
Social Studies	68 (--)	70 (--)	105	105	105	105
Arithmetic	136	175	175	175	175	175
Science	68 (--)	70 (--)	105	105	105	105
(Life Environment Studies)	(102	105	--	--	--	--)
Music	68	70	70	70	70	70
Art and Handicraft	68	70	70	70	70	70
Homemaking	--	--	--	--	70	70
Physical Education	102	105	105	105	105	105
Moral Education	34	35	35	35	35	35
Special Activities	34	35	35	70	70	70
Total	850	910	980	1015	1015	1015

Notes:
1. One unit school hour is a class period of 45 minutes
2. The numbers enclosed in brackets are the number of school hours for the new
    course of education to be enforced from April 1992.
Source:
Education in Japan 1989: A Graphic Presentation, 61.

each subject and under each grade represent the total required school hours for each course during a school year (one school hour = 45 minutes).

Information in the table indicates that Japanese elementary students spend about one-fourth of total elementary class time on "Kokugo," or the "national language." This great attention by educators to this subject has paid off handsomely. Between 95 and 99 percent of all Japanese are estimated to be literate. This is the highest rate for any of the world's countries.

High Japanese literacy rates are even more impressive considering the difficulty of written Japanese when compared to most of the world's languages. Japanese, described long ago by the sixteenth-century Jesuit missionary to Japan, Saint Francis Xavier, as "the Devil's Language," is considered by linguists to be among the world's most very difficult languages. Considering the formidable effort required to learn to read and write Japanese, the massive amount of time spent on language study in the classroom is perfectly justifiable.

One of the major problems with written Japanese is that learners must master three separate writing systems. Often the three appear together on the printed page. Two of the systems, hiragana and katakana, are phonetic syllabries consisting of forty-six basic symbols each, as well as additional symbols obtained through the use of diacritical marks. Each of the symbols represents a separate sound. Hiragana is used for particles, some nouns and verbs, and all endings denoting adjectives, adverbs, and verb tense. Katakana is used primarily for transliterated foreign words. Both syllabries are relatively easy to write, as the characters consist of only four to six strokes.

Such cannot be said for kanji, the characters originally imported to Japan from China. It is kanji that constitutes the most important and difficult element of the Japanese language. Kanji are ideograms, or pictorial representations of ideas. They can be quite visually complex. Writing an individual character might require from one to twenty separate strokes. If the position of a stroke is changed, the entire meaning of a character might change. Although there are said to be some 48,000 kanji in existence, around 4,000 characters are commonly used in writing. Mombusho has identified 1,846 kanji that are essential for basic literacy or the ability to read a newspaper. By the end of the sixth grade almost all Japanese children have learned, in addition to hiragana and katakana, well over one-half the kanji required for basic literacy.

Table 2

Examples of Japanese Writing

Kanji. Originally from China and used for main parts of sentences such as nouns and verbs and for Japanese names. Each character represents one word. For example, the second character in the row here means "river."

Katakana. Used for writing words in Japanese that came from other languages. Each katakana character represents a phonetic syllable. For example, the second character in the row here represents the phonetic syllable "shi."

Hiragana. Used for writing verb endings, adverbs, conjunctions, and various particles. Each character represents one phonetic syllable. For example, the second character in the row here represents the phonetic syllable "u."

Calligraphy by Setoguchi Aya .

Japanese elementary educators are so successful in their efforts to teach such a difficult language for a variety of reasons. Thanks to the efforts of millions of mothers what is called "readiness" by educators is present in Japanese children regarding language. Many children have learned hiragana by the time they enter the first-grade classroom.

There are also clear benchmarks established by the Mombushō for development of written language skills. These guidelines are closely followed by teachers throughout Japan. First-graders, in addition to being responsible for mastering hiragana and most katakana, are expected by school year's end to have learned seventy-six kanji, including words requiring two characters such as "teacher" and "school." Second-graders learn 145 new kanji. Third-graders learn an additional 195 new characters. This add-on by grade-level process repeats itself until students are responsible for having learned a total of 996 kanji by the end of the sixth grade. The combinations of kanji, hiragana, and katakana can be used to form many thousands of words.

Teachers and children learn their language through relatively uninspired but extensive and regular practice. Japanese students do repetitive writing drills and are frequently tested. Teachers don't use ability grouping in Japanese language or any other subject. Teachers often have the class read entire passages out loud in language lessons. This technique appears quite unusual, to say the least ,for the foreign visitor who has never before heard such a collective sound!

Virtually all Japanese adults have inculcated to some extent an appreciation for the written language and understand the great effort required to learn Japanese. Elementary youngsters, in their efforts to succeed in this mammoth childhood task, are supported by not only mothers and teachers but the larger society as well. Written Japanese is not only a means of communication, but is also an art form. Shuji, or calligraphy, has long been held in high esteem in Japan. Every elementary student as part of the writing curriculum learns to write with a brush and a pen or pencil. Displays of student shuji are a regular visual feature of the Japanese elementary school landscape. Communities and cities sponsor calligraphy competition involving all schools. The aesthetic as well as utilitarian emphasis that Japanese educators place on the written language fosters in many children a widespread appreciation for their written language.

Several national newspapers publish daily editions for elementary students that are delivered to homes throughout Japan. The newspapers contain articles for both lower and upper elementary school students and provide invaluable language skills reinforcement. The results of this massive literacy effort speak for themselves.[16]

Japanese elementary children are known worldwide for their consistent top-ranking performance on international mathematics tests. Although time spent on arithmetic is similar in Japanese elementary schools to those of other nations, mathematics classroom instruction in Japan is relatively sophisticated.

As with the language, the task of Japanese teachers in assisting students to master arithmetic is made much easier by parents and the larger society. The Japanese economic "miracle" is in part due to the high mathematics ability levels of ordinary people. Most Japanese consider mathematics knowledge to be a crucial survival skill. Many parents send elementary youngsters to private juku after school for instruction in mathematics and Japanese language. Radio and television programs on arithmetic for elementary youngsters are broadcast throughout the nation.

A major reason for the world-leading performance of Japanese students in mathematics is that elementary teachers are in general quite competent in the subject. In an interview with the author, one Japanese university mathematics education professor contended there was little difference in the mathematics ability level of the typical first-grade teacher in his country when compared to that of a typical Japanese high school teacher.[17] Also, because of the high pay and prestige of teaching there is no shortage of qualified mathematics instructors in Japanese elementary schools.

Teachers are assisted in mathematics instruction by the clear guidelines established by the Mombushō. The guidelines provide for a step-by-step sequential pattern of instruction during the elementary years. Once they begin first grade, Japanese children are introduced to mathematics concepts at earlier

---

[16] Description of national elementary-level reading campaign based on Duke, The Japanese School: Lessons for Industrial America, 51-81; and Harold Stevenson, "Learning to Read," Child Development and Education in Japan, 217-235.

[17] Interview with mathematics education faculty of Aichi University of Education, Aichi Prefecture, at Aichi University Attached Elementary School, June 1, 1990.

ages than is the case in the United States. Japanese children have learned multiplication tables through unison rote chanting by the end of the second grade. Decimals and fractions are also taught to children in Japan at an earlier age than American youngsters.

In addition to collective chanting of multiplication tables, there are several other unique aspects of Japanese elementary mathematics instruction. Beginning in first grade, teachers place a great deal of emphasis upon students working problems without pen and paper. By third grade Japanese children in calculations employ the abacus, or soroban. The soroban is an ancient device where beads are manipulated by hand. Although such a device seems archaic, Japanese educators believe the process visually reinforces arithmetic concepts in the minds of children. Surprisingly, given the amount of repetition employed in most Japanese instruction, elementary teachers assign students few repetitive math problems. Mathematics textbooks tend to not include numerous examples of similar problems. Japanese teachers spend significant amounts of time in class explaining concepts rather than in engaging children in solving a large number of similar problems. Elementary educators assume that if a child is having difficulty with a particular kind of problem he will receive extra help on the concept at home without the teacher being required to give an additional assignment.

The long Japanese school year and relatively short summer vacation also help students to retain mathematics as well as other subject matter. Teachers spend almost no time in the beginning of a school term upon review of the previous year's work.[18]

In addition to Japanese language and mathematics, science and social studies are the other two major academic subject areas studied by all elementary grades. Beginning in 1992 science and social studies were abolished as separate subjects for the first two grades and a new course entitled "Living Studies," was implemented in Japanese elementary schools. The living studies course is intended to be an integration of science and social studies. Curricular emphasis is placed upon practical problems such as pollution, transportation, and the preservation of certain animal species and wilderness areas. Given the classroom strategies elementary teachers in science and social studies courses have

---

[18] Duke, The Japanese School: Lessons for Industrial America, 81-120; and Japanese Education Today, 31.

employed in the past in both the lower and upper grades, it is likely that living studies will consist of more than just textbook learning.

Year after year Japanese children in international science tests rank at or near the top. Researchers in science education identify two major reasons Japanese children do so well. Elementary teachers strongly emphasize experimental and lab-oriented science in classroom instruction. It is estimated that in the elementary years children spend one-third of their science class time conducting experiments. Also, Japanese elementary teachers put forth considerable effort to develop positive feelings in children toward science.

The elementary science curriculum in the lower grades begins with rudimentary information pertaining to plant and animal life and progresses to more sophisticated earth and life science by the fifth and sixth grades. Typical Mombushō primary level science objectives contain language such as the following statement: "Pupils should notice the ways of living and growth of the living things, and experience the pleasure of intimacy with them while searching for and raising living things found in their surroundings." Mombushō officials emphasize practical science for young children. Teachers are encouraged in the written guidelines to have students understand how living things grow and experience the pleasure and intimacy of raising living things in the classroom environment.[19]

Virtually every lower elementary class learns rudimentary zoology lessons by keeping pet fish or hamsters. The teacher ensures that all children work with the animals by making different groups of students responsible for their care and feeding. It is also quite common for elementary classes to learn valuable lessons about botany through cultivating flower and vegetable gardens or even rice paddies on the school grounds. Japanese educators believe that a practical approach to science instruction helps many children to be more comfortable with the subject later in life.

The cultivation of positive attitudes toward science in children is also enhanced by other factors outside school. Throughout Japan a series of magazines on science for elementary schoolers is widely available. The monthly circulation of one of the most popular magazines series, Kagaku no Zasshi, or Science

---

[19] Course of Study for Elementary Schools (Tōkyō: Ministry of Education, Science, and Culture, 1983), 57.

Magazine, which also features an accompanying kit, is between fifty-five and sixty million! Researchers estimate that Kagaku no Zasshi reaches about one-half of the households who have elementaty school children.[20]

American Occupation officials imposed social studies upon the Japanese after World War II. Occupation authorities believed that social studies, including civics, "problems of democracy," and economics, was more appropriate to building a democratic society than the study of only history and geography, which had been the case in prewar schools. In many ways contemporary Japanese social studies resembles the American version of the subject. Beginning in third grade, social studies is a separate subject from science. During the first three years they study the subject, Japanese children learn about the geography of their community and about the economy and government of their local region. Sixth-graders learn Japanese history.

International comparative achievement data on social studies is extremely rare compared to subjects such as science and mathematics. However, classroom observations indicate that contrary to what occurs later in the careers of Japanese students, elementary social studies instruction includes numerous group projects, hands-on activities, and field trips such as the community mapping exercise described at the beginning of this chapter.

The foreign media often depicts Japanese education as largely a process of rote memorization on the part of students. While in the case of writing and, to a lesser extent, mathematics this stereotype is true of elementary schools, much less rote memorization occurs in the first years of schooling in Japan than at the secondary level. A visitor to a typical elementary Japanese science or social studies classroom with a preconceived notion that Japanese education consists entirely of rote memorization and submissive students is likely to be quite shocked by the constant hustle and bustle and buzz of student activity. Most Japanese youngsters in these subjects seem to have fun as they learn.

Perhaps because of publicity about Japanese literacy and mathematics achievement and about the "examination race" many foreigners have the impression that Japanese schools neglect subjects such as music, the arts, homemaking, and physical education. While these subjects get less attention in

---

[20] Presentation by Professor Kay Michael Troost of the North Carolina State University Sociology Department to the National Science Foundation in Washington, D.C. on April 13, 1983.

some Japanese junior and senior high schools, this is not the case in elementary schools.

Music in particular is an integral part of the elementary school core curriculum. Music teachers are elementary educators who have formal music training even though they might teach other subjects in addition to music. Topics include singing, instrumental performance, and an appreciation of both Western and Japanese music. All Japanese elementary children learn to play small wind and keyboard instruments. All students also hear a common core of Japanese composers' work as well as such Western music as Bach, Handel, Beethoven, and Schubert.

Japanese elementary children study art and physical education. Elementary students learn printmaking, sculpture, and drawing and a variety of games and sports including swimming. The large majority of Japanese elementary schools have pools. Two hours a week of instruction for both fifth- and sixth-grade boys and girls in homemaking, and the one-hour-per-week class in moral education described earlier, complete the formal curriculum which every Japanese youngster studies during the elementary school years.[21]

But in schools anywhere, the formal curriculum is only one part of what a child learns in school. The attitudes of teachers, parents, and even older students about not only what is important to know but what constitutes appropriate behavior as well is a portion of schooling that educators call the informa, or "hidden" curriculum.

A large amount of agreement exists in Japanese society about what should constitute the informal curriculum. The Japanese educator's attempt to socialize children to appropriate behavior is usually quite formal and structured. There is great continuity between the highly regarded societal values adults stressed to preschool children and how elementary Japanese children are taught to conduct themselves.

---

[21] Description of music and physical education taken from Japanese Education Today, 31; and Frank Abdoo, "Music Education in Japan," Music Educator's Journal 70, no. 6 (February 1984): 52-56.

Learning Appropriate Behavior in Japanese Elementary Schools

One American researcher who spent extensive time in Japanese first-grade classrooms described the entire experience as "...at times more reminiscent of a scout meeting or of Sunday School than of a first-grade classroom."[22] This reaction is accurate. Even though teachers introduce academic subjects to first-graders, they also spend a large amount of time in the first year of school and in the lower grades inculcating in youngsters what most Japanese consider to be appropriate values.

Usually Japanese feel the learning process consists first and foremost of mastery of the "right" procedures. Much more than in many countries, every art, skill, or subject has a right technique. Before a student can advance, he or she must spend much time mastering the "right" fundamental procedures. The same is true for the art of being an elementary school student.

In one study almost all Japanese first-grade teachers mentioned nonacademic, procedural skills when asked what were the most important things children needed to learn during the first month of school. Examples include appropriate ways to store a cap, arrange a desk, wash hands, use the bathroom, walk in the halls, sit properly, and store and pack and unpack a backpack. Teachers reported they spend two to three weeks teaching first-graders to "...live at school" before even beginning academic work.[23]

Teacher and parents consider the inculcation of an enthusiastic attitude in children for work, regardless of the task, as very important. Japanese children learn early in elementary school to exhibit the appropriate amount of enthusiasm and effort. School periods begin and end with opening and closing greetings by the class to the teacher. Teachers encourage children to almost shout these greetings in order to demonstrate their enthusiasm. The same is true of the morning roll call with each child expected to answer in a loud voice, "I'm here," when his or her name is called. If the response is too soft, a teacher might ask the child if he or she is feeling well.

[22] Catherine Lewis, "Japanese First Grade Classrooms: Implications for U.S. Theory and Research," Comparative Education Review 32, no. 2 (May 1988): 170.

[23] Ibid., 166-167. Japanese elementary students don't usually wear uniforms, but have identical caps and satchels.

The stress on enthusiasm and right effort in elementary school reflects a deep societal ideal that Japanese adults often point out to youngsters. Everyone has about the same ability, but those people who succeed in life are particularly enthusiastic and put forth greater effort than those who fail.

Just as in preschool, student groups are an integral part of the affective and cognitive life of the Japanese elementary school student. Each kūmi, or class, of forty to forty-five youngsters is with the same teacher for two or sometimes three years. Teachers divide the kūmi into hans, or small groups, of five or six children. Hans usually remain together five to six months before rotation. The kūmi and hans constitute self-contained units through the school day, learning, eating, and playing together. Teachers deliberately place students of different socioeconomic backgrounds in hans in order to assist them to feel more at ease with groups that contain different kinds of youngsters. Teachers assign both homework and chores to hans. Hans transport food to and from the classroom, clean parts of the room, and perform other jobs on a rotating basis. Each han has a child leader who is usually elected by fellow han members. Han leaders are responsible for checking small group attendance in various situations such as field trips. Han leaders also organize class reports the teacher assigns to the group.

Japanese youngsters learn to function in small groups through membership in the kūmi and han. Lessons about the importance of hierarchy also constitute important components of the kūmi-han arrangement as Japanese children learn to respond to the commands of their peers who are in leadership positions. As in kindergarten, much of the discipline in Japanese elementary schools is peer discipline. The teacher usually exercises authority indirectly whenever possible. Japanese elementary children who are reminded by a peer to prepare day packs correctly or to not be slow when picking up the class food from the lunchroom are likely to find such admonitions much less threatening than if an adult were making similar demands.[24]

Even though hierarchy and deference to leaders is important in Japan, so is the development of a spirit of egalitarianism. Japanese believe such a spirit is vital to an individual if he or she is to contribute to team play and group harmony. The policies of Japanese elementary schools support this value. Not only are

---

[24] Ibid., 168-172. For an indepth discussion of the kūmi and han in the elementary school see Duke, The Japanese School: Lessons for Industrial America, 25-49.

77

children not ability grouped, but virtually all children are passed through the grades. Japanese educators believe to hold youngsters back is to risk instilling feelings of inferiority in children. While these practices work well for the most part, they do create some problems. In almost every school there are a few students who find much of the content largely incomprehensible in their grade since they did not master previous material. In part because of strong societal beliefs about egalitarianism and group conformity, gifted children are not challenged in Japanese elementary classrooms.

The Elementary Juku Experience

Japanese elementary schools are generally pleasant environments for youngsters. However, the examination hurdles children later face in lower and upper secondary schools and some parents' desire to cultivate their children's skills in areas outside the elementary curriculum have caused the number of private after-school schools, or juku, to grow in Japan in recent years.

Recent Mombushō surveys indicate that while only a little over 6 percent of all first-grade children attend juku, the figure is 30 percent for all sixth-graders. Contrary to some foreign and Japanese reports, a large number of Japanese elementary youngsters do not attend juku to prepare for examinations. Instead they receive special instruction in piano, violin, tennis, or swimming. As a rule elementary students usually attend juku twice a week.[25]

Among academic subjects, the most popular elementary juku class appears to be conversational English. English is usually taught at this level, as illustrated by the case study at the beginning of the chapter, in an enjoyable manner. The objective is personal enrichment not examination success. Although most elementary students attend juku for enrichment purposes only, a very small minority of students are preparing for prestigious private junior high schools that offer excellent preparation for later entrance into elite secondary schools and universities. These youngsters take subjects such as Japanese language or mathematics in juku. Still, the pressure-packed juku of media fame usually affects the lives of junior and senior high Japanese students and not elementary youngsters.

---

[25] Japanese Education Today, 33.

78

The End of the Elementary Years

Just as a rather elaborate ceremony marks the child's entrance into the elementary school family, the same is true when he or she departs. In virtually every elementary school in Japan ,graduating students proceed into the graduation ceremonies in <u>kūmi</u> formation. At the ceremony the students are introduced as a <u>kūmi</u>, with their teacher reading individual names as each young person walks to the stage to receive the diploma. After the ceremony each <u>kūmi</u> goes outside for the final group picture. Graduation is a sad, yet happy time, for most elementary youngsters. [26]

The organization of the closing ceremony is again indicative of the important place value development holds in Japanese elementary education. The great two triumphs of Japan's elementary schools are that most students finish sixth grade understanding both academics and proper Japanese behavior. Many consider the fact that most Japanese elementary classrooms are warm and nurturing environments a third triumph. This warm classroom climate to a large extent disappears in the next stage of formal education in Japan.

---

[26] Duke, <u>The Japanese School: Lessons for Industrial America</u>, 39.

Questions for Comparison

1. Those in Japan who choose elementary teaching as a career are motivated in part to do so by the relatively high pay, status, and job security the profession offers. How do the factors listed above influence Americans who are considering elementary teaching as a career?

2. Comparisons of the mathematics knowledge of Japanese and U.S. elementary teachers indicate that Japanese teachers know substantially more mathematics. U.S. elementary teachers also fare poorly in mathematics knowledge when compared to their Western European counterparts? What might be several federal, state, or local public policy options to improve the mediocre and poor knowledge of mathematics of many U.S. elementary teachers?

3. Approximately 78 percent of Americans are functionally literate while estimates of Japanese literacy rates run as high as 99 percent. Based on your knowledge of American and Japanese early childhood and elementary education, can you identify any educational practices in or out of school that might contribute to Japanese national literacy success? Based on what you know of American early childhood education can you identify any American early childhood and elementary educational practices in or out of school that might inhibit the development of literacy?

4. In what ways does the administrative and financial structure of American public elementary education differ from what exists in Japan?

5. Based on virtually all comparative test data, Japanese elementary students do significantly better in elementary school than their American counterparts. How much is the performance of students in both countries a result of unique aspects of each society's culture? What are examples of cultural factors outside elementary school in both countries that influence academic performance.

Additional Reading

Although in the 1980s a large number of books were written about education in the United States, the sections on contemporary American elementary schools in John Goodlad, <u>A Place Called School</u>, McGraw-Hill, 1983, are particularly insightful. No single work on Japanese elementary schools is as helpful to the reader as the chapters on elementary schools in Benjamin Duke, <u>The Japanese School: Lessons for Industrial America</u>, Praeger, 1986; and Merry White, <u>The Japanese Educational Challenge: A Commitment to Children</u>, The Free Press, 1987.

Chapter Four

The Education of Japanese Adolescents

Introduction: Junior and Senior High Scenes

Kāmakurā is a beautiful city of 173,000 people overlooking the ocean and located less than one hour by train from Tōkyō. The small city was once the political center of Japan during the height of <u>samurai</u> influence and is still important in Japanese Buddhism. Kāmākura offers the many tourists impressive temples, beautiful gardens, the awesome Daibutsu, or Great Buddha, and wonderful scenes of the sea from atop verdant hills.

Although Kāmākura is popular with tourists year-round, the city is particularly crowded in the late spring. In May other tourists are greatly outnumbered by a sea of uniformed junior high youngsters. Even though the students visiting in Kāmākura are mainly from lower secondary schools, the uniforms are common attire for both junior and senior high students during all but the warmer months of the year. Boys wear black trousers and military-type tunics with stand-up collars and gold buttons. Girls wear navy blue sailor blouses and matching skirts. All the youngsters wear grade and class badges.

The daily Kāmākura scene is noisy each May with literally thousands of junior high students from throughout Japan being shepherded by teachers from one temple to another. These youngsters, almost all third-year students, are on a three-night and four-day excursion to famous places in Japan's history such as Kāmākura, Kyōto, and Nāra to learn about the history and culture of their country.

This excursion occurs in all Japanese junior highs. It is part of a series of messages adolescents learn in their formal schooling about what it is to be Japanese.

Other powerful messages about what it means to be Japanese and what constitutes culturally appropriate behavior are also conveyed to students every day in junior high classrooms. The following junior high classroom scene in Moriwa, a Nagoya suburb, is typical of almost any junior high throughout Japan.

The class is Japanese history for second-year junior high students. The forty youngsters are dressed in summer uniforms because it is June. The boys wear short-sleeve white shirts and black trousers and the girls are attired in navy blue sailor-type dresses. All students rise and bow as the casually dressed teacher, who is a young man about thirty, enters the classroom. Everyone but the teacher then sits down and work begins. Since it is early summer, the room is quite warm. Even though the school is located in an affluent community, there is no air conditioning. The classroom itself is a quite drab place with no art work or colorful bulletin boards on display.

The subject of today's lecture is the influence of early China on Japanese history. The teacher lectures throughout the entire period, pausing every few minutes to write names and dates on the board which students copy in their notebooks. Before the class is over the teacher has filled a large chalkboard at least twice with various historical facts, pausing to erase as youngsters finish copying the information.

Students follow the teacher's presentation in paperback history texts that are filled with graphs and charts as well as narrative. At no point in the fifty-minute class do any students ask questions, although the teacher stops three or four times and questions particular students. Each time a student is called upon, he or she rises to answer. All of the teacher's questions ask students to cite specific facts rather than to engage in more in-depth responses.

Although a few students look bored and there is some whispering in the back of the room, on the whole the class is quite orderly. At the end of the class the students rise again and bow to the teacher. Framed Chinese characters that admonish students to "Make a Strong Effort Without Fail" occupy a prominent place on the wall behind the teacher's desk. In addition to content, students receive, both from the routine they follow and the teacher's demeanor, clear value messages. In Japanese society, secondary students are expected to understand that schooling is serious business and demands continual concentration, attention, and effort.[1]

School becomes such a serious affair at the secondary level in Japan because it is then that the sorting process begins in earnest. Policy makers have designed secondary education in such a manner that stratification of young Japanese in order to determine future educational and vocational opportunities is one of the most important functions of formal education at this level.

The first official "sort" occurs during the last year of junior high school as students take examinations to determine what kind of high school they will be allowed to enter. Although approximately 95 percent of Japanese students go on to high school, the kind of upper secondary school one attends is a crucial determinant of the quality of later opportunities in life.

By 1988 almost 74 percent of high school students attended academic high schools or enrolled in academic programs at comprehensive high schools which prepared them for university. Approximately 25 percent of Japanese adolescents attended commercial or industrial high schools or enrolled in vocational programs at comprehensive high schools.[2] The latter schools and programs are designed to prepare students either for work after graduation or for advanced vocational training. The manner in which subjects are taught in academic and vocational high schools varies substantially. Some of the differences are illustrated in the following descriptions of English classes in an academic and a vocational high school.

Handā High School, located in a small town about one hour from Nagoya, is the most famous public high school in Aichi Prefecture. Many Handā students go on to top national and private universities. A majority of Handā students are male. The school building itself is austere looking, but impressive and well-kept. The first sight that a visitor sees upon entering is an enormous trophy case located near the principal's office. It contains numerous academic and athletic trophies.

---

[1] Descriptions of specific classes, teachers, and student life in this chapter, unless otherwise noted, are based on author's observations in Japan during May and June 1990.

[2] Education in Japan 1989: A Graphic Presentation, 26-27.

The forty-five students in a third-year English class at Handā are attired in summer uniforms almost identical to what students wore in the junior high described earlier. The class learns English by direct translation, the technique employed by the overwhelming majority of teachers in academic high schools. The teacher translates rather sophisticated written passages and the students quietly copy the translations in their notebooks. Students also translate written passages at their seats while the teacher monitors their work by walking around the classroom.

The classroom is characterized by complete order and no questions from students. During the entire period no one speaks English. Later attempts by the foreign visitor to speak English with students result in largely uncomprehending stares from these teenagers, all of whom are academically well above average by Japanese standards.

Teachers devote little time at Handā, or any other academic high school in Japan, to imparting conversational skills to students. Although virtually all Handā students will pass an English examination to enter a top-ranked university, presently only one prestigious public university has an English conversation test. Therefore, it is mastery of written not spoken English that is important to these students' futures.[3]

The visitor to Seiyrō Commercial High School, one of three Commercial High Schools in the large city of Nagoya, will quickly find that the school's physical appearance, classroom activities, and student body are quite different than Handā. Located in a poor section of the city, Seiyrō is a much older and dingier looking school than Handā. Also, 90 percent of the students are female. Most Seiyrō students go directly to work after graduation for banks, small companies, or if they are lucky, for Toyota Motor Company, which has major facilities in a nearby town.

The scene inside a third-year English class at Seiyrō is a lively one. The teacher, a young woman who spent time in the United States as an exchange student, has her students singing English songs. Several girls are not at all reluctant to try their English out on the foreign visitor. Although the level of spoken English is not particularly impressive, many more students attempt to

---

[3] Tōkyō University, as of the publication date of this book, had recently added a conversational component to the English language entrance examination.

speak the language than was the case with Handā students. The teacher also reports that she uses English language jokes and cartoons with students and includes a major conversational component in her classes. She is free to do this because, unlike Handa students, Seiyrō students' futures do not depend upon university examination scores.

The profound differences in academic and vocational programs--the educational sorting process, field trips for junior high students, rote memorization, and widespread use of uniforms--are not accidents. Adults have deliberately constructed these and other aspects of Japan's secondary educational system to, first and foremost, prepare each new generation of young people to do their part in keeping Japan prosperous. Although this preparation process begins when Japanese children are quite small, it first becomes extremely intense for most students during the junior high years. It is at that level we begin our overview of Japanese secondary education.

The Context for Junior High Education

During the Occupation the Japanese adopted the American concept of the junior high school. Chūgakkō, the Japanese name for junior high school may also be translated as lower secondary school. Since compulsory education is mandated throughout Japan through the ninth grade, which is the third and last year of lower secondary school, virtually the entire age cohort attends junior high school. Over 95 percent of lower secondary school students attend neighborhood public schools.[4]

Primarily because attendance is compulsory for all students in Japan, the administrative and financial organization of lower secondary school education is quite similar to that of elementary education. Despite Mombushō's great power, municipal school boards and local educational authorities also have substantial administrative responsibility for public lower secondary schools. These responsibilities include establishment, maintenance, and abolishment of schools; the adoption of textbooks based on a list of choices approved by Mombushō; and

---

[4] Education in Japan 1989: A Graphic Presentation, 22.

86

appointment, dismissal, and inservice education of teachers. Lower secondary school teachers, however, are certified at the prefectural level.[5]

Funding for lower secondary schools is divided into roughly equal portions among national, prefectural, and local governments. The national government, since it funds half the salaries of teachers in compulsory education schools, pays slightly over 31 percent of the total costs for public lower secondary schools. Prefectural governments fund slightly over 34 percent of public lower secondary school costs and local governments are responsible for the remaining 29 percent of total costs. Although instruction and textbooks in compulsory schools are free, parents of lower secondary school students in Japan pay the equivalent of about $600 annually per student. Parental contributions include various school fees and the costs of school uniforms.[6]

Japanese lower secondary school teachers by international standards are well paid, experienced, and highly qualified. The salary scales of lower secondary teachers are identical to that of their elementary counterparts. The basic national salary schedule is supplemented by a yearly bonus. Various allowances are also available for teachers based upon where they live, the number of their dependents, whether they commute, their housing costs, and other conditions.

In Japan, beginning teacher salaries are somewhat lower than those of teachers in several other developed nations. However, the steady climb in salary throughout a career causes average Japanese teacher salaries to be higher than those of several Western countries including the United States.[7]

Because of generous salaries and the high prestige of teaching, turnover rates among lower secondary teachers, as is true with their elementary and high school counterparts, is extremely low. Intense competition exists for positions. By 1989 approximately 60 percent of lower secondary school teachers had ten or more years of classroom experience. Although approximately 20 percent of present lower secondary school teachers entered the classroom after finishing two-year colleges, almost all of this group are older teachers. It is now virtually

---

[5] Ibid., 34.

[6] Ibid., 54.

[7] Willis D. Hawley, "The Education of Japanese Teachers: Lessons for the United States," in Fit to Teach: Teacher Education in International Perspective, ed. Edgar B. Gumbert (Georgia State University, 1990), vol. 8, 33.

impossible to obtain a lower secondary teaching job without a university degree. Slightly over two-thirds of all lower secondary school teachers are men. This is a significant change from the gender distribution ratio in Japanese elementary schools.[8]

Local school building-level administration is similar in the Japanese lower secondary school to both elementary and high schools. Two people, a principal and a head teacher, are responsible for school leadership. Almost all these positions are filled by men. Both principals and head teachers are, as is true of elementary administrators, over the age of fifty.

The Junior High School Curriculum: Subjects and Pedagogy

Japanese lower secondary students take a broad array of subjects. Mombushō, as is the case with elementary and upper secondary schools, determines what courses Japanese students take. In junior high, as in elementary schools, no tracking occurs. All students, regardless of their future plans, study the same subjects.

The following table depicts the Mombushō Course of Study which was formulated in July 1977 and implemented in April 1981. This course of study will be changed slightly in April 1993 as reflected in the bracketed numbers.

As in elementary school, the Japanese language, because it is so difficult, occupies the largest amount of student time of any other subject. Lower secondary students are required to learn another 1,000 kanji in addition to the 1,000 they learned in elementary school. This means that the young person who finishes nine years of school in Japan has theoretically learned 2,000 characters.

The ability to read and write hiragana, katakana, and 2,000 kanji, which Mombushō defines as basic literacy, enables a person to read a newspaper. In addition to kanji memorization, students in Japanese language class continue to study composition and grammar. Junior high students are also introduced to classical Japanese and Chinese literature and learn to read short, relatively easy passages in the archaic literary form.

Mathematics ranks second only to the Japanese language in the lower secondary school curriculum. In junior high all students study principles of

---

[8] Education in Japan 1989: A Graphic Presentation, 78.

88

Table 3

Prescribed Subjects and Number of School Hours
in Lower Secondary School

	Grade		
	I	II	III
Required Subjects			
Japanese Language	175	140	140
Social Studies	140	140	105 (70~105)
Mathematics	105	140	140
Science	105	105	140 (105~140)
Music	70	70 (35~70)	35
Fine Arts	70	70 (35~70)	35
Health and Physical Education	105	105	105 (105~140)
Industrial Arts and Homemaking	70	70	105 (70~105)
Moral Education	35	35	35
Special Activities	70 (35~70)	70 (35~70)	70 (35~70)
Elective Subjects	105 (105~140)	105 (105~210)	140 (140~280)
Total	1050	1050	1050

Notes:
1. One unit school hour is a class period of 50 minutes.
2. The numbers enclosed in brackets are the number of school hours for the new course of education to be enforced from April 1993.

Source:
Education in Japan 1989: A Graphic Presentation, 61.

algebra, probability, statistics, and some geometry. When they finish junior high, all Japanese students have studied algebra through factoring, the plotting of quadratic equations and the geometry of circles, the Pythagorean theorem, and some basic solid geometry.

During first-year lower secondary school science class, students study the properties of substances and their reactions, force, plant and animal ecology, and the solar system. Second-year students study atoms and molecules and their influence on chemical reactions, electricity, cellular processes, microscopic organisms, and weather change processes. Third-year students study the interrelationship of motion, energy, and work; ions and ionic substances; ecology; photosynthesis and bio-organic processes; and rock types and geologic formations. As in elementary school, the Japanese junior high science curriculum includes a great deal of experiments and other applied science activities.[9]

In junior high social studies first-year students study geography while second-year students take history. Although the emphasis in both years is on Japan, there are also international components. Students learn about Japan's relations with several foreign countries. Third-year lower secondary civics is actually a political economy class. Students study government and politics and the Japanese economic system.

A few years ago American and Japanese researchers conducted an extensive analysis of American and Japanese lower and upper secondary school social studies texts. Japanese texts, although they contained considerably fewer pages than American books, included many more sophisticated charts, graphs, and other quantitative data. For example, typical information common to a Japanese civics text might include graphs on rates of industrial output over the last seventy years for the five leading world economies or consumer prices in leading industrialized countries over the last twenty years.[10]

Although Mombushō requirements describe English as an "elective," nearly all lower secondary schools require three years of English language instruction. In Japan "electives" are often choices that are not made by students

---

[9] Japanese Education Today, 34-35.

[10] James Becker and Tokuyama Masato, eds., In Search of Mutual Understanding: Joint Japan-United States Textbook Study Project (National Council for the Social Studies, 1981).

but are courses selected by school principals according to prefectural guidelines. English is a widespread requirement in Japanese junior high schools for two reasons. The subject is part of high school and university entrance examinations. Also, Japan has extensive interactions with English-speaking countries.

Despite recent efforts of the Japanese government and Mombushō to place more emphasis upon spoken English, a student's written command of the English language is what counts on high school and university entrance examinations. Therefore, grammatical analysis, translation, practice with basic sentence patterns and vocabulary memorization are, by far, the major activities students engage in during lower secondary school English classes.

As in elementary schools, lower secondary school students take a wide variety of other courses in addition to "academic" subjects. These include moral education, music, fine arts, health and physical education, industrial arts, and homemaking.

Many Japanese are particularly proud of their public school music program. All lower secondary students take music from teachers who only teach that subject. Junior high students study and participate in such areas of music as singing, music history, theory, and conducting. In second-year lower secondary school, students study such great Western conductors as Claude Debussy and Ludwig Von Beethoven. They learn biographical information and listen to the greatest works of a composer. Students repeat the same process during the last year of lower secondary school. However, the major focus is upon traditional Japanese music and composition.

Even though both elementary and lower secondary school students take a wide variety of subjects, the teaching styles lower secondary school students encounter are substantially different than in elementary school.

The daily schedule is virtually identical in all Japanese lower secondary schools. From Monday through Friday there are six daily periods that each last fifty minutes. On Saturdays class schedules are reduced to fit the half-day schedule. Students, who are allowed a ten-minute break between classes, remain in one room and teachers move from class to class.

Activities within the junior high classroom, and even classroom decor, are quite unlike Japanese kindergarten and elementary schooling. Junior high students, unlike many elementary youngsters, tend to ask few questions. Junior high teachers lecture most of the time. In most Japanese junior high classrooms students lack almost any chance to express opinions about whatever is studied. Unlike elementary schools, student and teacher spontaneity is largely absent in the Japanese junior high classroom. Lower secondary teachers, although they only teach three or four classes a day and theoretically have time to construct creative learning activities for students, almost never develop such activities.

Instead, junior high teachers in class presentations make extensive use of detailed print teacher guides provided by Mombushō. In addition to teacher lecture, other student activities in lower secondary classrooms, regardless of subject, include drill, practice, and recitation. In contrast to elementary school, most lower secondary classrooms are purposeful, but more times than not, deadly dull places.

Even the physical surroundings reinforce the blandness of classroom activities. Although when viewed from the outside, both Japanese elementary and secondary schools have the antiseptic and colorless look of hospitals, many elementary classrooms are full of colorful artwork. With the exception of calligraphy, most Japanese secondary classrooms are quite drab. Many secondary teachers believe colorful classroom decorations disturb student concentration.

The physical surroundings and pedagogy of the junior high school are a reflection of both long-held views in Japanese society about the proper role and status of students and of modern examination realities. Confucian beliefs of the seriousness of education and the respective subordinate and superior roles of students and teachers still permeate contemporary Japanese educational institutions. Using Confucian logic as a point of reference, knowledge is to be imparted from teacher to student and is not something that adults and young people discover together. Therefore, there is usually no need for lower secondary students to ask the teacher questions in class. Instead, the proper student role is to listen, drill, practice, recite, and most of all, expend great effort. A good student is expected to soak up like a sponge information provided by teacher and textbook.

The examination system, described in detail in the next chapter, also profoundly influences teaching and learning in Japanese secondary school classrooms. Although during the compulsory education years there is no ability grouping and almost all students attend neighborhood schools, sorting begins with high school entrance examinations. All high schools occupy a clear rank on an unofficial but ever-present hierarchy present throughout Japan.

Admission to any high school is largely still determined by student performance on entrance examinations. The level of high school to which a particular student gains admission usually profoundly affects the rest of his or her life. Parents, young people, and other members of the larger society exert constant pressure on lower secondary school teachers and their high school teacher counterparts to concentrate on material that is included on high school and university entrance examinations.

Japanese secondary and university examinations overwhelmingly emphasize factual knowledge and not creativity of expression, analysis, or originality. Since doing well on future examinations is such a dominant goal for the majority of lower secondary school students and their teachers, "the facts" must be emphasized at the expense of other intellectual possibilities.

In junior high the educational results of classroom emphasis upon mastery of large amounts of factual material are mixed. As described earlier, graduates of Japanese lower secondary schools are, by international standards, quite well educated in subjects such as written languages and mathematics that are easily measurable by written examinations. However, there is tremendous concern by many Japanese that too little creativity is present in the secondary educational system because of this overemphasis on facts.

The Japanese value of groupism also exerts a powerful influence upon the intellectual lives of Japanese lower secondary students. Prevailing societal beliefs that Japanese as a people are more alike than different mean that in junior high all students are treated as having the same abilities. There are few provisions for diagnosis of learning disabilities or individualized instruction. Even though automatic promotion is an institutionalized component of compulsory education, every year a certain percentage of Japanese children fall further and further behind their peers.

These youngsters, called ochikobore in Japanese, which translates as "those who have fallen to the bottom," are often responsible for the increased school violence incidents in recent years in lower secondary schools. The plight of these students, along with the upcoming pressures of high school entrance examinations, makes the lower secondary school the most troubled level of Japanese K-12 schooling.

Still, youthful deviant behavior in Japan is far lower at all levels of schooling than is the case in other industrialized countries. A Confucianist heritage, as well as the importance of the secondary school experience as the major path to future success, causes order to be the rule rather than the exception in lower secondary schools. As described in earlier chapters, youngsters learn "appropriate" Japanese values at home and in their earlier school experiences. The process continues in lower secondary school. Along with parents, virtually the entire faculty of a typical lower secondary school engages in a constant effort to inculcate what are considered to be proper values in youth.[11]

The Lower Secondary School: Values and Student Life

Japanese lower secondary school students are organized into homerooms supervised by teachers. The homeroom teacher functions as advisor to the students and also assists in organizing various kinds of sports and music competition among homerooms. Although Japanese teachers lecture students on cultivation of proper values in homeroom meetings and the weekly moral education sessions, the total environment of the lower secondary school is probably an even more important influence on student value development.

Values such as group cooperation, loyalty, and appropriate deference to those of higher status are stressed in the daily routines of junior high schools. As in elementary and upper secondary school, all lower secondary students engage in weekly cleaning of the schools. The status and group cooperation lessons learned in kūmis and hans continue in lower secondary schools since students are still organized in these two divisions.

However, when lower secondary school life is examined, the importance of total individual effort regardless of the task, seems to receive particularly heavy emphasis. English phrases such as "total effort," or "commitment," are simply too weak to describe this value.

---

[11] Description of lower secondary school pedagogy and issues from Japanese Education Today, 35-37.

A better term is a Japanese one, gambare, which may best be translated as a combination of effort, perseverance, and tenacity. Not just in lower secondary schools, but throughout Japanese life, one constantly hears the exhortation, "gambere!," or "gambatte kudasai!." The importance placed upon memorization of factual material, the adult message to Japanese youngsters that they are all equal but it is individual effort that brings success, and the examples in moral education of famous individuals who triumphed over adversity all reinforce the importance of gambare. Such is also the case with Japanese extracurricular club activities. Club participation first becomes significant for youngsters during the lower secondary school years.

The typical lower secondary school has a variety of clubs. There are sports clubs including such traditional sports as judo, swimming, and Japanese fencing or kēndō, as well as Western team sport clubs such as baseball. Junior high schools also sponsor non-athletic clubs such as chess, flower arranging, tea ceremony, and music. There are two categories of clubs. Compulsory clubs, in which all students are required to participate, usually meet once a week. Voluntary clubs, which usually meet before or after school, are quite popular. Faculty members serve as sponsors or coaches of both compulsory and voluntary clubs.

It is in the voluntary clubs that the spirit of gambare is most cultivated. Since a major component of gambare is unrelenting effort, intense practice is an integral part of Japanese clubs. It is typical for voluntary clubs, whether basketball or theatre, to meet three to four days a week either before or after school, on weekends, and during summer vacation. It is extremely rare for a secondary student to belong to more than one voluntary club since to do so would be less than total commitment.

All club members are expected by both adults and peers to unquestionably accept all assigned tasks and exhibit total loyalty to the club. First-year lower secondary school students typically perform such menial tasks as retrieving foul balls in the baseball club or changing theatre sets in the drama club. They must do this enthusiastically and with no complaints. It is not unusual at all for young Japanese to develop such a sense of loyalty to a particular club that after graduation from lower or upper secondary school they return regularly to practices to assist or coach.

In addition to the values stressed through classroom academics and club activities, other special lower secondary school events throughout the year reinforce the "right" values in students and develop a sense of the uniqueness of being Japanese. Just as in elementary schools, the entry of new students to the junior high in the beginning of the school year is an occasion for special ceremony. The third-year class assumes responsibility during the first day for welcoming newcomers to the school community and assisting first-year students in orientation.

A major event for all third-year students which takes place in May is the three-night, four-day excursion to various parts of Japan ostensibly to study the history of Japan. This excursion, or shūgaku ryokō, which originated in the late 1880s is a universal rite of passage for Japanese. Uniformed students and their faculty chaperones visit such historic and cultural sites as Kāmākura, Kyōto, and Tōkyō. The deluge of facts about temples, shrines, and other cultural sites is probably peripheral to the affective lessons that are reinforced by this extracurricular activity.

The groupism lessons of Japanese schooling are applied in a new environment during the school excursion. The class moves through the excursion schedule in respective kūmis and hans with kūmi and han leaders and members engaged in mutual cooperation. Already existing bonds between classmates in each lower secondary school are strengthened by the excursion.

The individual's sense of being unique simply because he or she is Japanese grows as well because of excursions. The outing provides the opportunity each year for an entire future segment of the nation's citizenry to visit the most important national and cultural centers. Also, the excursion provides a last respite for the new third-year class before the stressful final year of lower secondary school in which preparation for senior high entrance examinations dominate all other considerations.[12]

Japanese students continue to do school work even during summer vacation since summer homework is compulsory in secondary schools. Club activities and class trips to resort areas are routine for first- and second-year junior high students.

---

[12] Kasāura Tatsūō, "A Century of School Excursions," Japan Quarterly xxxiv, no. 3 (July-September 1987): 287-290.

September 1 is the end of the summer vacation and the beginning of the second of three semesters in the school year. During the months that follow virtually every lower secondary school has an athletic meet and a school cultural festival. These events are largely planned by students. Group and status lessons, as well as the continual message of the importance of effort, are reinforced in the minds of youngsters as they spend long hours preparing for these highlights of the fall trimester.[13]

The final semester of the school year, which begins on January 8 and ends March 31, is marked by upper secondary school entrance examinations for third-year students and, finally, the graduation ceremony for that class. As they proceed to the ceremony in kumi formation, for most third-year students lower secondary school graduation is a particularly poignant occasion. Most will not be together again. The tracking process, thus far absent in Japanese education, begins the following year as students leave a homogeneous educational environment and enter one of two distinctly different tracks.

Upper Secondary School: The Transition

Even though the dropout rate after the compulsory education years is extremely low and over 93 percent of adolescents complete high school, upper secondary school structure in Japan is quite different than that of lower schools. Kōtōgakkō (in English, high school or upper secondary school) entrance is determined primarily by competitive examinations. There are different categories of high schools and the role of private high schools in Japanese education is substantial.

Although student preparation for entrance into a particular high school might start some time before, most young people make the most intense effort during the third year of junior high school. For third-year junior high students, club participation drops from over 90 percent to under 50 percent. Between 50 and 70 percent of third-year junior high students attend private after-school juku to prepare for high school entrance examinations. Even though the level of effort

---

[13] For an interesting first-hand account of life in Japanese lower secondary schools see Kāya Michiko, ed., The Life of a Junior High School Student (T ōkyō: International Society for Educational Information, 1985).

varies depending upon individual aspirations, many third-year lower secondary school students typically spend most of their summer vacations, holidays, weekends, and after-school time preparing for high school entrance examinations.[14]

Lower secondary school educators are most concerned about the upper secondary school entrance process of their third-year charges. Teachers of third-year students spend a considerable amount of classroom time either emphasizing content that is likely to appear on high school entrance examinations or administering practice tests to students. One researcher who closely monitored classroom activities of third-year students in a typical Japanese junior high found that third-year students took twenty examination practice tests in addition to examinations for grades and a Mombushō achievement test.[15]

Faculty efforts to assist students in the preparation process is not just limited to the classroom. Because the entry system is so structured that students can apply to only one public high school, teachers counsel a student to apply for the school to which he or she is most likely to be admitted. It is at this stage of formal education in Japan that status of schools by categories becomes extremely important.

·   Although during the Occupation the American goal was to institutionalize the comprehensive high school, this model is not dominant in contemporary Japan. Today approximately one-half of upper secondary schools are academic high schools. These schools, also known as general high schools, are designed only for those students who plan to attend university. Twenty-three percent of all secondary institutions are vocational high schools and only 28 percent of Japanese high schools offer both academic and vocational programs.

Currently in Japan the academic high school, or the academic program in a comprehensive high school, is the most common kind of upper secondary school experience for students. Almost 75 percent of students are enrolled in schools or programs where they are preparing for university. The large majority of the remainder of Japan's high school student population enroll in vocational high

---

[14] Japanese Education Today, 11 and 37.

[15] John Singleton, Nichū: A Japanese School; Case Studies in Education and Culture (Irvington Publishers, 1982), 39.

schools or programs. There are two major types of vocational high schools, commercial and industrial. A small percentage of young people are enrolled in other special schools.

Although in recent years, particularly in Tōkyō, the number of prestigious private high schools has increased, in general the more academically able students aspire to enter a public academic high school. Most public high schools have higher status and much lower costs than the typical private high school. The Japanese government, because of a belief by policy makers that all young people are not entitled to attend college preparatory secondary schools at public expense, deliberately limits the supply of public academic high schools. Only 40 percent of the five and one-half million students who attend upper secondary school can be accommodated in the public academic high schools.

Since most of the public high schools are administered by prefectures, each prefecture is divided into attendance zones. Each attendance zone contains a certain amount of public high schools and students who live in the zone usually choose one of the schools to attempt to enter. Although there are no official government rankings, in every attendance zone there is a clear hierarchy as to rankings of high schools. For academic schools the number of graduates who are admitted to prestigious universities is by far the major determinant of a school's status. A vocational high school's status is determined by where graduates are employed.

Examination construction for public upper secondary schools is primarily the responsibility of prefectural boards of education. The actual writing of questions is done by subject-area specialists who work for the board in each of the prefectures. Most prefectures test students in Japanese language, English, science, mathematics, and social studies. The examinations are held over a two-day period in late February or early March. Although the same examination is given at all public high schools in the prefecture, students sit for the examinations at the particular high school where they seek admission. The results are announced by each individual school about ten days to two weeks after students complete the examinations.

Although there are exceptions, those students who wish to attend a college-preparatory high school have two possible alternatives. The first and most preferable is to be accepted by a public high school by doing well on the entrance examination. If this objective is accomplished the student will save both his or her family considerable money and increase the chances of later gaining admission to a prestigious university. If a student who wishes to attend a general high school does not gain admittance to a public school, he or she can take an examination for a general private upper secondary school. The latter institutions are in general easier to enter than public schools, but are quite costly.

The combination of teacher counseling and student and family planning as to what school to attempt to enter usually works very well. As a rule because of counseling and a sophisticated practice test system, students know their odds of entering particular schools in their area quite well before they ever take examinations. Approximately 93 percent of all Japanese junior high graduates continue their education full-time in upper secondary school and another 2 percent of junior high graduates attend high school part-time. However, between 25 and 30 percent of students attend private high schools.[16]

Upper Secondary Schools: Administration and Teachers

The Mombushō is primarily responsible for setting national curriculum standards for high schools. However, unlike the case with elementary and lower secondary schools, the administration and financing of the large majority of Japan's public upper secondary schools is the responsibility of the 47 prefectural government boards of education. Prefectural governors are also empowered to approve the establishment or abolition of private schools.

National and municipal direct subsidies for public upper secondary schools and student fees account for only 14 percent of total costs. The prefectures finance the remaining 86 percent. Although private schools are largely self-supporting, the national government provides limited funds to the prefectures who, in turn, award grants to the private educational sector. Recent statistics indicate that each year parents of public upper secondary school students spend an average of $1,380 annually per student on school fees. In the case of

---

[16] Information about the transition from lower to upper secondary school from Japanese Education Today, 38-41; Education in Japan 1989: A Graphic Presentation, 22-27; Estelle James and Gail Benjamin, Public Policy and Private Education in Japan (St. Martin's Press Inc., 1988), 55-57; and David Berman, "A Case Study of the High School Entrance Examination in Chiba Prefecture, Japan," Theory and Research in Social Education xviii, no. 4 (Fall 1990): 387-404.

private schools the tuition paid by parents varies, but on average it is almost three times higher per student than is true of public schools. At the upper secondary school level these costs include textbooks. Unlike the situation in compulsory schools, high school students must buy their books.

Principals and teachers in public upper secondary schools are directly appointed by prefectural boards of education. A prospective teacher first obtains a certificate by meeting nationally established minimum requirements. He or she then must pass a rigorous prefectural examination to obtain an actual teaching position. As is true in lower schools, the relatively high salaries and prestige of teaching ensures a steady supply of applicants and intense competition for teaching positions.

Once appointed upper secondary school teachers, as is the case with lower school teachers, usually remain in the classroom. Currently almost two-thirds of all high school teachers have ten or more years experience. Salaries for upper secondary school teachers, which are based on national standards, are approximately 5 percent higher than their elementary and junior high counterparts.

Although it is still theoretically possible to obtain a second-class high school teacher's certificate with a junior college degree, virtually all new high school teacher appointees hold university degrees. Eighty-five percent of Japan's upper secondary school teachers now have university degrees and 6 percent hold master's degrees. High school teachers are much more likely to be male than their elementary and junior high counterparts. Men account for approximately 85 percent of the upper secondary school teaching force as compared to 26 percent of all elementary and 67 percent of all junior high teachers.[17] Japanese upper secondary school teachers also differ from their lower school counterparts in other respects. Although they take education courses and do student teaching during their university years, almost 90 percent of high school teachers, compared to two-thirds of junior high and one-third of elementary teachers, majored in an academic discipline other than education. High school teachers are much more likely than their lower school counterparts to think of themselves as subject matter specialists rather than professional educators.

---

[17] Education in Japan 1989: A Graphic Presentation, 78-79 and 82-85.

It is fairly common in Japan for high school teachers to do research in an academic field, write articles for professional journals, and to participate along with university professors in academic societies and organizations. In fact, a typical history or science teacher is much more likely to be friends with other history or science teachers in his community or city than with teachers of other academic disciplines in his school.

Even though variance exists among Japanese teachers as to intellectual ability, knowledge, and dedication, in general the nation's teaching force is its major educational asset. The following profiles of two teachers from the commercial and academic high schools described at the beginning of this chapter are illustrative of the abilities and personal characteristics exhibited by many Japanese high school teachers.

Kageto-sensei

Kageto Makoto is a friendly, stocky bearded man in his early forties who graduated from a prefectural university of education. He has taught microcomputing and business law for several years at Seiyō Commercial High School in Nagoya. Upon visiting Kageto's computer and business law classes the visitor is struck by how knowledgeable the teacher is of his subjects and of his genuinely kind and helpful interactions with his students, who are mostly young women. Although Kageto has a family and must commute over an hour one way to Seiyō, he often spends much extra time at the school assisting in extracurricular activities. During busy times, Kageto brings bedding material and occasionally stays overnight at school. Kageto was one of several Seiyō faculty who convinced school officials to allow students to have two school festivals rather than the once-a-year event common to most Japanese high schools. He argued the festivals helped school morale and provided Seiyō students a last opportunity to experience childlike fun before entering the world of work. The festivals which include art displays, student- and faculty-produced plays, skits, musical events, and sports are major affairs, and certain events are open to outside visitors. Kageto, who participated in a faculty singing group and organized several student skits, slept at the school several times during the last days before the spring festival began.

Kageto is impressive for his own intellectual accomplishments and aspirations, as well as for good teaching and positive interactions with students. Foreign languages are one of his hobbies. Kageto speaks creditable English and is extremely fluent in Chinese. Kageto learned the latter language on his own and through attending private classes. His desire is to not only speak Chinese but to also learn to read extremely difficult classic Chinese literature. He has accomplished both objectives through regular hard work on his own time. Kageto is also, unlike many younger Japanese, a serious practicing Zen Buddhist and rises every day at 4:00 a.m. to meditate in solitude for two hours. He feels this exercise is a vital foundation for cultivation of the appropriate warm relations with students.

Kageto worries that young Japanese know too little about Zen Buddhism and other aspects of traditional Japanese culture. He also feels Japanese youngsters watch too much television and that the latter medium is harmful to their creativity and willingness to learn.

Miyāhara-sensei

Miyāhara Satoru is a tall slender man in his late thirties who teaches contemporary society and politics-economics at Handā High School, one of the top public academic high schools in Aichi Prefecture. Miyāhara's contemporary society class on Adam Smith and basic market economics theory reminds the visitor of a university course. Miyāhara lectures on Adam Smith, the basic principles of The Wealth of Nations, and the contemporary significance of Smith's economics in a rapid but quite animated way. Unlike most classes in academic high schools, a few students even ask questions. Miyāhara, a graduate of the school where he teaches, also graduated from Nagoya University, one of the seven top public universities in Japan. He majored in economics while in university.

It is clear that Miyāhara, while a dedicated and popular teacher, thinks his academic interests require him to do more than simply engage in classroom instruction. Miyāhara is the author of several journal articles on economics and has co-authored economic education books used by other Japanese teachers. He is now working on his own book on economics. Miyāhara regularly attends and makes presentations at professional meetings. He has traveled twice to the United States to attend economics workshops at American universities and speak to American teachers and professors.

Miyāhara, although he has a wife and two small children, rises every morning at 4:30 a.m. and writes for two hours before leaving for school. The intense effort Miyāhara puts into his teaching and his scholarship epitomizes the Japanese belief in the importance of maximum dedication to all phases of one's work.[18]

Teachers such as Kageto and Miyahara can cultivate their intellectual interests in part because of flexible teaching schedules. Light daily teaching loads constitute a major difference in the schedules of Japanese upper secondary school teachers when compared to high school teachers in many other industrialized countries including the United States. A Japanese high school instructor's teaching load averages about fifteen hours a week. These teaching responsibilities are comparable to many American university professors. Relatively light teaching loads allow Japanese upper secondary school teachers the freedom to develop a high level of expertise in their academic disciplines, to spend large amounts of time counseling students, and to perform other non-teaching school work such as club sponsorship.

The fact that teachers are responsible for relatively few classes per week means there is always an adequate supply of educators to perform the kind of tasks that administrators or counselors are responsible for in American high schools. The administration of Japanese high schools usually only includes a principal and a head teacher.

A major reason high school teachers have light teaching loads is that in Japan classes are large when compared to those of other developed nations. Japanese high school classes typically contain about forty-five students. Even though the Japan Teachers' Union (JTU) complains regularly about large class size, most high school teachers don't seem particularly bothered by this statistic. It is important to bear in mind that because students are ability grouped by school and teaching usually consists of lecturing, it is easier to instruct a class in Japan than in nations with more heterogeneous classes and greater pedagogical expectations of teachers.

The principalship is usually a reward for thirty years or more of dedicated service by a teacher and includes a handsome salary, prestige, and much responsibility for communicating the goals of the school to outside groups such as parents and the business community. The daily life of the school is as a rule

---

[18] Shortly before publication of this book, Miyahara took a position as an economics professor at Nagoya Women's College.

directed by the head teacher who is usually between the age of fifty and fifty-five and is also recognized as an outstanding educator. Head teacher positions carry only a small amount of extra salary, but the position is looked upon as a stepping stone to a principalship.

Upper Secondary School: Subjects and Pedagogy

The following tables contain two curricula. The curriculum in Table 4 is that of a general or academic program while the curriculum in Table 5 is that of an industrial program where a student has decided to major in electricity. Although there are important curricular differences between general and vocational and commercial high school programs, students in all Japanese high schools are required to take a common core of academic subjects.

As is the case with elementary and junior high, Mombushō proscribes the national high school curriculum. First-year students, regardless of the high school they attend, study the same subjects. All first-year students take Japanese language I, contemporary society, mathematics I, science I, physical education, health, and elective courses in English and either painting, music, or calligraphy.

In Japanese I students continue to practice both reading and writing by studying contemporary literature and composition as well as classical Japanese and Chinese literature. In contemporary society students study contemporary issues, particularly from the perspectives of economics and political science.[19]

In first-year mathematics, students work with quadratic formulas and higher-order equations, graphing of quadratic equations, introductory trigonometry, complex numbers, sets, and algebraic proofs. In science I students learn of the laws of transformation and conservation of energy, basic chemistry and computation of chemical formulas, embryonic formulas, evolution, and genetics.

In most academic programs, second- and third-year students choose either a literature-social science, or a science-mathematics concentration, depending

---

[19] Beginning in April 1994, contemporary society will no longer be required of first-year high school students but will remain in the curriculum as an elective. A new course entitled geography-history will be required of all first-year students. Kobara Tomōyuki, "The Revision of the Social Studies Curriculum in Japan: A Crisis in Social Studies," The Social Studies Teacher 10, no. 1 (September-October 1988): 10-12.

Table 4

**Subject Areas, Subjects, and Standard Number of Credits
of Upper Secondary Schools**

Example of Curriculum for General Course

Subject Areas	Subjects	Grade I	II	II	Total
	Japanese Language I	5			5
Japanese	Japanese Language II		5		5
Language	Contemporary Japanese Language			3	3
	Classics			3	3
	Contemporary Society	4			4
Social	Japanese History		) 6	4	
Studies	World History		) (3x	(2x	10
	Geography		) 2)	2)	
	Politics and Economy			2	2
	Mathematics I	5			5
Mathematics	Algebra and Geometry		3	2	5
	Basic Analysis		2	2	4
	Science I	4			4
Science	Science II			2	2
	Chemistry		)	)	
	Biology		)3	)2	5
Health and	Physical Education	4	4	3	11
Physical Education	Health	1	1		2
	Music I	)	)		)
Art	Fine Arts I	)2	)1		)3
	Calligraphy I	)	)		)
	English I	5			5
Foreign	English II		2	3	5
Language	English IIB		3		3
	English IIC			4	4
Home Economics	General Home Economics	(2)	(2)		(4)
Additional Credits		2	2	2	6
Total For All Subjects		32	32	32	96
Special	Home Room	1	1	1	3
Activities	Activities of Clubs	1	1	1	3
GRAND TOTAL		34	34	34	102

Notes:
1. Thirty-five school hours or lessons per school year (one school hour is 50 minutes as a standard) should be counted as one credit.
2. Credit allocation to other subjects is prescribed by each establishing body of relevant upper secondary school.

Source:
Education in Japan 1989: A Graphic Presentation, 63.

106

Table 5

**Subject Areas, Subjects, and Standard Number of Credits
of Upper Secondary Schools**

Example of Curriculum for Electricity Course

Subject Areas	Subjects	Grade I	II	II	Total
Japanese	Japanese Language I	4			4
Language	Japanese Language II		2	2	4
	Contemporary Society	2	2		4
Social	Japanese History			)	)
Studies	World History			) 3	) 3
	Geography			)	)
	Mathematics I	4			4
Mathematics	Basic Analysis		3		3
	Differential and Integration			3	3
	Science I	2	2		4
Science	Physics			)	)
	Chemistry			) 3	) 3
Health and	Physical Education	2	2	3	7
Physical Education	Health		1	1	2
	Music I	)	)		)
Art	Fine Arts I	)	)		)
	Calligraphy I	) 2	)		) 2
	Craft Production I	)	)		)
English	English I	4			4
	English II		4		4
Small Total		20	16	15	51
	Fundamentals of Industry	4			4
	Practice		4	6	10
	Drawing		2	2	4
	Industrial Mathematics	2	2		4
Industry	Fundamentals of Electricity	6	2		8
	Electric Technology I		6	2	8
	Electric Technology II			5	5
	Automatic Control			)	)
	Information Technology I			) 2	) 2
Small Total		12	16	17	45
Special	Home Room	1	1	1	3
Activities	Activities of Clubs	1	1	1	3
GRAND TOTAL		34	34	34	102

Notes:
1. Thirty-five school hours or lessons per school year (one school hour is 50 minutes as a standard) should be counted as one credit.
2. Credit allocation to other subjects is prescribed by each establishing body of relevant upper secondary school.

Source:
Education in Japan 1989: A Graphic Presentation, 63.

upon what subject they would like to study later at university. However, once a student chooses a concentration there are few electives within it. Table 6 depicts the subjects taken by typical academic program students over three years of high school in each of the two concentration.

Despite the different concentrates, students graduate with approximately three full years of the five basic academic subjects: mathematics, science, social studies, Japanese language, and English.

As is the case with Japanese elementary and junior high students, Japan's high school students consistently rank one or two in the world in international tests of mathematics. All Japanese students, regardless of whether they are in academic or commercial/industrial programs, study algebra and geometry, vectors, and statistics and probability before graduating. Many students have also taken calculus.

In science, as can be seen from the tables, it is highly likely that even students in academic programs who do not plan to go into a science-related field will take biology and chemistry during high school.

In social studies all students study Japanese and world history, geography, and civics. Much of the latter two courses also contain significant economics content. Upper secondary social studies textbooks are similar to those found in junior high. The books contain a large amount of quantitative information. High school history textbooks however, have received intense criticism in recent years from both foreigners and Japanese because text authors largely ignore Japan's major role in instigating World War II and the atrocities committed by Japanese soldiers during that conflict.

Students continue to study both classical and contemporary Japanese language during their last two years of high school as well as some classical Chinese. In the study of English, students advance to more sophisticated grammar and sentence construction. Major emphasis is placed upon written translation instead of conversational skills. In addition to the academic subjects, all students take enrichment subjects such as physical education and art.

The four most popular types of vocational majors are commerce, industry, agriculture, and home economics. The differences between the Mombushō-proscribed formal curricula for academic and vocational programs are not that great.

Table 6

Academic Courses of Study

First Year	
All Students	Weekly Hours
Japanese I	5
Contemporary Society	4
Mathematics I	6
Science I	4
English I	6
Physical Education and Home Economics*	4
Health	1
Music or Calligraphy	2
Homeroom	1
Club Activities	1
Total Class Hours Per Week	34

Second Year			
Literature Majors	Weekly Hours	Weekly Hours	Science Majors
Japanese II	5	4	Japanese II
Classical Literature	2		Japanese History or
Japanese History	2	3	World History
World History	3	3	Algebra & Geometry
Basic Mathematical			Basic Mathematical
Analysis	3	3	Analysis
Biology or Chemistry	3	4	Physics
English	7	4	Chemistry
		5	English
Physical Education and			Physical Education and
Home Economics*	4	4	Home Economics*
Health	1	1	Health
Music or Calligraphy	2	1	Music or Calligraphy
Homeroom	1	1	Homeroom
Club Activities	1	1	Club Activities
Total Class Hours			Total Class Hours
Per Week	34	34	Per Week

*Boys take four hours of physical education and girls take two hours and two hours of home economics.

Table 6
(Continued)

THIRD YEAR			
Literature Majors	Weekly Hours	Weekly Hours	Science Majors
Modern Literature	4	3	Modern Literature
Classical Literature	4		Japanese History or
Japanese History	3	2	World History
World History	3		Integral and
Ethics or Politics	3	5	Differential Calculus
			Probability and
Basic Mathematical		5	Statistics
Analysis	2	4	Physics
Biology or Chemistry	2	4	Chemistry
English	8	6	English
Physical Education	3	3	Physical Education
Homeroom	1	1	Homeroom
Club Activities	1	1	Club Activities
Total Class Hours			Total Class Hours
Per Week	34	34	Per Week

Source:
Japanese Education Today, 43-44.

Of the thirty-four class hours a week taken by all Japanese high school students, only nine to eleven hours are devoted to vocational education in the schools containing students who do not plan to attend university. However, vocational high school teachers demand less of their students in academic subjects than is the case in general high schools. Textbooks also tend to be easier in vocational than in general high schools.[20]

Classroom instruction in the Japanese high school, as in lower schools, occurs six days a week. However, Saturdays are half days and students go to three instead of the normal six classes they attend the other five days. Although academic teachers use the lecture method more with students than their vocational counterparts, lecture with little or no student questioning or discussion is, by far, the dominant form of instruction in both types of Japanese high schools.

---

[20] Ibid., 44.

While Japanese high school teachers are among the world's most knowledgeable and hard-working educators, their instruction, with major exceptions, consists almost entirely of lectures. There are no small-group activities, student debates, projects and other kinds of classroom activities found in other nations' schools and even in lower Japanese schools.

The following case study of a world history class at Handā High School is a typical example of Japanese high school instruction.

A World History Class at Handā High

It is late June and forty-four second-year high school students, a slight majority of whom are boys, are laughing and talking with each other. Suddenly, the history sensei, a young man wearing a short-sleeved white shirt and a tie, walks into the class. The students, attired in summer uniforms, rise, give a greeting, bow, and are seated. Class now begins.

Today the teacher lectures on the years between the world wars. The teacher immediately begins a rapid fire lecture about names, dates, events, and causes and effects of various historical developments. As the teacher lectures, every minute or so he wheels around to the chalkboard directly to his rear and writes on the board. While the teacher is lecturing and writing, students are both taking notes in loose-leaf notebooks and underlining different parts of their textbooks.

In rapid succession the teacher describes the Versailles Peace Conference, the League of Nations, the Locarno Treaties, and the beginning of the Great Depression. The chalkboard is quickly filled with such names and dates as Woodrow Wilson, Lloyd George, Herbert Hoover, Mussolini, and 1929. After thirty of the fifty minutes in the class period have elapsed, no students have asked the teacher any questions. Several students whisper to each other as the teacher talks. Students are asking each other clarification questions about what the teacher has said or written.

The process continues for the last twenty minutes of the class. By the end of the class the teacher has filled the chalkboard three times with terms, dates, names and assorted historical facts and subsequently erased it after students hurriedly copy the material down word-for-word. Although two students ask the teacher questions in the last part of the period, the young people only ask for clarification of statements and not for analysis or elaboration from the teacher.

The teacher's lecture style during the class could in no way be described as inspiring. The teacher is dutiful but quite frankly dull!

There are a number of reasons for the dominance of factually oriented teacher lectures and the absence of questions in the Japanese high school classroom. The importance of impending university entrance examinations exerts a major influence upon the classroom strategies of teachers. Currently, over one-half of high school students take some form of entrance examination for post-secondary institutions. While many Japanese high school teachers would love to employ more varied pedagogical methods in the classroom, including encouragement of student questions and discussion, the structure of the educational system and public opinion inhibits them from using such techniques. Many Japanese believe a high school teacher's major responsibility is to prepare students to do well on university entrance examinations. While it has many disadvantages, didactic instruction is the most efficient method in preparing students to master the multiple choice and short answer questions that dominate university entrance examinations.

The existence of a national curriculum to a certain extent reinforces high school teachers' tendencies to accentuate facts in classroom instruction. Mombushō officials prepare a course of study for each subject that is taught in school and Japanese teachers are expected to closely follow the printed guide. Japanese textbooks, although written by private authors, very closely reflect the courses of study since they must be approved by the Mombushō. Courses of study and textbooks heavily emphasize facts at the expense of analysis or diversity of viewpoint. Teachers are expected to finish both courses of study and textbooks by the end of the academic term. Lectures are the most efficient way for a teacher to meet this expectation.

Since the majority of students will not take university entrance examinations, the atmosphere in the vocational high school classroom is somewhat more relaxed than that of the regular high school. Still, vocational high school instructors most frequently use didactic pedagogy. This is in part due to the fact that the same courses of study and many of the same texts are employed in vocational as regular high schools. Large classes in both vocational and academic high schools are also easier for a teacher to manage if he employs lecture than if alternative instructional strategies such as small-group activities are used.

Dominant societal values are also at work in determining teacher choice of pedagogical technique. Regardless of the type of high school program, a combination of factors, including Confucianism and the rigidly hierarchical nature of Japanese society, make student-teacher classroom relations more formal than elsewhere. Generally, students honor teachers but do not approach them on a casual basis or dispute points with their instructors. Japanese young people are not encouraged by adults to express their opinions. This causes Japanese students not to be particularly eager to voice their opinions or ask questions in the classroom. The teacher and student behaviors just described are less evident in elementary schools, somewhat visible during the junior high years, and extremely obvious in upper secondary schools.

High Schools: Student Life and Values

Japanese high schools, as is the case with elementary and junior highs are not inspiring physical structures. Almost all were built after World War II. Virtually all schools consist of two or three stories of concrete blocks that are painted white. Most schools have, by Japanese standards, large open spaces with a place for soccer and sometimes baseball as well. These open spaces, classrooms, and assembly halls are the sites where club activities take place in Japanese high schools. Club activities are, by far, the liveliest scenes in Japanese upper secondary schools.

Clubs are even more of an integral part of the social lives of Japanese high school students than is true with their junior high counterparts. In a recent survey about what secondary students found to be enjoyable, of those Japanese high school students who stated the most interesting things in their lives were school-related, a plurality named clubs.[21] In some high schools the achievement of a club can make a school famous throughout the region. Consider the case of the Seiyrō Commercial High School Rugby Club.

The Seiyrō club has been strong since shortly after World War II. In the history of the club only two faculty members have served as coaches. The rugby club has won the Aichi prefectural championships twenty-two times. In 1990 the Seiyrō club traveled to Australia and played matches as part of a sister city

---

[21] The Life of a Senior High School Student, 56.

program. The Seiyrō rugby club is so popular that between 60 and 70 percent of the approximately 200 boys in the school are members. Like Japanese sports clubs elsewhere, the Seiyrō team practices every day after school and many times on weekends and during vacations as well. However, the daily five-hour practice for the Seiyrō club is somewhat longer than would be the case in an academic high school in which students are concerned with university entrance examinations.

As one observes the Seiyrō rugby club practice, it becomes apparent that hierarchy and status lessons these teenagers learned earlier are reinforced on the playing field. Practice is organized by age groups and first-year students do very little rugby playing. Instead they fetch water, retrieve balls, and make sure there are plenty of towels for the upperclassmen. In every Japanese high school club, be it drama, chess, or baseball, first-year students prove their loyalty and recognize their subordinate status by performing menial tasks such as the ones described here.

Regardless of what club a high school student chooses, and options range from orchestra and drama to a wide variety of sports clubs, the value of individual commitment is imperative if an individual is to be a successful member. In other countries it is common for high school students to join a variety of organizations. In Japanese high schools membership in one, or at most two, clubs is typical for a student. Once in a club, a member is expected to be totally committed to the goals of the organization. As in junior high clubs, high school members must perform every task enthusiastically and with utmost effort.

For a large percentage of high school students the school club is an important group in their lives. Usually individual faculty members are sponsors. However, it is common for a faculty member to allow club members to make important decisions about activities. Often the friendships and commitment created through club activity endure after the high school years.

School sports and culture festivals are also important extracurricular events in Japanese high schools. Clubs and classes work long hours to prepare for these events. In most high schools there is one sports and one culture festival in an academic year. Class excursions also occur in upper secondary schools. Usually second-year students go on these excursions that are similar to those taken by junior high youngsters. The school excursions are not pleasure trips and the primary objective is to familiarize youngsters in one part of Japan with the

114

history and culture of another region of the country. Often in high school the class that is scheduled to take an excursion attends once-a-week lectures on the history and culture of the sites to be visited for months in advance. Often students are required to complete written reports afterward on what they learned during the excursion. The high school excursion is yet another lesson that all high school students receive that reinforces the idea of Japanese uniqueness.

Japanese teenagers engage in many of the same activities away from school as their peers in other industrialized countries including, most notably, watching television. However, there are some important differences between the lifestyles of Japanese students and those of high school students in the United States. For the academic high school student, there is the pressure of the impending university entrance examinations. Students know that failure or success in examinations will directly affect the rest of their lives. For the vocational high school student, there is also a direct relationship between high school performance and the future. Vocational students receive job offers from the best companies only if they have earned good high school grades. High school is very serious business for Japanese teenagers. One survey indicates that high school students in Japan average two hours each week night and about three hours each Saturday and Sunday doing homework.[22] It is a common sight on a Sunday morning for public libraries to be packed with students studying school assignments.

Japanese high school students who aspire to attend top- or even middle-level universities do even more work than this. Many Japanese high school students who plan to attend university attend yobikō, a special kind of private cram school designed to prepare its clients for university examinations, at some time during their upper secondary school years. The typical pattern is to attend yobikō two, three, or even four days a week after school, at nights, and on Saturday afternoons. Even during summer vacations high school students are required to engage in summer reading programs. Typically, they work with such books as Homer's The Odyssey, the Confucian Analects, and Dante's The Divine Comedy. Japanese high school students lead one of the most structured and stressful lifestyles of adolescents anywhere.

---

[22] Rohlen, Japan's High Schools, 275.

While high schools and the structure of the educational system cause adolescents to lead such structured lives, there are other important cultural elements at work as well. Japanese adults themselves seem to be most comfortable with highly structured and activity-filled daily schedules. Many Japanese feel it is particularly important to fill the lives of the young with meaningful activities. To the typical Japanese parent an after-school job for a teenager does not constitute "meaningful activity." Data from one study on teenage work in Japan and the United States indicates that only 21 percent of Japanese high school students work during the school term, compared with 63 percent in the United States.[23]

Also, Japanese adults tend to perceive high school students in many ways as large children instead of young adults. Students are not allowed to drive automobiles until they are eighteen years of age. While the opposite sexes are interested in each other, parents and teachers strongly discourage teenage dating. Most young people do not begin to date until after high school. Finally, for a variety of reasons, there are few drug problems among Japanese adolescents.[24]

The life of a Japanese high school student is in general not an easy one. For a large percentage of students the academic challenges have become too much. Student retention in a grade because of failing work is extremely rare and takes place only when parents pressure educators to have a student repeat a grade. Just as in junior high school, there are high school students who are behind enough in their studies they are often lost in class. Most Japanese high schools provide little if any opportunity for these students to improve upon their academic deficiencies.

Japanese high schools could not be described as pleasant places. International comparisons of high school students' attitudes toward their own lives and society indicate that Japanese adolescents are among the world's most pessimistic youngsters. In one survey, 70 percent of a national sample of high school students expressed dissatisfaction with their lives and Japanese society.[25]

---

[23] Japanese Education Today, 46.

[24] Ibid.

[25] The Life of a Senior High School Student, 42-44.

Although comparative attitudinal studies of academic and vocational high school students are not available, most probably students in academic schools or programs experience the most stress. University entrance examinations, private cram schools, and the abrupt change in demands that students encounter after entering universities all constitute important educational rites of passage for almost one-half of Japan's young people. All of these aspects of the education of this segment of the Japanese population are the subjects of the next chapter.

Questions for Comparison

1. A major aspect of secondary education in Japan is the inculcation of proper Japanese values. Are there identifiable values that are transmitted by most secondary educational institutions to American students? What are, in your opinion, dominant values transmitted to U.S. students through secondary schools?

2. In American secondary schools there are specialists who provide counseling to students. In Japan, teachers perform this function. Based on what you have read and your own experiences, is either nation's approach to counseling students more effective?

3. In the U.S. teachers teach more classes than in Japan but have smaller classes while the opposite situation is true in Japan. What are the educational advantages and disadvantages of these differing practices in each nation?

4. A major criticism of Japanese secondary education is that teachers overemphasize facts and lecture while ignoring in-depth treatment of subject matter and more innovative instructional methods. Based upon your own experiences would this criticism also apply to most American high school teachers?

5. Based upon the chapter you just read and your own experiences in American secondary schools, are there any elements of Japan's secondary education system that you feel would be appropriate for American educational policy makers to consider adopting?

Additional Reading

Paul George, The Japanese Junior High School: A View from the Inside, National Middle School Association, 1989, is an interesting short monograph on Japanese junior highs. The best work available in English on secondary education is Thomas Rohlen, Japan's High Schools, University of California Press, 1983. The Tōkyō-based International Society for Educational Information has published two excellent easy-to-read booklets entitled The Life of a Junior High Student and The Life of a Senior High Student. The former was published in 1985 and the latter in 1986. Kāya Michiko is the editor of both publications.

John Goodlad, A Place Called School, McGraw-Hill, 1984, is an excellent source for information on American junior and senior high schools. The best book in the last decade on American high schools is Theodore Sizer, Horace's Compromise: The Dilemma of the American High School, Houghton Mifflin, 1984.

Chapter Five

"The Examination Race" and the Japanese University

Introduction: The Race and the Vacation

Mr. Yāmato, the founder and president of Tōkaijuku is answering questions about this 25-year-old, private, for-profit "after-school" school. In his small office which can barely accommodate three visitors, Yamato is surrounded by stacks of standardized practice tests and seven closed-circuit television monitors. On each of the screens is a live classroom scene. Tōkai is a gakushū juku. This type of juku caters exclusively to elementary and junior high students.

Yāmato is a stocky self-assured man who is casually dressed in a striped polo shirt and smokes cigarettes as he talks. Yāmato is, for better or worse, a true educational entrepreneur. Directly behind this former commercial high school teacher's head is a framed calligraphy work which translated into English means "If You Want to Be Independent You Must Work and Get Money."

Yāmato left public school teaching after only a few years. Yāmato was resentful that even though he worked very hard, he received no more salary than some of his less industrious peers. Yāmato's school, while larger than most juku, is much smaller than the giant corporate educational institutions. Approximately 400 students attend Tōkaijuku either one, two, or three nights a week. Most of the students are in lower secondary school and are preparing for high school examinations. Each night for a total of two and one-half hours students study two

120

different subjects. Junior high students select subjects for study from English, social studies, Japanese language, and mathematics.

The first glimpses of classroom activities the visitor experiences are of the scenes on the closed-circuit televisions. Yāmato obviously utilizes them to make sure that teachers and students stay on task. Six of the seven teachers are male college students. The seventh instructor is a middle-aged woman. The instructors cover mostly the same material that is in the national lower secondary school curriculum. The primary classroom activities that students engage in are memorization of large amounts of information, recitation, and taking practice tests.

Classes are about one-half the size of Japanese junior highs with approximately twenty to twenty-five students in each section. Even though students are working in all of the classes, teacher-student relations in this juku are clearly more friendly and less hierarchical than is the case in lower secondary schools. Still, as the evening progresses, the students, all of whom spent a full day in school before juku, appear to be more and more tired. Many have not seen the inside of their homes since breakfast.

Yāmato runs a successful juku. The success or failure of all Japanese juku, except those that cater to elementary students, primarily depends upon one factor. Juku rise or fall based upon the number of students who successfully pass the entrance examinations for their preferred upper secondary school or university.

Kawaijuku's Nagoya branch is also a successful juku even though the physical surroundings could not be more different from Yāmato's gakushū. The Nagoya branch of Kawaijuku is headquartered in an attractive new four-story, high-rise building in downtown Nagoya. Kawai Nagoya is one of thirty-six juku branches in the Kawai Corporation. Ninety thousand students throughout Japan attend Kawaijuku. Kawai is one of the three largest corporate juku in Japan.

The sixty-year-old Kawai Corporation serves students ranging from elementary school youngsters to adult learners. However, the majority of Kawai enrollees are either upper secondary school students or "rōnin", those "masterless samurai" who have graduated from high school but failed the examination of the university of their choice. Rōnin study for a year or more before attempting to pass the entrance examination again.

Rōnin constitute over one-third of all entering university freshman each year and 50 percent or more of the annual class of freshman in Japan's most famous universities. Every year in Japan approximately 200,000 high school graduates spend a year of study as rōnin in a yobikō, or special juku. The purpose of yobikō is to prepare rōnin and upper secondary school students for university entrance examinations.

Tuition for Kawai rōnin and upper secondary students is not cheap, averaging roughly 585,000 yen or $4,500 for the three-semester term. Physics and English classes at Nagoya Kawai are held in large lecture halls with over 200 students attending each class. Instructors in almost all classes for upper secondary school students and rōnin are either university professors or high school teachers. They supplement their incomes by teaching part-time for Kawai.

What occurs in the Kawai classes is remarkably similar to the modes of instruction found at Tōkai and other Japanese juku. In physics class the teacher is working sample problems from old copies of university entrance examinations. Students follow him in their examination practice textbooks. The casually attired mustached English instructor appears to be about forty years old. He speaks Japanese to his two hundred students much more than he uses English. Students are learning no conversational English. They work in their practice books while the teacher makes comments on translating English paragraphs. The paragraphs are samples of what appears on university examinations. Kawai students also take frequent practice examinations.

As is true with the majority of the estimated 100,000 small and large private cram schools that dot the Japanese landscape, Kawai's success or failure rides on how well its students do on entrance examinations compared to other juku or yobikō. Based on its own accounting, the national yobikō division of Kawai is extremely successful. In the most recent year for which statistics are available more than 1,300 Kawai students successfully passed the Tōkyō University entrance examination, the most competitive in Japan. That year, Kawai students constituted 36.5 percent of all students accepted to the most prestigious university in Japan.

A visit to a social science class at Aichi University of Education, a mid-level public university near Nagoya, provides clues as to what constitutes the

122

work atmosphere for most of the 33 percent of Japanese 18- to 21-year-olds who successfully enter junior college or university.

The classroom is a lecture hall designed to hold one hundred people. It contains approximately forty-five students as class begins. The professor's lecture topic is social studies education in Japanese junior and senior high schools. While he talks a steady trickle of students enter the lecture hall and take seats. This continues for over twenty minutes of the one-hour class period. By the time the last student has wandered into class the total number of students is approximately sixty. After class the instructor remarks that there are ninety students on the roll. However, it is not uncommon for 25 percent or more of enrolled students to miss a given class.

During the lecture, Japanese university students behave in some ways that are quite similar to their high school counterparts. They take notes and there is very little interaction between the professor and the class. During the entire period five students speak but only three people ask questions. Two young people give answers to the professor's inquiries. Only one of the three questions requires an extensive answer from the instructor. The other two are points of clarification.

There are a few striking differences in the behavior of this university class and that of an upper secondary school class. During the entire hour there is a continual low buzz of conversation as students quietly but continually talk with each other. The conversations are not about the content of the lecture. Numerous students smile and even laugh quietly at the remarks of their peers.

The professor does not seem to mind the continual talk and goes on with his lecture. Such an apparent lack of attention on the part of so many students to what is actually going on in the classroom can only be found among Japanese preschoolers! A conversation with the professor and university students after class confirms the low level of student attention. After class, several students remark that their major concerns during university life are not academics but the social aspects of the college years, namely sports clubs, dating, parties, and other fun activities.[1]

---

[1] Descriptions of Tōkaijuku, Kawaijuku, and the university class are from author's field research in May and June 1990. Statistics on juku attendance from Kawaijuku publications, Kawaijuku, International Educational Center, 502013 Sendagaya, Shibūya-ku, Tōkyō 151, Japan.

The above vignettes are good indicators of what large numbers of Japanese young people do to try to win the "exam race," and what education is like for the winners after they enter university. The examination system, the multi-million yen juku industry the system has spawned, and university life receive the most criticism by Japanese of any aspect of education in the country. Yet, despite a barrage of condemnation that has existed for decades and recent public policy designed to change the status quo, "examination hell," juku, and a university system that is mediocre by the standards of developed countries continue to exist in Japan. The remainder of this chapter focuses upon these components of Japanese teaching and learning and their educational and social costs and benefits.

Educational Credentialism and Entrance Examinations

In order to really sense how pervasive the examination system is in Japanese life, one need only walk into any book store in the country. Books on how to do well on exams, practice manuals, advice-to-parent books, and even cookbooks containing recipes for student success occupy entire sections and whole floors of book stores. There are many other obvious signs of the popular culture's preoccupation with examinations as well. Buddhist temples and Shinto shrines obtain needed income from selling students good luck charms and prayers. One survey of 900 rōnin studying in Tōkyō, Nagoya, and Sendai revealed that 48 percent purchased such items from religious institutions.[2]

Spring is examination season in Japan. Every spring there are a few sensationalized newspaper and television accounts of parents or students attempting to bribe examination proctors or in some way cheat to gain advantage. When examination results are announced, newspapers give prominent coverage in listing successful entrants to prestigious universities. Throughout Japan, school and teacher reputations are made or broken on how well students do on examinations.

"Examination Hell," or the "Exam Wars," have been in existence in Japan for well over one hundred years. However, with the increasing number of young people who attend high school and aspire to university since World War II, what

---

[2] "Rōnin Fed up with Cramming," Japan Times, January 19, 1988, 2.

124

formerly only affected a small portion of the population is now much more widespread.

Gakurekishugi, or educational credentialism, is the fundamental reason why entrance examinations to upper secondary schools and universities are of such major importance to large numbers of Japanese. All societies place high priority upon a person's educational background. However, the Japanese seem to place the most intense emphasis of any country in the world on the educational institution that an individual attends.

As described in an earlier chapter, this is in part due to the fact that quite rigid hiearchalization of all enterprises is a strong Japanese cultural more. Whether officially designated as so or not, every Japanese knows there is a number-one flower arranging club in each of the 47 prefectures and, in turn, in each community. The same applies to educational institutions. However, the Japanese continue to emphasize educational credentialism for other reasons than simply a propensity to stratify all types of human endeavor.

Beginning in Mēiji times, policy makers designed Japan's educational system to be a vital component in a societal meritocracy. The quality of an individual's latter career possibilities was largely dependent upon the reputation of the school he, through effort and not family influence, could enter. The persistence of similar employment patterns today plays a major role in perpetuating this educational credentialism. In Japan, graduates of the best schools receive the choice job offers. In many other nations, the best graduates of all universities earn preferred slots in government or industry.

Based upon their own firm's place in the hierarchy, Japanese employers seek graduates from upper secondary schools, universities, and other educational institutions that have similar reputations in the education pecking order. A male graduate of Tōkyō University is virtually assured of being offered a position in one of the best companies or government ministries in Japan. By contrast, a graduate of a low-ranking private university can expect humble employment.

Despite much discussion about the negativity of extreme educational credentialism, the perpetuation of employment practices that support it continues. Recently, researchers examined the university backgrounds of both private and public sector employees in a variety of institutions and companies. Although nationwide, only 5 percent of university graduates are from Tōkyō University, 66 percent of all top executives in national government ministries and agencies are Tōkyō University alumni. In two of the most important government ministries-- finance and foreign affairs--80 percent of all employees who hold university degrees graduated from Tōkyō University.

Graduates of not only Tōkyō University but public universities in general hold great public- and private-sector employment advantages compared to most of their private university counterparts. High-status employment in Japan is usually to be found in a large company or government ministry while small enterprises offer second-rate positions. In a recent year, 80 percent of graduates of public universities entered companies with five hundred employees are more. Only 40 percent of private university graduates managed to enter companies the same size or larger.[3]

All Japanese realize the extremely strong relationship between the educational credentials a person obtains and the quality of future employment. In general it is much easier to graduate from Japanese universities than to pass the entrance examination and be admitted. Given this system, an ambitious young person will usually make an intense effort to pass the entrance examination for a prestigious university.

Educational credentialism in modern Japan began in the latter part of the 1800s. At that time the national government established the policy of legally exempting Tōkyō Imperial University Law Faculty graduates from the requirement of taking and passing the civil service examination to gain employment in ministries.[4]

By the turn of the century, it was common practice to award important public sector positions to graduates of the seven old imperial universities. Since only a small percentage of the population aspired to attempt to enter these elite institutions, educational credentialism and an emphasis upon entrance examinations affected only a few Japanese during the early part of this century. However, by the 1920s and 1930s increasing numbers of private companies were also selecting white collar employees based upon the status of their educational credentials.

---

[3] James and Benjamin, Public Policy and Private Education in Japan, 78.

[4] Beauchamp and Rubinger, Education in Japan: A Source Book, 139.

126

Most managers of large companies were not graduates of the imperial universities. However, individuals who were graduates of other select institutions had clear employment advantages. For example, graduates of the prewar commercial high schools, which offered a curriculum similar to today's university programs in economics or commerce, were favored as employees by large companies. By 1930, 72 percent of middle- and upper-level managers in private companies and 57 percent of engineers were graduates of commercial high schools.[5] As might be imagined, this development did much to make entrance examination results much more important for ambitious young people and their parents.

Although the importance of educational credentialism escalated at all levels after World War II, this was particularly true in high schools and universities. Today, well over 90 percent of all Japanese students attend upper secondary schools and one-third of the country's students attend university. Therefore, the majority of teenagers and their families are now affected by educational credentialism and entrance examinations.

Even though in recent years the national government and Mombushō have changed some aspects of the university entrance examination system, there is intense competition for all public universities and prestigious private universities such as Keiō and Wāseda. In a recent year 1.1 million students took university entrance examinations and 40,000 failed. Most in the latter category become rōnin and study for a year or more until they either pass the examination for their chosen university or give up.[6]

By the late 1980s a Mombushō-constructed, common, two-day standardized examination was established for all students who wished to enter a prefectural or national university. Students taking the common exam in January are tested in five subjects: English, mathematics, Japanese language, social studies, and natural science. Public universities and the more prestigious private institutions use the common examination as a screening device and not as the final determinant of a candidate's entry. In late February or early March, candidates

[5] Ronald Dore, introduction to Education and Examination in Modern Japan, by Amano Ikuō (University of Tōkyō Press, 1990).

[6] Nagāshima Hidēsuke, "Parents Struggle Financially to Assure Children's Future Success," Japan Times, weekly international ed., March 5-11, 1990, 5.

who make above the cut-off score established by a particular university for the common examination then take a second, one-day examination written by the university department they are attempting to enter. The most successful candidates on this second examination are then admitted to the university.

By far, the large majority of questions on both the common and university faculty-designed examinations consist of questions that require highly detailed factual answers but little analysis or critical thinking. The questions below are excerpted from an examination written by the politics and economics faculty of Wāseda University, a highly regarded private Japanese university. Students first read the following four descriptions of absolute monarchs in European History and must list the name of the monarch for each description.

a. Inherited a rich, powerful nation. Built up a standing army and arms industry, and reformed education. Tried to expand territory by invasion. Built a palace in the suburbs and was associated with many famous scholars and artists.

b. Born of ducal family of Anhalt-Zerbst. Brought to throne by a palace coup. Keen on Enlightenment philosophy. Codified laws in a constitution. Increased nobles' powers, provoking farmers' revolt. Annexed an Islamic country to the south.

c. Came to the throne aged 5, with mother as regent, while a cardinal held power as prime minister. Later ruled directly by decree. Established ministries, reformed army and industry. Fought many wars. Built a palace outside his capital, made it the center of political and cultural life.

d. Married to a duke of Lorraine. Her succession caused a war. She reformed finances, farming, commerce and industry. Allied with an old rival with whom her family had competed for European hegemony since the Middle Ages.[7]

On the Wāseda examination, in addition to naming each monarch, students were also required to answer other very detailed factual questions about European history. Since questions such as the above are the rule rather than the exception in Japanese entrance examinations, it is easy to understand why there is such great emphasis upon the memorization of enormous amounts of facts in both secondary

---

[7] "Japan's Schools: Why Can't Little Taro Think?", The Economist 315, no. 7651 (April 21, 1990): 22. The answers to the questions are: (a) Frederick II of Prussia, (b) Catherine II of Russia, (c) Louis XIV of France, (d) Maria Theresa of Austria-Hungary, Bohemia.

128

schools and in <u>juku</u>. In Japan, mastery of facts and details are the keys to climbing the educational ladder.

Even though the examination system receives much justifiable criticism in Japan, young people who do well on examinations are successfully performing traditional roles of Japanese students that are still much respected by many individuals and employers. Student mastery of many detailed facts was an important aspect of traditional Confucianist education. Written Japanese requires tremendous amounts of memorization. Also, many Japanese accept the belief that everyone is equal intellectually and it is strong individual effort that brings rewards. To many employers in contemporary Japan, students who have passed difficult entrance examinations for middle- and high-level universities have demonstrated they can make the supreme effort to achieve goals. Since many employers believe that passing a difficult university entrance examination is demonstrative of a person's character, they continue to support the examination system through their hiring practices.

Many employers and the public are attracted to the egalitarian nature of the Japanese university examination system. In Japan, to be the child of a wealthy alumni usually means nothing if a young person fails the university entrance examination. In a recent study comparing the ratio of poor to upper-income students attending elite universities in Japan, the U.S., and the U.K., Japanese universities had the highest ratios of economically disadvantaged young people who were students.[8]

The egalitarianism described above is largely true of the public universities. Because of examination schedules, students can stand for only one or two public university examinations a year. By contrast, if a student has the financial resources, he or she can take six or more of the private university examinations. Private universities hold entrance examinations at different times than public universities. Fees just to simply take private university entrance examinations are high. Based on 1990 calculations, if a student chose to stand for

---

[8] James and Benjamin, <u>Public Policy and Private Education in Japan</u>, 143-144.

two public university and six private university examinations, the total entrance fee costs would be $1,517 in U.S. dollars.[9]

What are vital considerations for a Japanese young person as to what university to attempt to enter? In Japan, it is quite important for prospective students to decide beforehand both the universities they wish to enter and what their majors will be if admitted. Japanese universities do not normally allow transfer from one university to another. Nor does the typical higher educational institution allow transfer from one university department to another without the transferee beginning study again. Public universities not only offer the best future employment prospects but are also cheap to attend because they are heavily subsidized by the state. Despite notable exceptions such as Wāseda and Keiō, private universities are easier to enter than public institutions, but are much more expensive and result in less desirable employment for graduates.

Costs among private universities vary tremendously. However, while a student at a national university will pay the equivalent of $2,600 in tuition for an academic year, his counterpart in a private university will pay over $7,000 for the same time period. The Japanese Government has deliberately kept the number of public universities smaller than the number of students who would like to attend them. Consequently, over 72 percent of all Japanese students attend private universities. Most private university students attend such institutions because they could not pass public university entrance examinations.[10]

Kyōiku Mamas and Anxious Young People

Educational credentialism is a major source of stress for many Japanese families. The percentage of students and their families who feel stress because of educational credentialism is greatest in homes containing third-year junior high students, since virtually all Japanese now attend high school.

Only a little over 20 percent of Japan's third-year high school students aspire to enter the top-ranking universities. It is these students who undergo the

---

[9] Seiichi Hirāi, "Japanese Education Costs Rising Rapidly," The Japan Times, weekly international ed., March 5-11, 1990, 12.

[10] Education in Japan 1989: A Graphic Presentation, 22-27 and 100-101. Dollar-yen conversion based upon 130 yen to one dollar.

130

most pressure. However, the postwar rise in the number of young people who wish to attend university means there now is at least some examination-related stress for the majority of high school students and their families.[11]

It has long been an expectation of Japanese society that mothers spend large amounts of time supervising the education of their children. The pressure on mothers has risen since World War II. The commitment to gain advantage for a child on the part of a mother takes a variety of forms. It might include gathering information about other students' work habits, objective fact-finding from numerous advice books, and approaching teachers directly to help a young person. If students don't do well on examinations it is typical for mothers to blame themselves. This is particularly true with mothers of boys since larger numbers of males apply to the more difficult universities to enter.

Consider the following case reported by an anthropologist who spent several months in a small town on Honshu. Each week one mother had her only son, a sixth-grader, commute four hours round trip for three days to a juku specializing in preparing students for entrance into the prestigious private Azabū Junior-Senior High school. The reason the child's mother was so interested in her son entering Azabū is that as many as one hundred of its graduates are accepted by Tōkyō University each year.[12]

The mother hired a school teacher who was not employed at the youngster's elementary school to tutor the boy in math each day the child did not attend juku. These sessions usually began in the middle of the afternoon and ended at night. As a result, the son could not perform the after-school cleanup to which all the children in his school were assigned. Since the teachers at the child's local school were unhappy with this situation, he was required to stay inside during lunch break while his classmates were playing and clean up part of the classroom. Although the son was jeered by his peers and the mother was

---

[11] Nishiō Kanji, "Reshaping Education for Today's Needs," Teacher's Manual for Video Letter from Japan II, Suburban Tōkyō High School Students (The Asia Society, 1988), 52.

[12] There are a few elite private junior-senior high schools in Japan where students can enter early through competitive examinations, thereby avoiding upper secondary school entrance examinations.

singled out for criticism at a local PTA meeting, the child eventually got into Azabū.[13]

Some analysts argue that the media has over-sensationalized the machinations of anxious mothers and that examination stress is limited to the middle class. While the former contention is to a certain extent true, the latter argument has less validity. From an income distribution perspective, Japan is one of the most "middle class" countries in the world. A majority of Japanese experience some examination-related stress.

One couple, whose son had twice failed examinations for a prestigious university, reported to the same anthropologist cited earlier that the situation almost caused life to reach the breaking point for the entire family. The mother and father found themselves talking of nothing but their son's study and often went out of the house so as not to disturb him when he was cramming for the examinations. The wife reported that the situation was so tense the couple had absolutely no time for normal husband-wife quarrels! Both adults regarded their son's examination crisis as the peak of their own life crisis. Fortunately, on the third try the son passed the entrance examination.

Obviously, entrance examination pressures have terrible costs for Japanese young people as well as their families. Some students take their lives after failure. However, when adolescent suicide rates for Japan and the United States were compared in 1984, only 5.5 of every 100,000 Japanese teenagers committed suicide. The American statistic was 9.0 suicides for every 100,000 teenagers.[14] Still, when evidence as to the causes of suicides can be found, Japanese young people are much more likely than American ones to have killed themselves because of school-related concerns.

Beginning in lower secondary school, when most youngsters are first exposed to the pressures of impending examinations, other negative manifestations surface. In recent years, increasing numbers of Japanese junior high students have begun skipping school. Educators and the media have named this much-publicized phenomenon "school refusal syndrome." Experts who study the problem identify entrance examination pressure as a major cause for this

---

[13] Lebra, Japanese Women: Constraint and Fulfillment, 203.

[14] Japanese Education Today, 79.

behavior. To a certain extent, "school refusal syndrome" has been over-sensationalized since fewer than one-fifth as many Japanese students skip school as American youngsters. Still, in a country such as Japan where discipline problems are rare, the recent school truancy rates are considered to be a very serious problem.

In high school the pressure on students competing to enter the most prestigious universities is legendary. A representative phrase bandied about by third-year high school students is "pass with four, fail with five," The phrase illustrates the relatively accurate belief that a student competing for an elite university is doomed to be a ronin if he or she sleeps more than four hours a night during the crucial final months of preparation.

There is evidence that examination stress is an important factor in shaping many Japanese high school students' views of their overall quality of life. In one study, national samples of Japanese and American high school seniors were asked questions about their lives. The two groups of young people were asked the same questions two years after they completed high school. One revealing statement in the survey which students were asked to either agree or disagree with was, "On the whole I am satisfied with myself." Only 30 percent of Japanese high school seniors claimed to be satisfied with themselves compared to 80 percent of the national sample of Americans.

Two years after high school there was no difference between the two samples' response to this question. Seventy-nine percent of both Americans and Japanese gave an affirmative answer. While it would be difficult to argue that pending examinations are the only reason for this evidence of low Japanese adolescent self-esteem, there is little doubt that they constitute a major cause for it.[15]

Although for most Japanese students examination pressures end with high school graduation, such is not the case with ronin. Most ronin tend to be disproportionately male. Estimates are that one-fifth of all male high school graduates become ronin each year. In response to surveys, ronin report daily

---

[15] Robert Evans, "The Transition from School to Work in the United States," in <u>Educational Policies in Crisis: Japanese and American Perspectives</u>, William K. Cummings (Praeger, 1986), 142.

feelings of anxiety about examinations. Many rōnin also claim to have low self-esteem.[16]

These feelings are even worse for the not inconsiderable number of students in this category who spend more than a year as rōnin. One such student was Miyāhara Satōrū, the teacher from the top-ranked high school in Aichi Prefecture who was described in a previous chapter. Miyāhara aspired to be accepted as a student in the economics department of Kyōto University. Kyōto University is generally regarded as second in prestige only to Tōkyō University, and the Kyōto University economics department is also highly regarded. This extremely bright and creative teacher spent two years after high school graduation studying for the examinations. Miyāhara, like many rōnin, lived at home and was supported by his parents. For a short time he commuted four hours round trip from his small town to a yobiko in Nagoya. Miyāhara stopped, however, when he found that the long transit time actually reduced the number of hours he could study.

Miyāhara gave up his dream of Kyōto University after failing the examinations for a second year as a rōnin. Miyāhara did pass the examinations of the economics department of the quite prestigious Nagoya University and went on to become a top student at that institution. Miyāhara, as is the case with almost all former rōnin, describes this time period as "the darkest in his life."

It is stories such as these, multiplied many times over, that lend credibility to statistics such as those reported by a major Japanese newspaper. Only 4 percent of a national sample of adults favored keeping Japan's examination system intact. Forty-five percent of those surveyed wanted significant changes and 38 percent favored outright abolition of the system.[17]

Even though many Japanese have very negative feelings about the entrance examination system, it is primarily responsible for the growth of a relatively unique kind of educational institution, the private juku.

---

[16] "Rōnin Fed up with Cramming," 2.

[17] James Fallows, "Gradgrinds Heirs," The Atlantic 259, no. 3 (March 1987): 20.

134

The Cram School Industry

Although Japan has a strong private school tradition, the growth of juku particularly in the last two decades has been phenomenal. Current estimates place the total annual earnings of juku at over five billion dollars in U.S. currency. Most of the estimated 100,000 juku are very small and operated in private homes. Then there are a few corporate juku such as Kawai that have branches throughout Japan and enroll thousands of students.

There were cram schools in Japan before this century, but only recently has juku use become so widespread. During the 1980s, estimates are that the number of children attending increased by one-half. There are no signs of abatement of growth. Approximately 16 percent of primary school students and well over 50 percent of junior high youngsters attend juku at some time while they are in each respective level of schooling. Students in urban areas are much more likely to attend juku than their rural counterparts.[18]

For a variety of reasons it is more difficult to quantify how many high school students attend juku. However, one estimate is that over one-half of urban middle-class families with high school students who plan to attend university send their youngsters to juku or employ a home tutor. [19]

Young people attend juku for several reasons. Although there are much-publicized exceptions, most elementary school juku tend to be similar to the enrichment courses to which many Western middle-class families send their children. In Japan, swimming, piano, and conversational English juku are all popular with the under-twelve set and their families. The majority of elementary juku are not designed to prepare students for entrance examinations and are almost universally regarded by attendees as enjoyable places to spend time.

Enrollees of gakushū juku attempt to keep up with other students in their classes or prepare for entrance examinations for a desired high school. High

---

[18] Carol Simons, "They Get by with a Lot of Help from Their Kyōiku Mamas," Smithsonian, vol. 17, no. 12 (March 1987): 44-53. According to a 1991 Tōkai Bank poll of students in Ōsaka, Tōkyō, and Nagoya, 37.7 percent of elementary and 65.9 percent of junior high students attended juku. Yoshida Ritsuko, "Harvest of the Standard-Score Greenhouse," Japan Quarterly 38, no. 2 (April-June 1991): 163.

[19] Merry White, "High School Students in Japan," Teacher's Manual for Video Letters from Japan II, Suburban Tōkyō High School Students (The Asia Society, 1988), 8.

school students and r̄ōnin attend yobikō. Almost all yobikō students are preparing for entrance examinations for universities or other post-secondary institutions. The curricula of gakushū juku and yobikō consist of courses such as Japanese language, English language, mathematics, science, and social sciences that are common to upper secondary school and university entrance examinations. Larger juku offer specialized courses such as a program designed to assist students to be accepted by the department of a particular university. Pedagogy in both gakushū juku and yobikō emphasizes the acquisition of large amounts of facts, examination taking techniques, and writing and problem solving.

Since entrance examinations are a primary reason for the existence of juku, large institutions such as Kawai are very much involved in administering and evaluating practice tests. The Kawai-run Japan Information Center for Examinations administers practice university entrance examinations for more than two million students annually. The center has access to a huge data base that it uses to conduct teacher guidance programs that assist educators to prepare students for entrance examinations.

Larger juku are very much involved in the publishing industry. Kawai produces a monthly magazine The Laurels of Victory that goes to more than a million high school student and r̄ōnin subscribers. The magazine contains articles and various tips for passing university examinations. Kawai publishes other periodicals for junior high and elementary students and floppy disks, compact disks, video cassettes, and over 160 textbooks.

Teachers in almost all juku are usually part-time. The typical juku faculty consists of university or high school teachers who are supplementing their incomes, college students, and housewives with teaching credentials. Teaching positions in large juku can be very lucrative. It is not uncommon for an instructor to earn annually the equivalent of $40,000 or more for twelve to eighteen hours teaching weekly.[20]

The juku industry is anything but static. Juku management is aware that, despite the recent massive growth in the industry, declining birth rates mean there will be fewer potential future students. Corporate juku compete fiercely for

---

[20] Juku teacher salary estimations from Robert August, "Yobik ō: Prep Schools for College Entrance in Japan," in Japanese Educational Productivity, eds. Robert Leestma and Herbert J. Walberg (The University of Michigan, 1992), 290.

students and produce very sophisticated print and video recruiting materials. The large juku are also expanding their modes of instruction on a regular basis as they compete for more students. Kawai now offers television courses where students can phone in questions for teachers. Several of the larger juku now offer courses in Japanese and other subjects for the increasing numbers of foreign students who come to Japan with hopes of eventually entering a university. Kawai as well as the other large juku are now opening other kinds of schools for students who wish to acquire a special skill such as business English. Juku are also investing in other countries. In 1989 Kawai opened a Japanese language school in Taipei, the capital of Taiwan.[21]

Despite the cultivation of flashy images and the diversification attempts of large juku, the entire concept of juku is quite controversial in Japan. This is primarily because juku are inextricably linked to the problems of educational credentialism and the examination wars. However, despite much hand-wringing from large segments of the public and the media about the evils of juku, actual Japanese feelings about these institutions are much more mixed than might be imagined. The Mombushō has taken an official position opposing juku and, if asked, most Japanese teachers and professors express the same sentiment. Yet thousands of teachers and professors throughout Japan supplement their income by teaching in juku. University students, for whom juku teaching is often very attractive, often hide the fact they are juku instructors from their universities who also officially oppose juku.

Many teachers, particularly older ones, argue that cram schools are not needed. These educators contend that if parents send their child to juku, they neglect their own responsibility to teach their offspring good study habits. Kageto, the commercial high school teacher who was profiled in an earlier chapter, thinks that juku is a bad idea because it destroys a student's will to learn something on his or her own. Kageto also strongly believes that juku children will only work hard if other students and a teacher are present.

The situation is somewhat different with many younger teachers who attended juku as students. One English teacher in Seiyrō Commercial High School argues that juku is only bad if parents force children to attend. The teacher

---

[21] Kawaijuku promotional materials.

believes it is fine for young people to attend juku if this is what they desire. The same teacher is grateful for her own juku experience. In her case she did not like to study until she went to juku and was stimulated by interesting teachers.

The young English teacher's latter point is reiterated by many Japanese students and parents. Many children, perhaps because of the more relaxed juku atmosphere compared to lower or upper secondary school, find juku instructors much more approachable, friendly, and stimulating than school teachers. It is common to hear from some students how much they like juku! Another argument made by both students and parents is that to not attend juku is to be lonely, since everyone's friends attend.

Many other parents and young people have quite opposite opinions about juku. The typical parent who sends children to juku does it with very mixed emotions. Many parents feel very sorry for what their children must endure, since they are regular witnesses to how tired their youngsters are after negotiating a full day in school, three hours of juku, and heavy homework assignments. The problem is that most Japanese parents want their children to have the best possible future opportunities. Since Japan is a society that places enormous emphasis upon the acquisition of the "right" educational credentials, many parents feel they are endangering the future quality of their children's lives if they don't send them to juku. The issues that surround the juku controversy are over two decades old and show absolutely no signs of resolution.

Juku would by-and-large probably cease to exist if not for the examination system and the growth of higher education in Japan. In a number of respects colleges and universities are just as controversial in Japan as juku. What are major trends in the evolution of this nation's somewhat troubled higher educational system?

Japanese Higher Education: From Mēiji to World War II

Although institutions of higher learning have existed in Japan since medieval times, the modern university system began to first take shape during the Mēiji years. In 1886 Tōkyō University, which had been created nine years earlier, was renamed Tōkyō Imperial University through the promulgation of the Imperial University Ordinance. From the very beginning graduates of the most prestigious

138

university in Japan have been the nation's favored few. Graduates of Tōkyō University, known in Japan as "Tōdai," have held a disproportionate percentage of important positions. This was first true in the highest reaches of government and later in the private sector as well. The government also created six other imperial universities in the years before World War II. These institutions constituted the apex of the prewar university system. While they are no longer categorized as imperial universities, these institutions of higher learning still rank at the top of Japan's public universities.[22]

Mēiji policy makers envisioned the imperial universities as organs of the national government. They were created first and foremost to assist in the attainment of the primary national government objective of the time--the modernization of Japan. That the universities were organs of the national government was made crystal clear in the language of the ordinance referred to earlier. The Imperial University Ordinance defined the purpose of higher education to be "the teaching of, and the fundamental research into, arts and sciences necessary for the state."[23] Japanese national universities were in the words of one scholar of higher education "... an indispensable sub-department of modern Japanese bureaucracy."[24] Faculty and administration of the universities were civil servants responsible to the Ministry of Education.

Mēiji political leaders dispatched fellow countrymen abroad to study the university systems of other countries. In addition, Mēiji leaders hired a number of foreigners to teach in Japanese universities. At first, Americans filled many university posts, but during the late Mēiji years government officials began to hire more and more German academics. By the time of the Imperial University Ordinance the German model most influenced the creation of the Japanese university system.

German universities were first of all major research institutions, and this function was copied in the Japanese imperial universities. Also, the Japanese emulated German universities in the creation of the chair system. In that system

---

[22] Beauchamp and Rubinger, Education in Japan: A Source Book, 138-139.

[23] Ibid., 138.

[24] Nakayama Shigēru, "Independence and Choice: Western Impacts on Japanese Higher Education," Higher Education 18, no. 1 (1989): 33.

one dominant full professor in each academic discipline is served by a number of assistants. However, there were important differences in the development of major Japanese universities when compared to their German counterparts. Unlike the Germans, Japanese policy makers created faculties of engineering and agriculture in the universities since such disciplines were considered vital to Japan's economic development. Also, while the Japanese adopted the bureaucratic aspects of the German system they did not embrace the concept of academic freedom as much as their German counterparts. Japanese students and faculty also did not enjoy the freedom of mobility between universities that was true of the German university system.

In prewar Japan the imperial universities were not the only components of the higher educational system, although they were clearly at the top of it. Several very good private universities such as Keiō and Wāseda were in existence by the latter Mēiji years. It was not until 1918, however, that the national government awarded official university status to these institutions. Almost from their inception the private universities were of a different character than the imperial ones. The private universities were more politically liberal than their government counterparts. Private institutions also concentrated on supplying graduates to organizations other than the government bureaucracy.

The prewar high schools, which any aspiring imperial university student had to first successfully negotiate, provided an education quite similar to that of a good American liberal arts college. The prewar higher educational system also included senmon gakkō or specialized post-secondary schools. Senmon gakkō trained people in professions such as medicine and engineering. Although senmon gakkō graduates could practice their craft, they were accorded less status than their university counterparts. Technical colleges and normal schools for the training of school teachers constituted other elements in the Japanese prewar higher educational system. Colleges for women also existed in the prewar system since females were not allowed to attend the same universities as males. In the early decades of the twentieth century all these institutions grew in number.

By 1940 there were forty-five universities in addition to numerous other higher educational institutions. The majority were private and the large majority of young men who attended university went to private institutions. University graduates made up a minuscule percentage of the population until after World

War II. Shortly before the beginning of World War II, less than 7 percent of the eligible male cohort were university graduates. Only 1 percent of the same group were imperial university graduates.[25]

The Effects of the American Occupation Upon Higher Education

As was true of all major Japanese institutions, higher education underwent profound changes during the American Occupation. Still, several fundamental aspects of the system remained unchanged. The Americans viewed the prewar system as too hierarchical, undemocratic, and elitist. American educational planners tried to change these perceived negatives through greatly improving access to higher education for all of ability regardless of sex or station in life. Occupation officials also attempted to decentralize national control over universities. While Occupation planners were extremely successful in expanding higher education opportunities to Japanese of both sexes and from all walks of life, most attempts to radically decentralize the system failed.

The old elite high schools that were prerequisites for university entrance were abolished and Japan adopted the American 6-3-3-4 system of education. The new constitution gave women for the first time the freedom to attend universities. As a result, female enrollees in Japanese postsecondary institution have steadily increased throughout the postwar era. Because of the general democratization of Japan during the Occupation years, academic freedom became more a part of the Japanese university than before the war.

The Americans wanted to both expand higher educational opportunities for Japanese and wrest control of universities from the Ministry of Education. In order to accomplish these two objectives Occupation authorities proposed that national universities be established in each of the then forty-six prefectures. These institutions, as well as the old national universities, were to be run by American-style boards of trustees.

University expansion was implemented and many prewar senmon gakkō and normal schools were hastily converted to public prefectural universities. In

---

[25] Beauchamp and Rubinger, Education in Japan: A Source Book, 138-143; and Philip Altbach and Viswanathan Selvarathnam, eds., From Dependence to Autonomy: The Development of Asian Universities (Kluwer Academic Publishers, 1989), 106.

addition to the expansion of public universities, the number of private universities grew as well. By 1955 the number of universities in Japan had grown to more than 245 compared to a total of only 49 in 1942. During the postwar years the number of American-style junior colleges grew as well. The junior colleges became particularly popular with women.

During the decades of the 1950s, 60s, and 70s the number of students attending postsecondary educational institutions in Japan continued to grow due to increased opportunities, rising national affluence, and a baby boom. By 1960, there were 525 postsecondary educational institutions attended by 710,000 students. By 1975, the numbers were, respectively, over 1,000 and 2.1 million.[26]

Despite stimulating higher education growth with their policies, the Americans were much less successful in decentralization and de-hierarchalization of Japanese higher education. The prefectural universities were created and categorized as national universities. The old imperial universities were also renamed "national," and in theory they were of no higher status than their new public counterparts. Nevertheless, today the old imperial universities have much higher prestige than the prefectural institutions. The prefectural universities do, however, enjoy higher status with the public than most private universities. The prewar educational stratification of "public as better than private" was unchanged by the Americans.

Japanese academicians and students fiercely resisted the American attempt to initiate board of trustee governance for each public university. Fought by Japanese professors on the grounds that business-dominated boards of trustees would attempt to impose right-wing agendas on universities, the trustee idea was eventually dropped. Today, a system exists whereby prefectural governments are responsible for significant funding of their public universities. Faculty exert substantial power over internal university matters. Mombushō sets general university administrative and curricular guidelines and provides some funding for higher educational institutions.

Before contemporary Japanese universities are considered, it should be reiterated that some basic elements of the system--the higher status of a few elite national universities and other public higher educational institutions compared to

---

[26] Beauchamp and Rubinger, Education in Japan: A Source Book, 143-147.

most private institutions, the employment advantages enjoyed by graduates of elite national universities, and utilization of examination systems to sort students-- are all aspects of the higher educational system that survived World War II and the American Occupation. All of these aspects of the higher educational system continue to profoundly influence contemporary Japanese universities.

Demography and Structure of Contemporary Higher Education

The expansion of higher education institutions and opportunities for young Japanese grew throughout the early years of the twentieth century, accelerated due to American-imposed postwar policy, and continued as a trend in the 1960s, 70s, and 80s. Between 1965 and 1988, a major expansionist period, the percentage of all Japanese enrolled in higher education soared from 14.6 to 33.5 percent of the nation's 18- to 21-year-old cohort.

By the late 1980s, there were over 2.3 million students enrolled in Japan's 490 universities and 571 junior colleges. The four-year institutions contained large majorities of males, as over 1,860,000 men were enrolled in four-year colleges and universities. This number represents 75 percent of all students enrolled in colleges and universities. Junior colleges had an enrollment of 445,000 students. Ninety percent of these students were women.[27]

Despite higher education's expansion, just as was true before World War II, the majority of Japanese college students attend private universities that are considered inferior to their public counterparts. By the early 1990s, Japan's national universities, including the newer prefectural and the former imperial universities, comprise only 19.4 percent of all universities. The remainder of Japan's universities are private.

When percentages of students attending public and private universities are compared, roughly 25 percent of university students are enrolled in public institutions while the remainder attend private universities. When Japanese women attend university, they are more likely than males to attend a private one. The majority of two-year colleges in Japan are also private. Among two-year colleges, 84 percent of all junior colleges are private and 90 percent of junior college attendees enroll in private schools.

---

[27] Education in Japan 1989: A Graphic Presentation, 18 and 26-27.

Even though Wāseda and Keiō and a few other elite private universities are exceptions, in general the resource gap between private and public universities and colleges is extremely pronounced. Public universities enjoy much better physical plants, computers, laboratories, and faculty than private institutions. By enjoying more economic resources for faculty, public universities are perhaps at the greatest advantage compared to private schools.

While a large majority of students attend private universities, when the percentages of instructors at private and public universities are compared, approximately 50 percent of all university instructors in Japan teach at public institutions of higher learning.[28] Not only are instructor-class ratios much higher in private than public universities, but private university faculty tend to be not as well qualified as professors in public universities.

Because governments subsidize public universities much more than private schools, tuition is much less expensive in public universities. A comparison of tuition fees converted into U.S. dollars indicates that while annual tuition at national universities averaged $2, 811 and tuition was only slightly higher at public prefectural universities, annual private university tuition averaged $6,580.[29]

Although governance of both private and public universities is a shared function, ultimate responsibility lies with the Higher Education Bureau of the Ministry of Education. The Mombushō is responsible for chartering and abolishing both public and private institutions, establishing general standards and policies, planning and advising on student welfare and student aid programs, and subsidizing private as well as public institutions of higher learning.[30]

Even though general policies are set in Tōkyō, public and private universities tend to have wide internal policy autonomy. Administrators and professors in national universities and most private institutions are legally appointed by the Minister of Education but chosen by faculty and staff of the particular university. The university hierarchy includes the president and

---

[28] Ibid., 22-23.

[29] Ibid., 100-101.

[30] Ibid., 32-33.

organizational units called faculties divided according to academic discipline. A dean is in charge of each university faculty.

Japanese university faculties are analogous in most respects to American university academic departments. For example, Tōkyō University now contains nine faculties including law, literature, education, economics, science, medicine, engineering, agriculture, pharmacy, and a college of general education. The professoriate exercises considerable power in university governance through the faculty senate which in principle is composed of the president, deans of each faculty and college of general education, some elected professors from each faculty, and the directors of the university library. Typically, it is this body that is responsible for nominating a new university president.

The various faculties each have organizations called faculty meetings. These bodies are responsible for both electing new deans and new professors. After the faculty meetings make their recommendations to the university president, he in turn nominates the employment candidates to Mombushō. Usually, it is standard procedure for the Mombushō to approve candidates for university faculty positions. Professors are awarded lifetime tenure upon being hired or shortly afterward. Guaranteed employment fosters a strong sense of professorial autonomy within Japanese universities.

Within the university faculty, the hierarchical nature of the larger Japanese society manifests itself yet again in the nature of relations between senior and junior faculty members. Most faculties consist of only one full professor. This professor holds tremendous power over the assistant professors and instructors who are his subordinates. The full professor's power includes determination of coworker research interests. Because so much power is allocated to one professor in the chair system, related problems of academic freedom surface periodically at Japanese universities.

University Life

Japanese universities compare unfavorably in several respects to university systems of other modern developed countries. When asked in a survey to rank their own universities compared to those of other nations, Japanese scholars gave their nation's universities relatively low rankings and selected American and European universities as the world's best.

The most famous universities worldwide obtain their reputations by creating a stimulating academic environment and producing outstanding research. Because the best universities in Japan derive considerable prestige from providing graduates for top government ministries and companies, university emphasis upon this function inhibits the development of a world-class intellectual or research environment.

Prestigious Japanese companies and government ministries usually limit their recruiting to a few, or even one or two, equally prestigious universities. Although a student's major can be important to employers, usually the reputation of his university is an even more critical variable.[31] Employers, many of whom hire university graduates for "life," have the incentive to train their workers on the job. Consequently, there is little pressure for students, particularly undergraduates, to work very hard at academics once they are admitted to a Japanese institution.

Students already know, based upon the status of the university to which they were admitted, the probable status of their future career. All they need do is complete their university degree. In Japan this is usually a fairly easy task. By world standards most Japanese universities are quite easy places from which to graduate. A very high 79 percent of all Japanese university students earn diplomas four years after entering college.[32]

In addition to a lack of pressure to work hard at college studies, the educational cultures of junior and senior high schools in Japan are other factors that make many university students not particularly interested in substantive intellectual work. For the last six years of their lives and even longer if they were rōnin, Japanese students were rewarded if they passively learned facts and deferred to teachers. Many continue to play the same student role in university by

---

[31] Engineering majors are popular with private-sector employers, and in the most recent year for which statistics were available engineering majors were the second most popular major among undergraduates. Social sciences was the most popular major. Education in Japan 1989: A Graphic Presentation, 26-27.

[32] Ibid., 66.

not asking questions or posing intellectual challenges to the assertions of professors.

The nature of the university entrance process also works against the cultivation of an inquiring attitude toward intellectual pursuits on the part of many Japanese undergraduates. Freshman who are suddenly free of the enormous pressure to do well on entrance examinations have a natural tendency to not work as hard as before they entered university.

Also in the Japanese system, university freshman are admitted to a particular faculty and not the university as a whole. For example, if a Japanese sophomore loses interest in his philosophy major and becomes attracted to science, he may not transfer from the faculty of humanities to the science faculty as would be true in many nations. The only courses of action available to the Japanese student is to either take a new set of entrance examinations or graduate in philosophy and re-enroll in science as a freshman or possibly as a junior. Nor are credits usually transferable between universities, even those of equal standing. Because of the structure of the entrance process, Japanese university students are denied the freedom to change intellectual interests and still progress through university. Such constraints work against strengthening the intellectual climate of Japanese universities.[33]

Research in leading world universities is produced by faculty, many of whom must demonstrate their productivity for several years to win tenure and promotion. By contrast, Japanese university faculty usually gain permanent employment upon appointment. Faculty at Japanese universities are often graduates of the university where they are employed and picked by their major professors. Many Japanese faculty do not have doctorate degrees. Because of the hierarchical nature of the Japanese university, junior faculty get along by following the lead of their superiors rather than initiating and pursuing scholarship on their own. Because in Japan junior faculty are so deferential to their superiors, the give and take of peer discourse which is essential to academic growth is quite constrained in universities.

Given these problems in Japanese higher education that affect the behavior of students and teachers, it should be no surprise that Japanese professors in the

---

[33] Martin Bronfenbrenner, "Economic Education in Japan at the University Level," Journal of Economic Education 16, no. 4: 270.

earlier survey did not rank their institutions as world leaders. The college classroom scene described in the beginning of this chapter is typical of a system that some critics say contributes little to national development. One widespread current media characterization of Japan's universities is "Leisure Land."[34]

Despite the fact that domestic and foreign analysts largely concur that based on the resources the country devotes to universities, Japanese higher education is the weakest link in the nation's formal educational system, some students learn a great deal in the classroom. Even larger numbers of Japanese undergraduates learn important values and interpersonal relations lessons outside the classroom during their university years.

Perhaps even more in Japan than in other industrialized nation, college is a welcome respite for young adults between "examination hell" and the pressures of full-time work. Japanese college students use the time to forge their own identities through dating and through developing relations with their peers in social activities and clubs. Because of adult pressure and impending university examinations, most Japanese high school students do not engage in serious relationships with members of the opposite sex. University students, with little pressure and time on their hands, actively take part in the dating and courtship rituals.

University clubs are extremely important in the lives of most college students. There is a tremendous variety of clubs at the typical university. Many Japanese students devote even longer hours each day to club activities than was true when they were high school students. Sports clubs in particular are popular and it is quite common for a table tennis or field hockey club to meet and practice five or six hours a day for six days a week.

The hierarchical pattern described in accounts of secondary school club activity repeats itself during the university years. First-year club members form similar relationships with senior club members. Kōhai use honorific language toward sempai, run errands for older members that include doing laundry and other personal favors, and perform menial tasks at club practices such as retrieving tennis balls or setting up props for theater practice. In return, seniors

[34] John Gittelsohn, "Japanese Universities Taking a Cue from National Politics, Now Face Their Own Crisis of Complacency, Analysts Say," The Chronicle of Higher Education 36, no. 3 (September 20, 1989): 45.A. Also, Albert Yee, "Why Asia's Schools Don't Make the Top Ranks," Japan Times, March 16, 1988, 286-287.

148

assist <u>kōhai</u> to become more proficient in the club sport or activity. More importantly, <u>sempai</u> often assist their former fellow club members after university.

Much of club activity in Japanese universities is a simple quest for fun by young adults. However, the intense dedication of so many Japanese college students to their clubs is significant in understanding the values lessons learned in Japanese universities, the nature of higher educational institutions, and the larger cultural environment in which universities exist.

The keys to the values lessons reinforced by club activity lie in the intensity of many clubs and the <u>sempai-kōhai</u> relationships. Although recently "hard training" sports clubs and other clubs that require four or five hours practice several days a week are falling out of favor with some university students, great intensity is still the norm for many university clubs.

For example, members of an intramural basketball club at one prestigious private university in Ōsaka meet in the locker room after any loss for over an hour. Each team member, including substitutes who see no action, gives a short and often emotional speech about how he should make more of an effort on the court or cheering from the bench. This group pep rally process is also repeated before and after practices. "<u>Gambare,</u>" or "persevere," is a cry that is as common in university as in secondary school clubs. Club members are often prized as much for their intensity, effort, and loyalty, as for their skills. Good club members also play the game of first deferring to their seniors and then later on assuming the role of strict but kindly senior to junior club members.

Like younger Japanese, university students continue to learn intensity of effort, loyalty, and respect for hierarchy. Since these personal characteristics are also prized in the adult work place, the club activities of a university senior who is applying for a position are often of great import to prospective employers.

A spokesman for Sumitomo Bank, one of Japan's most prestigious financial institutions, described the value of university club quite accurately in the course of explaining his bank's employment process.

> "In Japanese colleges, many students spend four years without doing much of anything, so it is a plus for a student if he can say he did something with devotion. If a student was a captain of the club, then he is likely to be trained in harmonizing the team to produce good teamwork and to work under pressure. We don't require them to submit grades. Even if grades are bad, it does not

necessarily mean that we don't want a student. We stress personal characteristics."[35]

It is common for students who are applying with large companies to be quite frank in emphasizing their dedication and the great time they devoted to a university club. This is particularly true with males who were members of team sport clubs such as baseball, field hockey, or tennis. Some private employers admit they consider a student who was a member of a baseball club to have more valuable experience compared to students who were members of a club such as mountaineering or fencing that stressed more individualistic skills.

The importance private employers place on university students' extracurricular activities is also indicative of both perceived and real shortcomings of Japanese universities. Much of classroom activity in the university is viewed by the rest of society as narrow and of little use in the adult work place. To both employers and other critics of Japanese universities, the character building of the club experience is more important than academics. It is common for employers to state that they are looking for the "right person." He can be taught what he needs to know at the work place.

The Japanese university student's commitment to the club instead of the classroom may also be interpreted as a sign that formal university education is failing to meet the needs of many young people. Many top-level Japanese universities with their large lecture hall classes offer no opportunity for student-professor contact that results in intellectual growth for young people. Japanese have even coined a phrase, "May sickness," for the disappointment many college freshman experience after the initial excitement of beginning study at their chosen university.

As described earlier, because Japanese universities are not difficult to negotiate, a large percentage of students graduate after four years. Many of the students who don't graduate after four years do so by choice. Many young people realize that after university they will be expected to work long hours and have few vacations. They deliberately prolong their university work an extra year because their campus offers a restful moratorium from societal pressure. Since most

---

[35] Susan Chira, "In Student's Game Plan, College Can Be a Racquet," Teacher's Manual for Video Letters from Japan II, The College Years (The Asia Society, 1988): 28.

150

students are not inspired by academics, they do clubs, lead active social lives, and even miss parts of semesters to travel abroad. All of these activities, while enjoyable and even positive experiences for most students, are evidence that universities in Japan are not nearly as inspiring to intellectual development as is the case with other formal educational institutions in the country.

The active social lives many university students lead and the failure of the institutions to challenge young peoples' intellects described above are offered as generalizations for a better understanding of higher education in Japan. It must be stressed that there are many exceptions, both on the part of university faculties such as Tōdai's Faculty of Medicine and others that demand much from their charges.

Among the millions of Japanese university students there are also a number of Japanese university students who are quite serious about their studies. Graduate education in Japan is limited compared to many nations and only accounts for 3 percent of the total higher education enrollment. Still, for most students graduate work is serious business and offers the kind of intellectual growth opportunities found in similar programs elsewhere.[36]

Changes in the University

Major changes are already occurring within Japanese higher education as a result of demographics, decisions by many young women to pursue four instead of two year degrees, and internationalization.

Japan, as is true of other modern industrialized nations, is experiencing a drop in the birth rate that by the early 1990s resulted in a decline in the number of eighteen-year-olds. Although there are a few exceptions, such as the University of the Air, an institution created in 1985 by the national government that broadcasts television and radio courses to primarily adult students, Japanese universities have focused exclusively upon the 18- to 21-year-old segment of the population. Already facing student shortages because of demographics, by the 1990s Japanese universities were studying, and in some cases implementing, programs designed to enroll more adult students. New potential students include

---

[36] Japanese Education Today, 49.

housewives and others who were previously never encouraged to pursue a university degree.

Many of the recent enrollment increases in Japanese universities are due to increasing numbers of Japanese women who are pursuing four year degrees. A number of women now attending university a few years ago would have enrolled in a private junior college. Until the mid-1980s, junior colleges, which are almost exclusively female, were a major postsecondary option for women. These institutions, in some ways like Western finishing schools of earlier times, offer students liberal arts curricula and such career possibilities as preschool teaching. However, according to the Association of Private Junior Colleges in Japan, junior college enrollment has substantially declined in recent years as women are now more motivated to seek better educational qualifications as a result of the 1985 enactment of the law to guarantee equal opportunity for women in jobs. As employment opportunities gradually open up for university-educated women, even larger members of this sex will probably enroll in institutions of higher learning.[37]

Internationalization of Japanese higher education also began in earnest during the latter part of the 1980s. Pressure by the Japanese government on institutions of higher education to internationalize and a desire by colleges and universities to increase or maintain student enrollments were the major reasons for internationalization efforts. By the end of the decade both the numbers of foreign students studying in Japan and Japanese university students who were willing to do a portion of their college work abroad had increased dramatically relative to 1980. Also in the 1980s, a number of Japanese and American colleges began various kinds of programs for students in each other's country.

Confronted with already occurring change and significant criticism from a variety of quarters, Japan's universities face perhaps the most critical times in their history. Any major changes in entrance procedures, student demography, and in the mission of Japanese universities will almost certainly have significant effects upon upper secondary education as well as the cram school industry.

Given the problems of universities described earlier in this chapter, it is not surprising that university reform is a key issue in a larger educational reform

---

[37] "Japan's Junior Colleges Being Absorbed by Parent Universities," The College Years: 40-41.

debate that has been the subject of much attention in Japan for almost ten years. The ramifications of reform efforts for the Japanese university and cram school industry which, along with the examination system, comprise the aspects of Japanese education under the most critical scrutiny, are discussed in more detail in the final chapter of this book.

Questions for Comparison

1.   The American secondary and higher educational systems are extremely different from Japan's regarding institutional entry. In the U.S. most high schools do not require entrance examinations and national standardized tests for university entrance measure aptitude more than content students have previously learned. What are the advantages and disadvantages to American education of a secondary and university entrance system that tends to, for the most part, de-emphasize examinations?

2.   One argument by many American educational reformers during the past decade is that there are no external incentives for American secondary school students to work at academics. Assess the validity of this argument based upon your own experiences in American schools and what you have just read about the Japanese.

3.   Recently in the United States there has been an expansion of private educational tutoring businesses. Is there a role for private "after-school" schools in improving American education or would the resources allocated to these American "juku" be better utilized by traditional public and private educational institutions?

4.   The following are three major criticisms of Japanese universities. They are too inflexible in their entry and transfer policies. The higher educational system as a whole does not effectively motivate students to develop intellectually. Cultural mores cause students and faculty to allow hierarchy and deference to interfere with academic freedom and inquiry. Based on your experiences are any of these criticisms applicable to American colleges and universities?

Additional Reading

Portions of the recommended books on Japanese education at the end of the previous chapter contain sound information on juku, the examination race, and educational credentialism. Those who are interested in learning more about the evolution of the examination system and educational credentialism in Japan should read Āmano Ikuō, Education and Examination in Modern Japan, which was published in 1990 by the University of Tōkyō Press and is available in English. Estelle Japames and Gail Benjamin, Public Policy and Private Education in Japan, is an excellent economic and social analysis of the relationship between the state, private education, and the Japanese examination system. The book was published in 1988 by St. Martin's Press. Although there is relatively little in English available on Japanese universities, the chapters on Japan in From Dependence to Autonomy: The Development of Asian Universities are highly recommended. The book is edited by Philip Altbach and Viswanathan Selvarathnam and was published by Kluwer Academic Publishers (the Netherlands) in 1989.

The question of the relationship between examinations and student performance in an American context receives excellent treatment in Arthur Powell, Eleanor Farrar, and David Cohen, The Shopping Mall High School: Winners and Losers in the Educational Marketplace, Houghton Mifflin, 1985. John Bennett and J.W. Peltason, eds., Contemporary Issues in Higher Education, is, in general, a good overview of the problems facing American higher education. The book was published in 1985 by Macmillan. An even more readable book which describes and analyzes the American undergraduate experience is Ernest Boyer, College: The Undergraduate Experience in America, Harper and Row, 1987.

Chapter Six

Education in the Japanese Work Place

Introduction: Case Studies in Human Capital Development

Sēnsōji Temple is located in Asakusa, a colorful, bustling, and somewhat old-fashioned area of Tōkyō. Sēnsōji is a good place for Japanese to meet foreigners. Each day thousands of Japanese as well as visitors from other nations visit the temple with its massive gate and fierce-looking immense guardian statues. In addition to the temple itself, there are numerous open-air shops that sell a variety of trinkets, souvenirs, and food stuffs. The shops are located on both sides of the half-mile pathway leading up to the temple entrance.

These days, amidst the crowded and noisy bazaar area, a foreigner who appears to be from an English-speaking country is quite likely to be approached by a Japanese man. The Japanese is an English teacher and will ask in that language if the visitor will do his students a favor and speak with them in his or her native language. If the foreigner agrees, typically, seven to nine Japanese who appear to be in their early twenties will encircle the tourist. They will ask questions in English such as "Where are you from?," "Do you like Japan?" and "Are you interested in Japanese culture?". Most of the young people in the group are likely to be young women. Only two or three students will speak really intelligible English, but everyone in the group will usually try a question or two.

156

The students are all recent high school graduates and are enrolled in a nearby two-year school of foreign languages. They are preparing for careers where it is important to speak English. These future foreign tour guides and airline stewardesses are carrying out an assignment intended to provide them with practical English speaking experiences.

Even though the July vacation period is about to begin for all schools in Japan, including Nagoya's Seiyrō Commercial High School, several faculty members of that institution still face some very long summer meetings. Throughout June a number of companies visited the school. Among the companies that sent representatives to Seiyrō were several prestigious firms such as Toyota, Coca Cola-Japan, and Mitsui and Tōkai Banks, as well as many firms of lesser stature. Company representatives visited classes of students who had just begun their third year of high school and left information about their firms.

Shortly before summer vacation, third-year students who plan to enter the work force immediately after high school left wish lists with teachers of the top three companies they would like to enter upon graduation. In their visits each company representative informed teachers of these students exactly how many openings for new recruits from Seiyrō High would be available in the firm beginning in April of the next year. After receiving this information, a select faculty committee recommends new recruits for each of the visiting firms based upon both the wishes of businesses and students and teacher assessments of individual student achievement and capabilities. Companies receive the lists of suggested future employees from the school each September and a large majority of employers follow the faculty suggestions as to whom to hire.

The small city of Nagaoka, located near Kyōto, is the site for a two-day quality control circle convention attended by 350 employees of both large and small Japanese companies. Quality control circles are small groups of business and industrial employees who usually work in the same department or section. The small groups meet two or three times a month and exchange information about how to do their jobs more efficiently and work on commonly agreed upon problems.

Although the two-day itinerary includes plant tours and one lavish cocktail party and dinner, most of the convention attendees' time is spent either making or listening to the sixty-two presentations which are arranged in four concurrent blocks. Two-man teams are responsible for each of the presentations. The presentations are extremely diverse, but each consists of a fifteen-minute oral case report followed by a five-minute question and answer period. Presentation topics range from the best ways to teach statistics to fellow employees to how a QC Circle in one plant thought of a better waste disposal system which was later implemented by the company. During the two-day conference over one-third of all attendees make presentations. With the exception of ten managers who coordinated the conference, all attendees and presenters are production workers who completed their formal education upon high school graduation.[1]

Economists use a term called human capital investment for actions that increase productivity of workers by improving their skills and abilities.[2] A major reason Japan is an economic super power is that the nation's public and private sectors are extremely successful in human capital development. Much of this development takes place within elementary and secondary schools and colleges and universities. However, millions of Japanese also learn skills and other valuable work-related information in a variety of other settings than the institutions already described in earlier chapters of this book.

The major focus of this chapter is upon education and training for the Japanese work place. Since human capital development in Japan takes a variety of forms, a number of public and private institutions are major actors in the vocational educational process.

Educational Institutions for the Work Place

Even though the entrance process and academics of vocational high schools were described earlier in this book, in examining the preparation of future Japanese workers it is useful to begin with the demography and vocational curricula of these schools. Seiyrō Commercial High School is just one of several types of vocational high schools under Mombushō's general administrative

---

[1] Robert Cole, Strategies For Learning: Small-Group Activities in American, Japanese, and Swedish Industry (University of California Press, 1989), 285-292.

[2] Campbell R. McConnell, Economics: Principles, Problems, and Policies, 10th ed. (McGraw-Hill, 1987), 15.

authority and financed by prefectures and locales. Vocational high schools, which are almost all public, enroll approximately 26 percent of all Japanese high school students. Although commercial and industrial high schools are the two most common types of secondary vocational institutions, there are also vocational high schools of agriculture, home economics, nursing and fisheries.[3]

Several specialty programs exist within vocational high schools in addition to the academic curriculum. In industrial high schools, machinery, electricity, electronics, architecture, and civil engineering are the most common specializations. Other programs exist in such fields as automobile repair, metalwork, and textiles. In commercial high schools such as Seiyrō, popular student concentrations include general commerce, data processing, accountancy, and administration.[4]

Vocational high school enrollment has declined in recent years. Since 25 percent of academic high school students go directly to work upon graduation, there is some evidence that certain employers prefer graduates of the latter institutions over their vocational counterparts. Still, vocational high schools provide Japanese business and industry with large numbers of workers. Over 75 percent of vocational high school graduates are immediately employed upon finishing their studies.[5]

Approximately 37 percent of academic high school graduates and 15 percent of vocational high school graduates enroll in a variety of other special educational institutions rather than going directly to work or attending university.[6] These institutions in order of prestige include koto senmon gakkō, or technical colleges, senshū gakkō, or special training schools, and kakushu gakkō, or miscellaneous schools.

Presently there are sixty-two technical colleges in Japan. Even though their enrollments total only about one-twentieth of the number of college and university students, technical colleges are considered by government policy

---

[3] Education in Japan 1989: A Graphic Presentation, 26-27.

[4] Ronald Dore and Sako Mari, How the Japanese Learn to Work (London: Routledge, 1989), 34.

[5] Ibid., 19.

[6] Ibid.

makers to be quite important. Fifty-eight technical colleges are operated by the national government. All colleges of technology are under the authority of Mombushō. Colleges of technology recruit students at age fifteen and annually enroll approximately 9,500 boys and 350 girls. The 50,000 or so technical college students, usually in five-year programs, complete both a high school education and specialized technical training in all branches of engineering and in such manufacturing technology fields as industrial chemistry. Most colleges of technology have close ties with industry. Japanese companies provide some faculty for the colleges and three-week summer assignments in factories for students.

Although a technical college engineering graduate has less general expertise than his university counterpart, technical college graduates are highly valued by industry. The technical college movement, which dates back to the late 1950s and early 1960s, grew from a perceived need by industry for personnel who would possess technical skills below the university graduate level but above that of vocational high school graduates. Employers consider college of technology diplomas to be the equivalent of junior college credentials. While a few technical college graduates go on to university to complete engineering degrees, most go directly to manufacturing employment.[7]

Special training schools serve primarily high school graduates. These institutions are both more numerous and heterogeneous than colleges of technology. Unlike colleges of technology, special training schools are usually private. Government-run institutions account for less than 10 percent of these institutions. Approximately 700,000 students attend special training schools. This number represents considerably more students than the total enrollment of Japan's junior colleges and is about one-third the number of students who attend Japanese universities. While Mombushō has certification power over almost all special training institutions, other national government agencies such as the Ministries of Labor and Health provide subsidies and in some cases have administrative authority over a few special training schools.

In recent years special training schools have grown at the expense of traditional junior colleges. The primary reason is that, unlike the junior college,

---

[7] Ibid., 45-46.

the mission of all special training schools is clearly a vocational one. Special training school curricula are extremely varied. Examples of subjects that might be studied in special training schools include English, dental technology, automobile mechanics, business, data processing, cooking and dietetics, electronics, accounting, and secretarial science. Average ages of special training school students are similar to that of university students. However, because it is easier for an older student to enter a special training school than a university there is more age variance among students of the former institutions. Even with this variation, many young people who attend special training schools made the decision while still in high school. Other young people choose the special training school route as an alternative only after failing university entrance examinations or not securing employment with a desired company.

National government standards require the duration of all special training school courses to be at least one year. While special training school program lengths range from one to three years, the most common programs are of two-year duration. There is great variance in the quality of special training schools. The trend among employers who hire special training school graduates is to classify these workers as having the same educational credentials as that of junior college graduates. Special training school faculty have educational backgrounds as varied as the institutions in which they work. Depending upon the major program or programs of a particular special training school, its faculty are holders of graduate degrees, university graduates, or master practitioners of a craft or skill. Special training school tuitions vary also because of the wide range of institutions. The typical special training school student, however, pays $6,000 to $9,000 annually to attend.

Private miscellaneous schools constitute the final broad category of vocationally oriented institutions in Japan. Miscellaneous schools are not under the jurisdiction of Mombushō and they provide students with many of the same kind of vocational programs as special training schools. However, program length in the typical miscellaneous school is much shorter than that of the average special training school. Miscellaneous school course lengths vary from three months to one year or more. Unlike their special training school counterparts who hold high school diplomas, many miscellaneous school students left Japanese public educational institutions after completing junior high school. Miscellaneous school faculty tend to be master practitioners of the craft or vocational skill that is the core of the particular school's program in which they are employed. Since miscellaneous schools have lower status than special training schools, enrollment in recent years has declined while there have been increases in the number of students attending special training schools. As a result many miscellaneous schools are now in the process of attempting to be reclassified as special training schools.

In both special training and miscellaneous schools, open admission is the general policy. Although some of the former institutions employ entrance examinations, usually they are for placement purposes only. The barriers faced by students who finish courses in either of these institutions occur after graduation. Usually before a graduate of either type of institution can secure employment in a particular field, he or she must pass vocational licensing examinations. These examinations are either required by government or by practitioners of the particular occupation a student desires to enter.[8]

Because special training schools in particular are now a major part of the formal education of a large portion of Japanese high school graduates, it should be useful to consider one such institution, the Nagoya-based Trident School of Languages of Trident College, in some detail.

The Trident School of Languages

In Japan, it is quite common in places like train stations or shops to hear Supremes songs on the radio or other English language expressions. Even during a nationally televised Japanese major league baseball game, the end of the commercial and the resumption of play will be indicated by a booming voice in English announcing, "and now back to the Friday night game!" Perhaps no people in any country employ as many expressions from a foreign language or seem as interested in learning another language as is true of the Japanese with English.

Some Japanese have been interested in learning the English language ever since the mid-1800s when Commodore Perry opened the country to the rest of the world. Recently, however, the tremendous amount of business that Japanese

---

[8] Ibid., 52-75.

companies now conduct in the English-speaking world, the attraction of American pop culture in Japan, and a growing government emphasis upon internationalization have all stimulated an English boom that is now at least a decade old. Currently, estimates are that at least twelve million people, or one out of every ten Japanese, are engaged in the study of English. A substantial portion of students studying English are doing so to prepare for occupations that require English. The large majority of these students take an English program in a special training school. Trident School of Languages is in many ways a typical English language special training school.

Trident School of Languages is one of three major divisions of Trident College, a special training school operated by Kawaijuku, the large Nagoya-based private educational corporation whose yobikō was described in the previous chapter. Although the languages school adopted its present name in 1986, the school has existed since 1970. Except for small foreign student and night programs that serve both sexes, Trident School of Languages' student body is entirely composed of women. Trident School's day enrollment has averaged between 800 and 900 students in recent years. The day students are, by far, the major sources of income for the institution. Full-time students at Trident School of Languages pay an average in U.S. dollars of nearly $7,000 annually in fees. While many special training schools serve as many men as women, with the exception of gender, Trident's student body fits the profile of "typical" special training school students. Trident School of Foreign Languages' enrollees are almost all recent high school graduates who will complete the school's two-year program and then go on to become full-time employees with mostly area-based companies.

As is true of almost all special training schools, Trident School of Languages markets itself based on the practicality of the school program. This institutional thrust is reflected in the curriculum of the school. While some Trident graduates secure jobs as interpreters or translators based exclusively on their language training, most of the institution's students are much more employable if they study business-related subjects as well as English. Although there are two different general majors, English language or business, and several different tracks within the majors, all students must take both English and business subjects such as word processing, computer programming, and typing.

There are 130 part-time teachers in the day program. Most of these instructors are Japanese and teach business courses. Seventeen full-time university-trained native speakers teach the language courses at Trident..

The majority of the school's students enter two-year programs and take English language and combinations of secretarial and office-related courses. There is, however, a special three-year course that features a one-year abroad program where students spend a year at an American or Australian junior or four year college campus. Three-year students take a few more courses on the cultures of English-speaking countries than other Trident students.

Trident has excellent facilities including language laboratories, language information centers with videos, microcomputers, and other state-of-the-art equipment. Trident is relatively easy to enter. Applicants are given a written and conversational English examination and the results are used for placement purposes. Applicants who do poorly on the entrance examination are placed in special classes rather than denied admission. Trident instructors seem to employ quite innovative language instructional techniques on a regular basis. Students participate in English language festivals, read novels and other high-interest literature to improve their vocabulary, and have English-language theme lunches with their teachers. Even though more innovative English language instruction appears to exist at the Trident School than in the typical Japanese high school or university, faculty also work hard to prepare students for examinations such as the Test of English as a Foreign Language (TOEFL). Some students need to do well on the TOEFL to qualify for highly coveted positions such as airlines stewardess.

As is true with most special training schools, Trident staff devote large amounts of time and energy in assisting students to find employment and the school operates an extensive placement service. School officials are quite proud of the fact that 95 percent of the students who want a job obtain one. However, staff report a certain amount of unhappiness on the part of some Trident graduates who fail to secure positions where they use English. The typical graduate of Trident School is employed as an office or a clerical worker in the private sector. The school takes pride in the fact that employers such as Toyota, Sumitomo, and Coca Cola-Japan hire their graduates. As mentioned earlier, the most prized position in the minds of most Trident students is that of airline stewardess, but only one or two students from Trident each year score well enough on the TOEFL test to qualify. Other desirable jobs include English-speaking tour guide positions for Toyota or for the numerous pottery companies in the Nagoya area that cater to foreign tourists.

Despite superb facilities and a seemingly dedicated and competent faculty, the average Trident first-year student comes from the lower 50 percent of all Japanese high school graduates. In this respect Trident is quite similar to most special training schools. Approximately one-half of Trident students graduated from vocational high schools while the other half attended academic secondary schools. According to school officials, most young women who are Trident students either gave up the prospect of university entrance early or took company or university entrance examinations but were unable to enter the firm or university of their choice. Attempted conversations with Trident students in English confirm the above generalizations. Most are unable to carry on an English language conversation except at the most rudimentary level. Still, Trident School of Languages enrollment has grown or remained stable throughout the history of the institution. Enrollment and the school's relatively impressive placement record are indicators that Trident School of Languages is successful as a special training school. Its graduates are securing positions with respectable firms.[9]

The best special training schools enjoy regular relationships with major Japanese firms who hire their graduates each year. The best special training schools also provide their graduates with both superior training and employment advantages compared to young people who have only high school diplomas. However, researchers of vocational education in Japan contend there are a number of special training and miscellaneous schools who exploit students and are barely short of fraudulent in pursuit of profit. The great differences in the quality of these educational institutions cause Japanese firms to have quite varied reactions to graduates seeking employment. Data from one survey of large Japanese companies indicate that while most firms give credit to special school training, 13 percent of all firms reported that they counted high school and special training school graduates as having the same educational credentials.[10]

---

[9] Information on Trident obtained by interviews with staff in June 1990.

[10] Dore and Mari, How the Japanese Learn to Work, 71-73.

While Japanese elementary and secondary schools, universities, and the vocational institutions just described all educate students in part for future employment, in any society most workers continue to learn important information and skills after they become full-time employees. No country is as well known as Japan for creating a high-quality work place learning environment. It is to that learning environment that we now turn.

Education in the Japanese Work Place: An Introduction

Leila Philip, a young American woman interested in Japanese art, spent two years in the 1980s as the apprentice of a master Japanese potter. The potter and his family lived and worked in Mīyama, a small village of six hundred people in Southern Kyushu. Ms. Philip lived in the home of the potter and his wife which was adjacent to their pottery workshop. For months after arrival Ms. Philip's primary activities consisted of housework chores, serving tea to visitors, and workshop duties such as preparing clay and firing the pottery kiln. Ms. Philip's teacher eventually allowed her to work first on simple cups and later on more complicated art such as rounded bowls and plates.

The village of Mīyama is well known for pottery and contains fourteen workshops. Even though the young American woman traveled half-way around the globe to learn about Japanese pottery, her hosts did not consider visiting other artists' work places to be a major part of Ms. Philip's educational program.

The Japanese word for apprentice is <u>deshi</u> which also may be translated as "younger brother." As a <u>deshi</u>, Ms. Phillip in a sense "belonged" to the particular potter and his family to whom she was apprenticed. Even though most of the Mīyama artists enjoyed cordial relations, it was not considered exactly appropriate for an apprentice of one artist to spend time in another artist's work place.[11]

Today, the apprentice system is a work place environment that touches the lives of only a few contemporary Japanese. However, the values that impacted Ms. Philip's experience and define appropriate behavior for a learner in a new job are still very much present in the Japanese work place of today. In order to understand on-the-job education in Japan, it is important to explore the

---

[11] Leila Philip, <u>The Road Through Mīyama</u> (Random House, 1989).

relationship between traditional values and the organization of contemporary Japanese enterprises.

Through most of this century the Japanese experienced intensive economic growth. Japan's enterprises have continually expanded, modernized, and developed new and more sophisticated goods and services. During the 1950s and 1960s, the decades in which the most rapid growth took place, many large Japanese firms adopted the so-called "lifetime employment" system. By the 1950s and 1960s the public sector had been providing permanent employment for some time. As early as shortly after World War I, a few Japanese companies had begun experiments with the concept as a means of keeping skilled employees from taking advantage of an expanding economy by constantly switching jobs in order to make more money. In the years before and after World War II Japanese management often desired to maintain a stable work force. In order to achieve this objective, management in many firms developed a set of incentives for employees including guaranteed permanent employment, attractive fringe benefits, regular bonuses, and promotion by seniority. The general intent of this incentive package was to entice employees to remain with a particular firm for most or all of their working years.

Other forces besides economics were at work as well. The "lifetime" employment system also became widespread among Japanese firms because dominant values of the larger culture were quite congruent with this system of enterprise organization. As was true of the traditional Japanese apprentice system, deeply held cultural beliefs in the importance of group loyalty meant a disproportionately high number of Japanese workers found the idea of belonging to one firm for life quite attractive.

This interaction of values with economics also influenced expectations of both employers and employees regarding mutual obligations. Today, permanent employees of firms such as Sony and Nissan are not as much a part of a work "family" as was true with apprentices. However, they are much more members of such a unit than is the case with employees who expect to be with a firm for only a few months or years before switching jobs. Employers also treat lifetime workers differently than employees who will more than likely leave the company in the near future. A realization of the mutual obligations of the lifetime employment system makes it easy to understand why, just as was true of traditional apprentices, today's permanent employees in Japanese firms are expected to learn many different jobs instead of only mastering one task. Job rotation is one important educational process of most large Japanese firms.

The Low Transaction Costs of the Japanese Work Place

The lifetime employment system impacts how Japanese employees learn in much more general and profound ways than the job rotation system for which Japanese companies are famous. Economists who study human capital development within the private and public sectors in different societies often apply the concept of "transaction costs." Transaction costs include both direct financial costs as well as other important costs such as time which managers of any organization incur in communicating all sorts of information to employees.[12]

If a firm's or organization's transaction costs are high, then employers or managers will not consider it in their best interests to spend extensive amounts of time on widespread dissemination of information. Faced with a high transaction-cost environment, managers usually confine the information they provide to a particular worker to essential information that enables him to do a specific job. For example, if an automobile manufacturing company hires an employee whose assignment is to mount and align tires on a vehicle, this is all he or she will be taught to do. Normally, a firm or organization that expects a large work force turnover rate on a regular basis faces high transaction costs. It makes little sense from a manager's perspective to invest extensive money or time providing information for workers who will soon change jobs.

Because of the lifetime employment system in Japan, many firms and organizations have low transaction-cost environments. Since employers expect workers to be with an organization for long periods of time, a substantial investment in the dissemination of as much information as possible to everyone is a sound managerial strategy. If the automobile manufacturing plant discussed earlier is Japanese, a worker assigned to the tire section might work in that section for awhile but also be trained in welding and rotate periodically between the two

---

[12] Hashimoto Masanori, The Japanese Labor Market in a Comparative Perspective With the United States: A Transaction-Cost Interpretation (W. E. Upjohn Institute for Employment Research, 1990), 14.

sections. Often the firm might find it advantageous to train an employee who already knows how to mount tires and weld to assemble engines as well. Future production might very well be improved by shifting this worker and others to the engine assembly section.

Many Japanese firms do not just confine education and training to teaching employees to perform more than one job. Management often provides workers with constant information about the company even if the information has no direct relationship to any job the employee might ever perform. For example, salesman who work for a manufacturing plant might receive weekly briefings on the operating ratios on the shop floor. Production workers might learn information about new employee recruiting efforts on a regular basis. Many large Japanese companies provide for joint consultation sessions between labor and management and circulate memos to large numbers of employees that describe proposed company plans. Both of these practices are designed to insure that as many employees as possible are privy to information on company affairs.

There are several positive effects of widespread attention in Japanese firms and organizations to maximizing the knowledge levels of all employees. Although it is difficult to measure, there is significant anecdotal evidence that employees appreciate the fact that superiors provide them with all sorts of information about the organization. General company morale is boosted as a result. Also, the understanding that an organization's employees possess about what is happening elsewhere in the agency or firm helps individuals better realize their parts in the whole. Since Japanese organizations commonly engage in liberal distribution of information, the odds are high that a member who really needs to learn something will not accidentally remain ignorant of important information. Finally, as described earlier, a disproportionately high number of members of Japanese organizations can perform more than one job. The ability on the part of a worker to fulfill more than one task is often of great economic benefit to the firm in which he is employed.[13]

---

[13] Rodney Clark, The Japanese Company (Yale University Press, 1979), 129.

Lifetime Employment: Ideals and Reality

Earlier, when the term lifetime employment was first used it was enclosed in quotation marks in order to indicate that the term must be qualified. By no means all, or even a majority of the Japanese work force have, or even desire, permanent positions with one company. Estimates as to the numbers of Japanese permanent employees vary and data collection is difficult. However, a reasonable estimate is that approximately 50 percent of the Japanese work force are lifetime employees if public as well as private sector employees are counted. This statistic is only tabulated for non-family employees who do not work for themselves. The 25 percent of Japanese workers who are self-employed or family workers are excluded from these calculations.[14]

Gender and private sector firm size are important determinants of whether an employee is permanent or subject to lay-offs during economic hard times. Particularly within the private sector, few women have permanent employment. The traditional Japanese belief that a woman should be family- rather than career-oriented is one major reason women have difficulty obtaining lifetime employment. Also, employers expect most women to leave employment when they have children. It is estimated that women make up 10 percent or less of the permanent private sector employee work force.[15] According to one survey even university-educated women were offered positions by only 22 percent of Japan's five thousand largest companies.[16] The typical job that a woman receives in a company consists of very low-level work and most companies pressure women to leave when they marry.

The lifetime employment system is much more widespread in larger firms. Small firms lack the economic resources to retain workers during recessions. The results of one study examining employment practices of firms with over and under one thousand employees indicate that while over 70 percent of employees of the

---

[14] Dore and Mari, How the Japanese Learn to Work, 76.

[15] Although data on percentages of public-sector permanent employees who are women are unavailable, the percentages are probably double that of the private sector since there seems to be greater opportunities for women in the public sector in Japan. For example, a majority of public elementary school teachers are women.

[16] Linda Wojtan, ed., Introduction to Japan: A Workbook (Youth for Understanding, 1986), 57.

170

first-category firms could be classified as permanent, the percentage of permanent employees in the second-category firms averaged about 20 percent.[17]

Evidence also exists that younger workers find the idea of lifetime employment less attractive than their older colleagues. Data from one recent poll indicates that while over 40 percent of a sample drawn from the entire Japanese work force felt they would be willing to change jobs in the future, 66.3 percent of men in their twenties said they would be willing to change jobs.[18]

Still, despite the fact that lifetime employment by no means includes the entire work force, the concept exerts a powerful impact upon attitudes and personnel policies throughout the entire economy. Although formal lifetime employment exists primarily in large companies which are only 1/2 of 1 percent of Japan's total companies, these large firms employ over one-fourth of the total work force and produce nearly 50 percent of the nation's GNP. The high status of the large firms means that to a large extent their personnel policies will be supported by the public and, when possible, emulated by smaller firms.[19] For example, surveys indicate that about 80 percent of the Japanese population strongly believes in lifetime employment. Support is so widespread that, in the words of one scholar of Japanese management, "Lifetime employment is the goal towards which both firms and individuals have to direct their efforts-or their apologies...."[20]

Also, when the amount of work force job change in Japan is compared with the same phenomenon in other industrialized countries, the data indicates that not only large Japanese firms but small ones as well retain employees for relatively long periods of time. Whether officially classified as permanent employees or not, on average Japanese change jobs less than their counterparts in other nations. In a recent study comparing job change in Japan and the United States, it was found that the typical Japanese male will hold about five jobs before

[17] Arthur Whitehill, Japanese Management: Tradition and Transition (Routledge, 1991), 130-131.

[18] "Poll Reveals New Attitudes in Japan Toward Work and the Home," News From Japan (Washington, D.C.: Japan-U.S. News and Communications Center, March 14, 1988).

[19] Japanese Education Today, 57.

[20] Clark, The Japanese Company, 175.

retiring while his American counterpart will hold about eleven jobs. Researchers in the same study found that Japanese females, usually not privy to lifetime employment, changed jobs a little over five times during their working years while American women changed a little over ten times during the same period.[21]

The strong influence of lifetime employment in Japan means that managers and agency heads are much more likely to look for traits that indicate a job recruit will be comfortable with learning how to do several kinds of work over the course of a career. Their counterparts in other nations will be more likely to hire applicants who are narrow specialists. Because of the permanent employment system, many Japanese workers must often be lifetime learners in a very real sense.

Linkages Between School and Work

In Japan clear linkages exist between formal educational institutions such as high schools, vocational schools, and universities and the agencies and companies in which graduates of the former educational institutions will be employed. The linkages between these two types of organizations often determine the environment in which a Japanese will work and learn.

In the opening section of this chapter a short case study was presented on a vocational high school's role in the employee selection process. The role Seiyrō faculty played in determining student employment and the relationships of the high school with various "client" firms are examples of quite widespread Japanese educational/business linkages.

The typical pattern is that individual vocational high schools and academic high schools where a significant portion of students do not elect to attend university will develop and maintain long-standing relationships with agencies and firms. Japanese secondary school reputations within the community or prefecture are in large part determined by the perceived quality of the employers who hire graduates from a particular educational institution. The great amount of time many high school educators spend on selecting the right students for a particular company is completely reasonable behavior considering that the

---

[21] Hashimoto, The Japanese Labor Market in a Comparative Perspective with the United States, 88.

172

school's reputation may rise or fall upon how satisfied employers are with the graduates they recruit. As a rule, the more prestigious a particular high school the higher the number of large companies that will recruit from it.

Employers also value a long-standing relationship with a particular high school since, if the arrangement has been satisfactory for years, the school is a reliable source of good employees. It is common practice for a company who has enjoyed a long relationship with a school to hire some graduates from the school every year, even if economic conditions do not actually justify hiring anyone in a given year. Company management views this kind of gesture as important in maintaining a valuable linkage.

The process described earlier in Seiyō High School is typical. Shortly before summer vacation, which marks the end of the first of the three-semester Japanese school year, third-year students are told how many jobs particular companies are allocating to the school. Students then make their choices and a faculty committee matches individual students with employers. In the fall, companies then interview candidates during the students' next-to-last semester of high school. Future workers are then hired before the school year ends. Data from studies of this process indicate that over 80 percent of the time, employers hire the initial candidates recommended by school faculty.

While school staff base student employment recommendations on several criteria, grades are the primary determinant in the nomination of a young person for a position with an agency or firm. Japanese teachers report that generally the quality of an individual student's grades are both the most objective selection procedure and the best indicator of how well a student will later perform as a worker.

The high school/employer linkages just described have existed with some secondary schools and firms since before World War II. Since the majority of special training and miscellaneous schools are new and often employers are suspect of the quality of some institutions, these kinds of linkages are not as widespread. However, well-respected special training and other kinds of vocational schools have recently developed similar long-term relationships with employers.[22]

---

22 James Rosenbaum, "Linkages Between High Schools and Work: Lessons from Japan" (Policy Studies Associates, Inc., 1989).

In Japan, employer recruitment of university graduates is, with certain exceptions, more similar than different from the process by which Japanese workers who do not attend university are hired. Recruitment of college seniors begins about the same time and particular universities, like secondary schools, have linkages with specific agencies and companies. These linkages are actually even more established at the university level. Because of employer preference for male permanent employees, the major focus of the university/employer linkage process is upon the recruitment of young men as lifetime employees.

Grade point averages or individual majors tend to be less important for a university student than the particular university from which he will graduate. Although engineering, economics, and law undergraduate majors are popular with recruiters, as a rule the particular university from which one graduates carries at least as much status as what subject was studied. Leading companies and government agencies tend to recruit employees almost exclusively from two or three prestigious universities. As described in an earlier chapter, Japanese companies are also quite interested in the kinds of extracurricular activities potential employees concentrated on while in university.

Japanese university placement services do much of the work performed by high school teachers in the secondary school recruitment process. The university placement service director is an important contact for many Japanese undergraduates. Placement services screen and determine who will have priority in interviewing with certain companies before the firms visit a campus. Many major corporations also administer examinations to potential recruits. The major purpose of these examinations is to measure such individual characteristics as general knowledge, motivation, and leadership potential rather than a candidate's specialized knowledge. In most Japanese universities, individual professors establish relationships with specific employers and are called upon year after year for recommendations.

Since many organizations tend to recruit from a few universities, linkages are established between university cliques of employees in agencies and companies who were students together and their old campuses. These networks serve as sources of vital information for employees about potential recruits.[23]

---

[23] Whitehill, Japanese Management: Tradition and Transition, 133-134.

Long-time Japanese practice based on widely held cultural beliefs causes employee quality to vary among work places of differing prestige. However, the care and time spent on the recruiting process by both educational institutions and employers means that the most prestigious company and government agency employers can make certain assumptions about new employees, be they high school or university graduates. In both tracks new workers have won the recognition of high school or university educators as being outstanding among their peers and deserving of high-status employment.

If the new employee in a major agency or firm is a high school graduate, managers may safely assume that he or she will not need basic remedial education. If the new employee of a company such as Sony or Nissan is a university graduate, management is aware he or she worked very hard to pass a highly competitive university entrance examination and, while in university, impressed faculty, staff, and classmates. These assumptions of the most prestigious employers also hold true to a lesser extent for employers in Japanese agencies and companies that are regarded as middle tier. The cumulative result for high and middle level Japanese employers is that a very large percentage of new employees will fit the description of "lifelong learner."

Work Place Education: University Graduates

Typically, new recruits fresh from university are welcomed to a company or agency through a formal ceremony in which the company president or some other top leader addresses the new class. While practices vary by agency or company, these ceremonies are similar in many respects to the rites of passage for new students in Japanese schools that were described in an earlier chapter. It is not uncommon for families of employees to attend this rather formal occasion.

During the first few months on the job--anywhere from one to five months depending upon the company--new employees go through an induction program. Again, although practices vary there are orientation sessions where employees learn procedures, are introduced to the various departments in the company, and receive other general information. There are also sessions where management articulates dominant organizational values to new employees. Members of the new class are expected to get to know each other extremely well during this time period. Some companies require the new men to live in a company dormitory during the initial training sessions.

Most firms and government agencies also emphasize the same traditional Japanese values to new employees that they first learned in school. Some companies require trainees to engage in physically demanding experiences such as twenty-five mile walks with enforced silence so as to encourage the value of perseverance. Many of these activities are quite stressful and bring to mind aspects of military basic training. Some companies use outside organizations for a portion of university recruits' induction time. One such private training agency publishes large daily advertisements in the <u>Daily Nikkei</u>, Japan's most prestigious economic journal, offering two-week courses of "training in hell," which features such activities as bellowing in groups and singing at a local railroad station.[24]

Meditation, which is believed to cultivate the greatly admired virtue of concentration, is popular enough with Japanese companies that annually thousands of new recruits spend a portion of their induction time in Zen Buddhist temples as lay trainees.[25]

During induction periods it is quite common for junior-senior relationships to develop between older members of organizations and recent inductees. Often the senior and junior employees will have graduated from the same university. Often for many years of an employee's career his senior will serve as a teacher and advisor about various aspects of the company.

The next stage of a typical university graduate's on-the-job education and training, which is much more lengthy than the induction phase, is a period of job rotation. The job rotation stage might last anywhere from eighteen months to two years.[26] This phase in the education of university graduate employees consists of a series of practical, on-the-job work experiences. An economics graduate might spend a month in a clerical position in the shipping and receiving department of the company. An accounting major might work for a short period of time in the

---

[24] Peter Tasker, <u>The Japanese: A Major Exploration of Modern Japan</u> (E. P. Dutton, 1987), 82.

[25] Daizen Victoria, "Japanese Corporate Zen," in <u>The Other Japan</u>, ed. Patricia Tsurumi (M. E. Sharpe, Inc., 1988), 131.

[26] Dore and Mari, <u>How the Japanese Learn to Work</u>, 25.

marketing section of a firm. A university graduate who goes to work for a large bank might serve as a teller in a smaller branch for a period of time. In manufacturing firms, engineering majors are placed in front-line shop floor situations where they can actually see a product constructed by assembly line operators.

Japanese managers view this time-consuming job rotation process for university graduates as having a number of benefits. New employees are likely to develop a holistic understanding of the company because they have done a number of different jobs. Also, when university-educated employees advance to management and supervisory positions, their abilities to communicate information are likely to have been enhanced because of prior associations with employees of varying educational levels and skills. The long-held belief by Japanese that self-development is an end in itself is manifested in the dynamic learning process of job rotation. Also, since often there is an expectation that an individual will be with a company for years to come, job rotation means he is more likely to be useful in a number of different work capacities rather than only in the specialty in which he was educated.[27]

It is important to understand what relatively little emphasis Japanese management places upon the university major compared to management in other societies. This holds true even in such specialized fields as accounting and engineering. The results of one study of the accounting sections of major Japanese corporation indicated that only 34 percent of the university graduate employees in accounting divisions majored in accounting in college. Only 7 percent of the respondents with university degrees in accounting sections had spent their entire careers in accounting departments without experiencing job rotation to another section.[28] A similar study of Japanese engineers concluded that within two to three years of hiring more than 40 percent of engineering majors worked in a job that required a technical specialty substantially different

---

[27] Ibid., 90.

[28] Hiramatsu Kazuō, "The Role of Accounting Education and Research in Japanese Corporations," The Sixth International Conference on Accounting Education (Kyōto, Japan, October 8, 1987), Appendix ii.

than what they studied in college.[29] Although there are major exceptions, Japanese university graduates have inculcated the expectation that they are generalists who work for a company. Large- and medium-company employees introduce themselves to strangers not as engineers or lawyers but as employees of Sony or Nissan.

In addition to job rotation, university graduates, particularly if they have been identified as potential candidates for top-management positions in an organization, are placed in many other learning opportunities during their careers. It is common practice for company employees of this educational level, particularly section chiefs in their early thirties, to write the equivalent of a graduate-level thesis on some aspect of the company under the supervision of a senior manager. Also, managers often enroll in a variety of correspondence courses on specialized topics and, from time to time, the company will pay for someone in management to enroll in a course such as advanced statistics at a nearby Japanese university. It is also common practice in some of the more prestigious Japanese companies to send younger employees who have been with the firm for several years to top-ranked universities in foreign countries for graduate study. Japanese companies involved in international business also often go to great lengths to assure that managerial personnel have extensive language training.

It might seem surprising that studies which compare the amounts of money spent on education and training in Japanese firms with expenditures of foreign organizations conclude that Japanese companies spend less money on education of their employees. However, an examination of comparative Japanese and foreign expenditures on education and training is a poor indicator of the substantial investment Japanese organizations make in employee education. It is not a usual practice of a Japanese firm to rely heavily on outside organizations or consultants for employee training. It is also much more common in Japanese firms than in many foreign organizations to expect employees to bear at least some of the financial costs of correspondence courses and other special training that might be needed for work.

---

[29] Dore and Mari, How the Japanese Learn to Work, 52-55.

The enormous amount of time Japanese employees spend in informal teaching and learning situations, while not counted in formal training budgets, still represents a tremendous commitment to work place education. In fact, Japanese organizations devote substantially more time in work place education efforts than foreign firms without spending an enormous amount of money on outside consultants and institutions.[30]

Work Place Education: High School and Vocational School Graduates

It is Japanese management's creation of a lifelong learning environment for blue-collar workers similar to the experiences of university-educated employees that has attracted great attention all over the world. Japanese blue-collar workers enjoy the reputation of ranking among the most motivated and productive employees in the world. One reason is the generally excellent job secondary schools in Japan do with all students. The high school graduate who enters a large Japanese firm possesses numeracy and literacy and is well situated to learn what fellow workers and managers have to teach. Also, because of lifetime employment, high school graduates who work for large companies have similar incentives to learn as their university-graduate coworkers. Frequent retraining is the norm in a blue-collar worker's career if he works for a large or medium-sized company.

Initial experiences of high school or special training school graduates who work for large companies are similar to that of university graduates who enter the firm. However, blue-collar and clerical workers' initial training periods are shorter and somewhat less varied than in the university track. An assembly line worker's induction period might last a month. Although he will go through job rotation, it is likely to last about a year rather than longer. Like the university graduate, employees with high school educations in Japanese firms are privy to a constant information flow about various aspects of the company.

A major method by which high school-educated employees receive such information is the joint consultation system. In this system, management and worker representatives discuss a broad spectrum of issues ranging from investment plans of the firm to proposed revisions of company housing

---

[30] Ibid., 81-84.

allowances. The joint consultation system became widespread in the 1950s as part of an effort by Japanese firms to improve communications between management and workers. All signs are that this objective has been achieved.[31]

Also, blue-collar as well as white-collar workers often take correspondence courses in various subjects. This is in large part because since the 1950s the national ministries of education and labor, prefectural governments, and even some individual firms have developed perhaps the world's most elaborate system of qualification certificates for various kinds of jobs including boiler maintenance, crane slinging, handling dangerous materials, forklift truck driving, safety inspection, motor assembly, English proficiency, and many other skill areas. Successful certification at a skill, which is determined by examination, depends upon the applicant's satisfactory performance on both written examinations and on demonstration of competence in the skill. Since often a candidate's performance on a skill test determines whether he is promoted or paid a higher salary, the tests act as a powerful incentive for workers to be well prepared by enrolling in correspondence courses. The data from one survey of fifty large Japanese companies indicated that during the year when the survey was conducted 74 percent of all employees were engaged in some kind of work self improvement/study program.[32]

Another innovation in work place learning that directly involves assembly line workers and other high school graduate employees is the Quality Control Circle, or QCC. QCCs are perhaps the most publicized aspect of Japanese company personnel techniques and were first begun in Japan in the 1950s. QCCs are small factory- or office-based groups where between five and eight workers in the same department or section meet two to four times a month to engage in job-related problem solving. A key to much of QCC activity is the use of applied statistics in problem solving. Workers are taught such techniques as fishbone and Pareto diagrams, histograms, and normal statistical distributions as they work at solving problems relating to improving both their own section and the companies' efficiency, productivity, and quality control. QCCs make suggestions to

---

[31] Lester Thurow, ed., The Management Challenge: Japanese Views (MIT Press, 1985), 60-61.

[32] Dore and Mari, How the Japanese Learn to Work, 106-109.

management and, if they are accepted, members often are given financial rewards. In addition to the benefits that the company derives from actual problems that are solved through QCCs, the circles serve as ongoing educational and motivational mediums for many members.

Although W. Edwards Deming, an American statistician and university professor, is credited with fathering the QCC idea, it is the Japanese who first made QCCs famous. The QCC movement in Japan was fostered by the Japan Union of Scientists and Engineers (JUSE), a powerful organization with close ties to major companies. JUSE built a nationwide network of QCCs in the postwar decades. By 1987 there were 250,000 registered QCCs with over two million workers involved in the movement. The large majority of these employees were high school or vocational school graduates.[33] The QCC convention described at the beginning of this chapter is one of thousands of such activities that occur in Japan each year. Japan is probably the only nation on earth that has developed such a sophisticated information sharing system for non-management level workers. In fact, there is little doubt that QCCs and other educational techniques employed in Japanese firms with clerical and assembly line workers are a major factor in the country's postwar economic successes.

Conclusion: Lifelong Learning Environments

QCCs, job rotation, correspondence courses, the superb basic education most Japanese receive before they begin work, and the permanent employment ideal have all helped to create lifelong learning environments in large companies and government agencies and, to a lesser extent, their smaller counterparts. However, because of Japan's Confucian heritage and other cultural influences, lifelong learning is an obsession with many Japanese that transcends the work place. Many Japanese make a continual and ardent effort during their adult years to learn a variety of different subjects and skills, both for personal development and to improve the quality of leisure time. In the next chapter this second aspect of lifelong learning in Japan will be examined.

---

[33] Cole, Strategies for Learning, 280-281.

Questions for Comparison

1. In Japan a network of vocational schools exists for students who have completed or dropped out of secondary schools. What are their equivalents in the United States? What are typical curricula for these American schools? How difficult are such American schools to enter? How are these institutions viewed by American industry and the public?

2. Assess the effect of widespread linkages between Japanese high schools and universities and employers upon the effort Japanese young people make to learn while in school. To what degree do similar linkages exist between American high schools and universities and employers in this country?

3. American companies and government agencies are much more likely to be characterized as "high transaction" organizational environments than their Japanese counterparts. How does the American situation affect work place learning?

4. One clear advantage Japan enjoys when compared to the United States is that its non-university educated workforce is better educated than their American counterparts. What are some possible ways this situation might be improved in the U.S.?

5. Millions of Japanese put forth great effort to learn English for utilization in work-related situations. Does a changing world economy now warrant similar efforts by Americans to learn foreign languages?

Additional Reading

The best single work on education for the work place in Japan is Ronald Dore and Sako Māri, How the Japanese Learn to Work, Routledge, 1989. The book focuses upon every aspect of vocational education in Japan. Readers who desire to understand more about high school vocational education in the U.S. should examine Arthur Powell, Eleanor Farrar, and David Cohen, The Shopping Mall High School: Winners and Losers in the Educational Marketplace. The book was published by Houghton Mifflin Company in 1985.

One of the most stimulating books on the relationship between human capital and economic success in both Japan and the United States is The Management Challenge: Japanese Views (1985) which is available through MIT Press and edited by noted American economist, Lester Thurow. The book consists of eleven articles by Japanese economists and business people and Thurow includes very interesting comments for each piece in which he compares American and Japanese experiences. Robert Cole, Strategies for Learning: Small-Group Activities in American, Japanese, and Swedish Industry, University of California Press, 1989, is an even more detailed comparison of the relationship between learning and economic productivity in three nations. Also, portions of The Japanese Economy and The American Businessman by Daniel Metraux contain information on learning, culture, and Japanese management. The Edwin Mellen Press published Metraux's book in 1989.

The educational backgrounds of managers and workers in Japan and the United States also receive extensive treatment in David Halberstam, The Reckoning, which was published in 1986 and is available in paperback through Avon Books. Halberstam's work, perhaps one of the most readable books on the corporate cultures of the two countries, focuses upon the histories of Nissan and Ford motor companies.

Chapter Seven

Adult Learning as Self-Development

Introduction

Seven women gather for a discussion inside the living room of a comfortable house in Togo, a small town about an hour from Nagoya. They sit on the floor on pillows around four low tables arranged so that those present will face each other. The women, whose ages range from about thirty-five to fifty-five, all have copies of an introductory Jungian psychology textbook with them. Some attendees also have notebooks. The women are members of a Jung discussion circle which meets for about three hours one morning a month in a different member's house. The women founded the circle four years earlier. At the time, several members of this group served on a town task force to recommend children's books for the town library. In working together, the women found they shared a mutual interest in Carl Jung.

One of the women is a trained psychologist and she serves as the group's leader. Each month on their own, circle members read twenty to thirty pages from the text. When the group gathers, the circle leader answers any questions members might have based on the reading. While the leader occasionally asks questions, she truly functions as a seminar leader and does not present a lecture to the other members. A wide-ranging and lively discussion occurs during the entire time of the circle meeting. Virtually all the women either contribute real-life anecdotes or talk of books or movies that confirm or refute the assertions of the famous Swiss psychologist about human action. In this particular session, at least thirty minutes is devoted to applying Jungian principles to the behavior of several adults toward children in the American movie, "The Dead Poet's Society."

The scene is much more formal in the Japanese literature class that is about to begin shortly after lunch one weekday in the Nagoya City Lifelong Education Center. The center is an impressive multi-storied building built in 1988 in the downtown section of this bustling city. Minutes before the class begins the forty people who, about evenly divided by sex, engage in the usual behavior of students anywhere. They talk with each other, open books, and arrange notebooks. However, the class shares one unusual characteristic. Every student is at least sixty years of age or older and is enrolled in the college for the elderly, which is a division of the Nagoya Center.

There are approximately 500 students in the college for the elderly and most enrollees take two years to complete their chosen courses of study. There are four major courses of study offered in the college: life studies, which is the study of such subjects as consumer economics and civil law; cultural studies, where students take courses in literature, history, and foreign languages; gardening; and ceramics.

As the teacher, who is a professor from a nearby university, enters the classroom two students walk by each row of desks calling names. The students who are attending the class respond quite enthusiastically when their names are called. The class begins after the monitors give their reports to the instructor. During the lecture on Heian literature that follows, students ask more questions than in the typical Japanese high school or university classroom. Students are quite attentive during the class period, which lasts over an hour.

In conversations with the foreign visitor after class, several senior citizens give reasons for enrolling in the cultural studies program of the center's college. One woman, who had been a housewife all her life, mentioned she always wanted to learn about Japanese culture but never had the chance. A retired business executive, who many years before had graduated from university with a natural sciences major, argued that his education had given him no opportunity to study the humanities.

It is Sunday afternoon, which is a busy time of the week for most Japanese book stores. This is certainly the case in Tōkyō's Kinōkuniya Book Store, located in the bustling Shīnjuku section of the city. The sixth floor of the multi-floored book store is entirely devoted to foreign books. There are 40,000 books in English available on this floor. Kinōkuniya features both fiction and non-fiction works on virtually every imaginable subject. A prominent biography section includes not only books on famous and infamous Japanese, but also translated biographies of such Western luminaries as Lee Iacoca, Prince Charles, and Madonna. Recent books about Japan occupy almost one-half of one floor and include not only books by Japanese on Japan but translations of books by a host of foreigners on the same subject.

Even though Kinōkuniya is one of the largest book stores in Japan, it has two things in common with most book stores in that nation. Like Kinōkuniya, most Japanese book stores tend to be crowded since spending time in them is a major Japanese hobby. Also, it is quite typical for patrons of Kinōkuniya or any Japanese book store to pick up a book and spend an hour or even several hours reading the book while standing or kneeling in front of the shelf from where it was selected. As often as not, readers return the book to the shelf rather than buy it. Japanese book store proprietors and staff, regardless of what their true feelings might be about this kind of customer behavior, never seem at all bothered by it.

Adult clubs, "colleges" for the elderly, and the widespread hobby of book store browsing are but three of many examples of the lifelong learning in which many Japanese engage. The line between learning for personal enrichment and acquiring new information or skills that result in job-related advancement often blurs. However, many adult Japanese spend a great deal of time pursuing both formal and informal educational activities that do not relate to career or economic advancement.

Perhaps in no society on earth is interest as high in learning for intrinsic reasons as in Japan. Confucianism, as influential in shaping contemporary Japanese attitudes as the nation's religions, is permeated by respect for teachers, scholars, and learning. Also, the average Japanese adult is well-equipped to pursue new knowledge and skills due to the superior performance of elementary and secondary schools in providing most of the population with a basic education and an appreciation of such subjects as the fine arts and physical education.

In addition to a heritage of respect for learning and a sound educational background, other aspects of Japanese society stimulate an active pursuit of new

186

knowledge by adults. Many Japanese educators and parents view large amounts of unstructured free time as harmful for children and deliberately involve youngsters in as many activities as possible. The widespread Japanese adult propensity to seriously pursue hobbies seems to be a carry-over effect of this earlier socialization process. Also, Japan is one of the world's most middle-class nations if income distribution and respondent self-selection are two primary determinants of social stratification. In most societies it is the middle class that often strongly defines personal growth in terms of learning new knowledge.

Adult Japanese learn through individual effort and through joining small groups or by utilizing formal educational institutions designed for adult learners, such as the old peoples' college described earlier. It is to individual and small group learning in Japan that we now turn.

Individual and Small-Group Adult Learning in Japan

Perhaps the most individualized way for a person to learn is by reading a book, magazine, or newspaper. As implied in an earlier description, the Japanese have a special relationship with the printed word. The large number of books published annually is a quite striking aspect of book consumption in Japan. In a typical year approximately 35,000 different new titles might be published in Japan. In absolute terms, this is almost as many books as are published in a typical year in the United States, a country with about twice Japan's population.[1]

A large number of books published in Japan are of Western origin. A best seller in the U.S. or Great Britain is almost sure to be translated into Japanese. This occurs for two reasons. While often personally uncomfortable with foreigners, many Japanese are quite curious in an intellectual sense about the rest of the world. Foreign books have long been a window through which Japanese might view other lands. Therefore, a large variety of both foreign fiction and nonfiction is translated and published in Japan. Also, many Japanese are intensely eager to find out what the rest of the world thinks of them. Consequently, virtually any book written anywhere in the world about Japan is almost sure to be translated into Japanese.

---

[1] Christopher, The Japanese Mind, 194.

Among Japanese adults, fiction is more popular than nonfiction. While Japanese read their own famous novelists such as Mishima and Kawabata and such Western writers as Faulkner and Joyce, much fiction read in Japan is of little literary value. Still, the large number of foreign books purchased by Japanese caused one American journalist who is a long-time student of the country to argue that, as a result, Japanese adults can keep abreast of current world artistic and intellectual developments without knowing how to read a foreign language. People elsewhere would have a difficult time acquiring such knowledge since it is not common practice in most countries for such a large amount of foreign works to be published in the native tongue.[2] Japanese have a love affair with magazines as well. As is the case in most modern industrialized countries, there are a staggering number and variety of magazines available in Japan. As of the late 1970s, approximately 3,000 different magazines were published annually, and that number has probably grown in recent years.[3] Many of the most widely read magazines in Japan are anything but educational in nature. For example, adult comic books that contain great amounts of sex and violence are extremely popular. However, several magazines that enjoy wide circulation are "high brow" by the standards of other modern industrialized countries.

For example, there are several monthly magazines, Bungei Shunjū being the largest and most well known, which contain articles on everything from politics and sociology to the arts. The monthlies, which feature relatively sophisticated articles often written by professors, enjoy almost as much of a monthly circulation in Japan as weekly news magazines such as Time or Newsweek in the United States.

Weekly news magazines such as the American ones just mentioned do not exist in Japan. This is in large part because the Japanese consume an enormous number of newspapers. Japanese newspaper consumption is estimated to be twice as high per capita as in the U.S. An estimated 93 percent of Japanese read a daily newspaper. In worldwide per capita sales of newspapers, Japan ranks second only to Sweden. The largest Japanese newspapers, the Asahi, Mainichi, and Yomiuri papers, enjoy national circulation.

---

[2] Ibid., 195.

[3] Ibid., 201.

188

The major newspapers are published each day and offer evening editions six days a week. These newspapers employ extensive numbers of reporters in every part of the globe and provide comprehensive analysis of both international and domestic affairs. In addition to coverage of politics and economics, by world standards, culture and the arts receive comprehensive treatment in the major Japanese papers. Typically, the major papers carry a daily serialized novel which is often by a leading Japanese author. Once a week, major newspapers publish a high-quality color reproduction of a famous Japanese or foreign painting along with a detailed commentary.[4]

Japanese television includes both private and public channels. While television serves up the typical light fare found in affluent countries throughout the world, it also provides substantial educational programming. Approximately 8,500 of Japan's almost 12,000 broadcasting stations are operated by the Japan Broadcasting Corporation, or Nippon Hōsō Kyokai (NHK). One-half of NHK's stations offer only educational and cultural programming. Even the NHK "general interest" stations devote less than 30 percent of programming to entertainment.

In addition to documentaries and arts-related programs, standard fare on NHK stations includes panel discussions by academics and experts on a variety of topics. It is common for panel discussions to be scheduled immediately after the airing of a classic Japanese or foreign film. The guest academic or film critic panelists then analyze the film, often for rather lengthy periods of time.[5]

"Shumi," which in Japanese means both "hobby" and "taste," is an important medium that individuals utilize in learning throughout the adult years. Japanese adults pursue a wide variety of hobbies. Popular hobbies in Japan range from Western activities such as golf and classical music to traditional Japanese arts, sports, and literature. Some of the more popular traditional Japanese pursuits include bonsai or miniature gardening, ikebana or flower arranging, martial arts such as judo, kēndō, and karate, and haiku and tānka poetry. An annual national tānka contest is held featuring a set theme. The winning thirty-one syllable tānka

---

[4] Descriptions of the Japanese press and magazines fromTasker, The Japanese: A Major Exploration of Modern Japan, 110-112; Edwin Reischauer, The Japanese Today: Change and Continuity (Belknap Press, 1988), 219-221; and Christopher, The Japanese Mind, 196.

[5] Christopher, The Japanese Mind, 203-206.

poems are read in the emperor's presence and, traditionally, the emperor himself contributes a poem.

Hobbies are pursued in every culture in which people are affluent enough to have leisure activity. However, the Japanese seem to have a deeper level of interest in their hobbies than is true of people in equally affluent cultures. Most Japanese have a personal literary, artistic, or performing skill which is often a means to both self-expression and self-identity. The well-known American Japanologist, the late Edwin Reischauer, wrote that "The ardent pursuit of a hobby is almost necessary for self-respect in Japan...."[6]

Individual pursuits of hobbies in Japan often takes place within the context of the small group. The Jung study group described earlier is simply one of many such examples which may be found in Japan. Clubs and associations seem to exert a larger role in the lives of many Japanese than is the case with similar entities in other societies. The Jung Study circle is a little unusual in that it is a single club and is not part of an elaborate hierarchy. Many Japanese adults who cultivate a sport, art, or literary pursuit join a club that is part of a regional and national network of similar organizations.

Traditional Japanese beliefs about the importance of hierarchy and status exert great influence upon how individual Japanese pursue their hobbies. It is common for many Japanese to pursue hobbies by working with a teacher who has received licensure in the particular subject, whether it is karate, haiku poetry or bonsai cultivation. Usually, the teacher will hold a certain rank within a regional or national organization. Students of a particular teacher are usually quite aware of his or her rank compared to other teachers of the subject.

The following description of a koto teacher and her work specifically illustrates how adult learning in Japan takes place within the context of individual and small group interaction.

The koto is a traditional instrument that first came to Japan from China. The koto was part of the emperor's court as early as the 11th century. The instrument, although there are variants, is a thirteen-stringed, wooden half-tube, semi-cylindrical plucked zither. The koto player sits in front of the instrument in the same manner as an American steel guitar or dobro player. Koto musicians

---

[6] Reischaucer, The Japanese Today: Change and Continuity, 165.

use both hands to play the instrument. With the left hand the <u>koto</u> player manipulates moveable bridges for each string. The bridges raise the pitch of strings or modify tone. Simultaneously, the <u>koto</u> player uses three picks to pluck the strings with the right hand. The picks fit upon the thumb and the first two fingers. The sound of a <u>koto</u> is stately, evocative, and somewhat haunting.

On the second floor of a Togo suburban house in midsummer, the sounds of two kotos coupled with the heavy humid air produce an almost dream-like effect for listeners. The players are Mrs. Ōka, a graceful Japanese housewife in her mid-thirties, and one of her students who is also a housewife but a few years older than Ōka. A third student sits nearby in the traditional Japanese manner and listens intently. The musicians sit side-by-side with sheet music propped up on a holder between them as they play the <u>kotos</u>. Soon, a third student comes up the stairs of the house and joins the group.

Mrs. Ōka has a long relationship with the <u>koto</u> and began to play the instrument when she was in elementary school. Even as a young girl, Mrs. Ōka became familiar with the organizations and hierarchical structures developed by players of the instrument. Ikūtaryū and Yamadaryu are the two major schools of <u>koto</u> in Japan. Mrs. Ōka learned from a teacher of the Yamadaryu school, which focuses upon instrumental music. Practitioners of Ikūtaryū sing as well as play. Although both schools are highly respected, Ikūtaryū, in part because it is larger, is more famous than Yamadaryu. Within the national network of Yamadaryu associations there are five grades which indicate various skill levels, as well as two additional grades associated with the procurement of a <u>koto</u> teaching license.

Mrs. Ōka holds grade seven, which is the highest rank. For Mrs. Ōka, obtaining the highest rank for <u>koto</u> performance and teaching was a long and arduous process. In order to receive the grade seven rank, Ōka had to convince a panel of <u>koto</u> masters of her technical playing, practice experience, and, more intangibly, of her good character as a teacher. The requirement that an aspirant demonstrate appropriate character before being licensed to teach Japanese traditional or martial arts is a typical rite of passage. In Ōka's case, association judges took such matters into account as how many local <u>koto</u> concerts she attended as a listener or player, and her students' opinions of her teaching abilities, before they awarded her a rank of seven.

Ōka began her home-based school over ten years ago. Currently, she has five students who each receive instruction for about an hour once each week. Ōka's students are all adult women, as is now the case with most <u>koto</u> devotees in Japan. Her students pay 5,000 yen, or about $38.50 a month, for the lessons. When asked why they decided to learn <u>koto</u>, Mrs. Ōka's students cited such reasons as an affinity for the sound of the instrument, a desire to learn more about a classical Japanese music form, and the need for a satisfying hobby to enrich their lives. Mrs. Ōka and her students not only play at the Ōka home, but also give at least one recital a year at the town hall and play in such places as homes for the elderly. Throughout the entire lesson, both teacher and students exhibited a relaxed but purposeful and focused attitude as they played and listened.[7]

Formal Educational Institutions for Adults

Since they work less hours outside the home, more Japanese women than men join clubs, hire teachers, and stand for skill tests in endeavoring to master a particular hobby. However, large numbers of men as well as women engage in such behavior during the adult years. So many adult Japanese make serious and sustained efforts to learn more about a subject or hone a skill that small groups alone do not satisfy national demand. Throughout Japan, both private and public educational institutions exist to meet the needs of adult Japanese who seek self-development through learning. One category of institutions that has enjoyed tremendous growth in recent years is the privately owned cultural center.

Located in downtown Nagoya, the Chūnichi Cultural Center occupies a complete floor of a skyscraper owned by one of Japan's major newspapers. A visitor who strolls through the center on a Saturday morning might look in one room and see between thirty and forty men and women engaging in oil painting. As the adults labor over their canvases, an instructor walks around and works with individual students. In the room across the hall twenty-five women are busily sewing kimono. In a third class forty people engage in ballroom dancing to the music of a CD player. Since there are slightly more women than men in the dance class, some women dance with women.

---

[7] Description of <u>koto</u> class based upon author's field research in May and June 1990.

Cultural centers, which began in 1969 with the establishment of the Asahi newspaper's center in Tōkyō, are now big business in Japan. Currently, all major newspapers, as well as some large department stores, operate centers. The popularity of cultural centers such as Chūnichi and Asahi is impressive. In 1990, the Chūnichi Center offered 1,000 different classes and 25,000 students enrolled at its main Nagoya branch and in thirty-five other branches located throughout Japan.[8] Sixty-five thousand students take classes each year in the Asahi Center, which has major branches in both Tōkyō and Yokohama. According to recent statistics, there are 400 cultural centers throughout Japan that are operated by thirty-eight newspaper publishers, twenty-two broadcasting companies, and forty-one department stores. In a recent year, a total of 400,000 people took classes in Japan's cultural centers.[9]

Cultural centers, which are patronized primarily by adults, offer an incredible variety of courses. The large cultural centers offer subjects ranging from novel writing to scuba diving. Cultural centers require no entrance examinations and award no diplomas. The typical class will meet two hours, once a week for three months and cost students between $90 and $130 in U.S. dollars. Although cultural centers have an administrative staff, most instructors work on a part-time basis and their backgrounds are as varied as the courses available in centers. Depending upon the course, a cultural center class might be taught by a university professor, a professional photographer, or a seamstress.

Who enrolls in cultural centers and what are their motives? Patrons of cultural centers first pay a one-time membership fee and then tuition to enroll in particular courses. A majority of students tend to be housewives in their thirties or forties. However, cultural centers do not serve just this clientele. Studies of enrollments in such centers as Asahi indicate that males constitute 20 percent of all students.

When asked why they pursue work at cultural centers members respond with a variety of answers. However, cultural center students often mention a

---

[8] Statistics gathered by author in a visit to Chūnichi Cultural Center in Nagoya on June 6, 1990.

[9] Morōoka Kazūfusa, "Continuing Education: The Japanese Approach," in Bulletin 28 of the UNESCO Principal Regional Office For Asia and the Pacific (Bangkok, Thailand: United Nations Institute, September, 1987), 58.

desire for self-improvement as a motivating force behind their decision to enroll in courses. Also, many middle-aged housewives were quite poor as children in the years after World War II and had no extensive opportunities for learning and study. Many of these women now feel the need to make up for lost time by attending cultural center classes. A desire to be with old friends and meet new ones constitutes yet another reason members cite for spending time in cultural centers.

While the majority of courses are for individual life enrichment and not to improve human capital for the work place, almost all the centers offer some courses on such topics as preparing for the airline stewardess examination. Therefore, cultural centers perform, to a limited extent, some of the same functions of the special training schools that were described in the last chapter. The curriculum of the Chūnichi Center is typical of that of a large cultural center. Below is a sample of courses listed in a recent Chūnichi Cultural Center brochure.

1990 Sample Course Listing, Chūnichi Cultural Center

Classical Japanese Literature	Speech
Haiku	Accounting
Tanka	Typewriting
Fortune Telling	Driving
English Classes (varying levels)	Word processing
Spanish Language	Oil painting
Arabic	Water color painting
Korean	Black ink drawing
Chinese	Folk dancing
French	Koto
German	Choral Music
Flower Arranging (9 kinds)	Violin
Cooking (various kinds)	Bonsai
Modern Dance	Yoga
Martial Arts	Novel Writing

Cultural centers are not without their critics in the electronic and print media. Some journalists argue that the centers just exist to take money from bored housewives. Other writers condemn the centers for not contributing to national productivity. Despite what their critics think, cultural center enrollment has grown steadily since the institutions first began in the late 1960s. Most probably the growth has occurred because the centers serve some real needs of

194

their members. Japanese secondary education, with its emphasis upon preparing
for university examinations or the work place, does not offer students much
latitude to pursue individual interests. Also, only a few Japanese universities have
recently begun to encourage adults to take courses or provided any kind of
programs whatsoever for this segment of the population. Based on their past
growth and current popularity, private cultural centers will probably remain a
permanent part of the Japanese educational landscape for some time to come.[10]

Public Adult Educational Institutions

It is not only private cultural centers that provide adults of all ages with
the chance to learn. In fact, despite the popularity of private institutions such as
cultural centers, in Japan the large majority of opportunities for adult education
occur within public institutions.

Beginning in the late Mēiji period, some public sector policy makers
realized the need to establish continuing education programs for adults. However,
during the first half of this century other priorities took precedence. Until after
World War II, adult educational opportunities were scant in Japan. The few
available adult education programs were administered by national and local
governments. Especially during the 1930s and 1940s, adult education programs
were more often designed to promote government propaganda than to fulfill their
avowed function. However, one important trend in adult education began in the
prewar years and still exists today. Despite recent policy changes by a few
Japanese universities, institutions other than higher educational institutions have
primary responsibility for adult education.

Since the promulgation of the Shākai Kyōiku, or Social Education Law
of 1949, a wide variety of adult education public sector centers have come into
existence in Japan. Today, government administered centers include citizens'
public halls, public libraries, women's education centers, and, most recently,
lifelong learning centers. All of these institutions originated because of national
government directive, operate according to guidelines emanating from the

---

[10] Shigēkane Yōshiko, "Learning for Joy at a Cultural Center," Japan Quarterly XIII, no.
4 (Tōkyō: Asahi Shinbun, October-December 1985): 412-417.

Lifelong Learning Bureau of the Ministry of Education, and, for the most part, are funded and staffed by prefectural and municipal governments.

Citizens' public halls are the most prevalent adult educational institution in Japan. Most public halls were built in the 1970s and 1980s as a result of national government encouragement which included startup subsidies for facility construction. As of the late 1980s, 17,400 citizens' public halls existed throughout Japan. Local government employees and volunteers administer and staff public halls. Although the public halls provide learning opportunities for citizens of all ages, adult classes are the most common type of programs. Japan's 1,801 public libraries are often operated as part of a public hall complex.[11]

The Togo Public Hall is a typical example of this type of adult educational institution. The hall itself is a modern three-story building. Facilities include classrooms as well as space for basketball, volley ball, badminton, weight-training, and archery. The town hall has a full-time staff of six employees and ten part-time teachers. Funds for the hall come from both local taxes and grants that the Ministry of Education provides for prefectural governments. The prefectural governments in turn disperse funds to the local halls. A town social education board also participates in the administration of the hall and from time to-time submits reports to the prefectural government and to Mombushō.

The curriculum of the hall is divided into classroom courses and outdoor sports training. Examples of the former include introduction to video making, bird watching, local history research, gardening, crafts, folk dancing, and introduction to personal computing. Sports classes offered through the Togo Public Hall include kēndō, badminton, tennis, aerobics, Japanese archery, gymnastics, table tennis and boating. Classes usually meet once weekly and the length of courses vary from six to ten weeks. Because of public subsidies, course fees are quite low and average in U.S. dollars approximately $30 per student. In the most recent year for which statistics were available, 580 Togo citizens took courses at the public hall.

The public hall philosophy of learning for personal development rather than for personal gain is reflected in a framed motto which hangs on the spacious paneled office of the director of the Togo hall. The English translation of the

---

[11] Education in Japan 1989: A Graphic Presentation, 116-117.

motto is, "My activity is limited by my self interest so I should live to free my self from self interest."[12]

The development of women's educational centers in Japan dates back to the 1970s when the first such institutions were established. While not as common as public halls, women's educational centers may be found in many larger towns and cities throughout Japan. Although private as well as public centers exist, as of 1991 local governments operated about one-half of the two hundred women's educational centers that had been established.

One example of a public center is the Nagoya Women's Center. The Nagoya center opened in the late 1970s and today is housed in a medium-size three-story building. The center services about three hundred women each day on an annual budget of approximately $377,000 in U.S. dollars. The thirteen-member staff includes a director, three full-time teachers, a small counseling staff, and clerical employees. The center also employs part-time instructors, many of whom are university professors. Yamāmōto Fukiko, a middle-aged woman who is a junior college graduate, is Director of the Nagoya Women's Center. According to Yamāmōto, the purpose of the center is to provide adult women with education which will improve their daily lives. The center's major focus is neither vocational education, as is the case with special training schools, or education for leisure, as is true with cultural centers.

Examples of courses offered by the center include child care methods, historical and contemporary problems of women, parenting, psychology, sociology, and introduction to volunteer activity. Center facilities include a library and day care center, as well as a coffee shop. Women often meet at the coffee shop for discussions before or after classes. Courses usually meet once a week for ten to thirteen times. Fees are quite low because of local government subsidies. The typical student at the women's center is a married housewife who feels she needs to better understand her own life, make more friends, or develop skills so as to engage in voluntary community activities. Courses in volunteer work are offered and the center sponsors a number of volunteer projects. The latter include aiding needy children and working with the rehabilitation of prostitutes.

---

[12] Information on Togo Public Hall obtained by author during a visit on June 6, 1990.

Both the nature of Japanese formal education and cultural expectations about the role of women mean most center attendees have heretofore not been involved in open and free-wheeling discussion. Almost all center classes are structured so that women may actively participate in seminars. When this author visited a sociology class and a class on effective PTA membership, he found that almost all of the ten to twelve women in each class participated extensively in discussion.

The origin, administration, and funding of women's centers in Japan is somewhat different than that of public halls. Whereas the impetus for public halls emanated from Tōkyō, women's centers were more of a grassroots movement. They were created because in the 1970s many feminists groups exerted pressure on local governments to provide such facilities. Although the Mombushō operates one national center for women and contributed about 10 percent of the construction costs for the Nagoya facility, generally funds for women's centers come almost entirely from municipal and, to a lesser extent, prefectural governments.

While the Nagoya Center serves primarily housewives, there are already centers in Japan that are beginning to cater to working women. With the immense changes that Japanese women are now experiencing at home and in the work place, a need will most probably continue to exist for such adult education facilities.[13]

The most recent development in Japanese adult public education has been the creation of lifelong education centers by prefectural governments. Most prefectural governments are now constructing such centers because of increased national government attention to the needs of adult learners. This attention emerged as a result of a report issued by the special education reform commission that Prime Minister Nakāsone created in the mid-1980s. The report included two major criticisms of adult education. For various reasons, Japanese education in general was too oriented toward pre-adult students. In the report, commission members also called for more coordination among various actors involved in adult education, including national government ministries, prefectural and local governments, the private sector, and higher education.

---

[13] Interviews by author with Nagoya Women's Center staff on June 26, 1990.

Several policy developments resulted from these concerns. In the late 1980s, the powerful Mombushō Central Council for Education undertook an extensive study of how to promote lifelong learning. The final result of the study and ensuing report was a special law passed by the Japanese Diet in June 1990. The Lifelong Education Promotion Law authorized the establishment by Mombushō of a new council on lifetime and social education. This council would promote and enhance lifelong education by coordinating the efforts of other national government ministries such as the Ministry of Labor and prefectural governments. It was specified in the same legislation that similar prefectural-level lifelong education councils be established throughout Japan. The prefectural councils would engage in similar coordination efforts at the prefectural and local levels. The legislation also called for the establishment of lifelong education promotion centers in prefectures where they did not already exist.

A final but important feature of the Lifelong Education Law was the provision of favorable national tax incentives for private educational enterprises in order to encourage these institutions to create more opportunities for adult learners. While the law did not include major funding or a budget, Japanese adult education advocates view it as an important first step in creating a public national adult learning network.[14]

Even before the passage of the law, fourteen prefectures and several of Japan's major cities had already established lifelong learning centers. Two major goals of the centers are to provide programs that are beyond the scope of the citizens' public halls and to coordinate and enhance the activities of the halls and other local adult learning centers. The centers are primarily funded by prefectural governments with some Mombushō assistance. A closer examination of the Nagoya City Lifelong Learning Center, the institution which sponsors the college for the elderly described earlier in the chapter, provides specific examples of how lifelong education centers attempt to achieve the above goals.

The Nagoya Center was established in 1988 by the Nagoya City Government. The center's staff includes a director, approximately fourteen other full-time staff, and over twenty part-time instructors. The center's annual budget

---

[14] Interview by author with Kitāmura Yukīhisa, Director of the Ministry of Education Bureau of Lifelong Learning on June 28, 1990. An extensive discussion of the National Council on Educational Reform is included in the final chapter of this book.

excluding salaries is about $700,000 in U.S. dollars. While Mombushō provided sizable initial subsidies for the construction of the large multi-story building which houses the center, both program and personnel costs are borne by the Nagoya Municipal Government's Board of Education. The center shares the building with a night vocational high school which is administered by a separate division of the board of education. Both the center and the night high school use a well-equipped multi-media educational resource center also located in the building.

The Nagoya Center seems to provide exactly the type of activities envisioned by the recent legislation described earlier. For example, center personnel with the help of a team of local university professors conducted a major survey of Nagoya residents to investigate attitudes and awareness about lifetime learning options in the area. In Nagoya there are seventeen centers that provide various types of courses for adults. The Nagoya Center facilitates information exchange among these smaller centers through a variety of activities including newsletters as well as radio and television. Through careful coordination with the Nagoya Board of Education the center also makes its state-of-the-art computer center available to approximately 18,000 Nagoya commercial high school and academic high school youngsters. As of 1990, the high school students spent about twelve hours an academic year working on computer-related design projects at the center.

In addition to coordination responsibilities, the center provides an average of twenty night and day adult educational enrichment classes each year. Examples of subjects offered through the center include both beginning and advanced English, French, art history, Japanese literature, and city planning. Between three hundred and four hundred adults, who are mostly women and older men, take advantage of the courses offered by the center each year. Center students pay about the same low fees as charged by the public halls. Classes at the Nagoya Lifelong Education Center typically meet one and one-half hours once a week for twelve to fifteen weeks.[15]

Besides these adult classes, a major center program is the old peoples' college described in some detail at the beginning of this chapter. The old peoples'

---

[15] Interview by author of Inagaki Tsūyoshi, Assistant Director of The Nagoya City Lifelong Learning Center, on June 6, 1990.

college is the most popular adult education program offered by the center. Currently, there are twice as many eligible applicants as there are spaces in the college and the five hundred elderly students consider themselves quite lucky to participate. Throughout Japan both lifelong education centers and public halls are now devoting extensive time to planning and implementing similar programs for the elderly segment of the population.

Many Japanese consider the issue of providing a high quality of life for Japan's aging population to be one of the most important questions facing the country. Already Japan has, on average, the longest-lived population in the world.

However, other demographic and sociological trends relating to aging insure that the question of how to provide for the old will be a problem in Japan for years to come. Although presently several countries, including Germany and the United States, have higher proportions of elderly than Japan relative to their total populations, Japan leads the world in the rate of growth of its proportion of elderly relative to the rest of the population. By the year 2000 it is expected that 15.6 percent of Japanese will be over sixty-five. By the year 2020 Japan is expected to be second in the world only to Sweden in terms of the proportion of elderly to all other residents.[16]

The problem of an increasing elderly population in Japan is sociological as well as demographic. Japanese are socialized to a greater degree than many people in other cultures to particularly value work and to judge both individual worth and that of others based upon occupation. Despite the recent transition, Japan retained the extended family as an institution longer than many of the Western countries. As the number of extended families now contracts, many Japanese elderly already face the dual problems of living alone or in a home for senior citizens and becoming accustomed to deriving personal rewards for activities other than work.

One of the strengths of the Japanese public sector is its far-sightedness. Various government commissions have studied issues related to Japan's aging population for the last two decades. Several programs, including courses for the elderly at public halls and the concept of a "university" for the elderly, have been

---

[16] Tasker, The Japanese: A Major Exploration of Modern Japan, 106; and Randall S. Jones, "The Economic Implications of Japan's Aging Population," in Japan: Exploring New Paths, ed. John Choy (Washington, D.C.: Japan Economic Institute of America, 1988), 80.

implemented as a result of government initiative. The earliest "university" for the elderly in Japan, Ināmino Gakuen, was founded by the Hyōgō Prefectural Government in 1969.

Ināmino Gakuen is located on the site of a former public agricultural junior college. Ināmino Gakuen's curriculum is similar to that of the Nagoya program except it is of four-years duration. Ināmino recently opened a two-year graduate school. By the mid-1980s there were already 221 graduates of the institution, and many of them have gone on to work in other elderly education programs throughout Japan. Although the private cultural centers and the public town halls, lifelong education centers, and universities for the elderly represent a good beginning, demographics indicate that the provision of learning opportunities for the elderly will be a major part of lifelong education efforts in Japan for the next few decades.[17]

Older people also make up a significant percentage of students who have enrolled in Japan's University of the Air. University of the Air was founded in 1983 under the auspices of Mombushō's Bureau of LifeLong Learning. This unique university, which has its own broadcasting system located in the Tōkyō area, is utilized by at least 21,000 adults. As of 1990, 2,207 people had graduated from the University of the Air.

The university features classes that are broadcast at all hours of the day so that students can juxtapose their work with the acquisition of further education. As part of their work through the University of the Air, students also complete readings and take examinations for credits at six separate study centers. Currently, three curricular programs are offered: science for everyday life, industrial and social studies, and humanities and natural sciences. Approximately 12 percent of students in 1988 were in their 50s with 7 percent of the enrollees in University of the Air courses either sixty years of age or older.

The establishment of the University of the Air in Japan is significant because it represents the first serious public or private sector attempt to provide higher educational opportunities for adults of wide-ranging ages who are past the

---

[17] Takashi Fukuchi, "The Founding of a University of Senior Citizens," in World Perspective, Case Descriptions on Educational Programs for Adults: Japan, ed. Morōoka Kazūfusa (Battle Creek, MI: Kellog Foundation, August 1989), 126-145. Also available through United States Department of Education Office of Educational Research and Improvement ED3111176CE053020.

traditional university attendance years. Two-thirds of the students enrolled in the University of the Air are over the age of thirty. While Japanese higher educational institutions lag behind several countries in the provision of such programs as continuing education and extension courses, the situation is beginning to change. As of 1990, at least five Japanese colleges and universities had established extension classes for adults. Because of a decline in the traditional university student population and government pressure, many other colleges and universities are now seriously studying establishing programs for adults.[18]

In spite of the fact that universities are only beginning to provide for adult learners, in general there are widespread opportunities in Japanese society for people to engage in lifelong learning. Given the large variety of opportunities for continuing education that exist in Japan and the large number of motivated people who take advantage of such chances, the Japanese may perhaps lead the world in lifelong learning.

---

[18] Information on the University of the Air from Education in Japan 1980: A Graphic Presentation; and from June 28, 1990 Kitāmura interview.

Questions for Comparison

1. Although a large variety of adult clubs certainly exist throughout the United States, American participation in such organizations seems to be limited when compared to Japan. What are some culturally based reasons fewer Americans choose to participate in clubs than Japanese?

2. Available evidence certainly indicates that the adult reading public in Japan is more widespread and, despite the popularity of adult comics in that country, more sophisticated than in the United States. What are some possible reasons for this phenomena?

3. In the U.S., the adult education programs that are not of a remedial nature are primarily administered by continuing education divisions of colleges and universities. What are some factors that led to this development in the United States?

4. The Japanese public sector has been quite involved in developing educational programs for old people. Is there any evidence that governments in the United States are engaging in similar activities? Should the American public sector develop comprehensive programs to meet the educational needs of older citizens?

Additional Reading

Readers who are interested in the relationship between learning and hobbies and club and group activities in Japan should examine Robert Christopher, The Japanese Mind, Fawcett Columbine, 1983. The section on adult hobbies in the late Edwin Reischauer, The Japanese Today: Change and Continuity, Belknap, 1988, is particularly informative. Readers who are particularly interested in how adult women use leisure time for learning should consult Takie Sugiyama Lebra, Japanese Women: Constraint and Fulfillment, University of Hawaii Press, 1984. Non-University Sector Higher Education in Japan, International Publication Series No. 3, Research Institute for Higher Education: Hiroshima University, is a research report which should be of particular use to those readers interested in adult learning.

Ernest Boyer in College: The Undergraduate Experience in America, The Carnegie Foundation for the Advancement of Teaching, 1987, describes recent adult higher education trends in the U.S. Although the book was published several years ago, Carol Aslanian and Henry Brickell, Americans in Transition: Life Changes As Reasons For Adult Learning, College Entrance Examination Board, 1980, is an excellent and very readable overview of many aspects of U.S. adult learning, both within and outside of colleges and universities.

Chapter Eight

Reform Efforts and the Future of Japanese Education

Introduction: The Future of Education in Japan

If international comparisons are an indicator, the Japanese should be quite proud of their educational achievements. Based on achievement tests, Japanese are among world leaders in mathematics and science knowledge and national literacy levels. Although many Japanese are quite proud of the nation's accomplishments, there is also widespread discontent about the failures of the educational system.

Many problems in Japanese education, including school violence and school refusal syndrome in the junior high years, the general extreme over-emphasis on entrance examinations, and a higher educational system that is mediocre by world standards, were described in earlier chapters. In the 1980s, great concern by many Japanese about the above problems and other education-related issues precipitated the most serious effort to reform education since the American Occupation. Although the intense concern of the last decade has somewhat subsided, major educational problems still exist and basic reform efforts continue in Japan.

Although future economic and social trends will change the ways adults learn in and out of the work place, attention in the past few years in Japan has focused upon reforming schools and universities so that these institutions might better meet the needs of Japanese in the twenty-first century. In the concluding chapter of this book, schools and universities are re-examined in light of recent reform efforts. Particular attention is devoted to the internationalization of Japanese education and to university reform, since changes are now occurring in these two areas. However, in order to understand recent changes in education and unresolved educational issues that will probably pose problems for Japan well into the next century, the broader context of the recent educational reform movement should be first examined.

The Background of Reform Efforts of the 1980s

The roots of the intense reform effort of the 1980s first emerged in the late 1960s. Even then, there was a strong feeling among many Japanese, including top business and political leaders, that while the educational system had many attributes, Japan's schools were too rigid and overcentralized. Such constraints upon schools would serve the nation poorly in the future unless reform occurred. In response to both the ruling Liberal Democratic Party (LDP) and a mandate from the Minister of Education, Mombushō's Central Council for Education (CCE) studied educational reform possibilities from 1967 until 1971.

In 1970, the Japanese government also called upon the twenty-four nation Organization of Economic Cooperation and Development (OECD) for an outside review of its educational institutions and policies. The writers of the OECD report praised Japan's many accomplishments in education. However, they criticized the overly centralized control of Mombushō, an overemphasis on conformity within the system, the extreme institutional hierarchy among educational institutions, and the overemphasis upon entrance examinations and educational credentials.

In 1971, the CCE issued a report addressing some of the same issues included in the OECD document. The CCE report called for, among other things, university reform, elimination of excessive uniformity in schools, reform of the entrance examination process, and promotion of alternatives to the 6-3-3-4 system.

While the reform attempts of the 1960s and 1970s brought about some changes, including expansion of kindergartens and government aid to private universities, efforts to bring about more flexibility in Japan's schools, entrance examination system reform, and general university reform completely failed.

There are several reasons educational reform efforts largely failed. The liberals and progressives resisted much of the 1960s and 1970s reform attempts because they distrusted both Mombushō and the business leaders calling for reform. Also, within Mombushō, there were deep divisions among bureaucrats who favored reform and those who did not. University administrators and faculty feared reform would destroy their sovereignty and organized against change. Even business and political leaders who were LDP members were divided as to the specific nature some of the educational changes might take. After the failure of the 1967-71 efforts to reform the system, education was not an important political issue for over a decade.[1]

In the early and mid-1980s, Prime Minister Nakāsone was the political leader who again brought national attention to bear on educational reform. Nakāsone first focused public attention on the issue in 1982 by including education as part of a plan to lead Japan to play a new and stronger role in international affairs commensurate with its new economic power. In 1983, Nakāsone continued to publicize the education issue by appointing a special advisory group chaired by the founder of the Sony Corporation. The report of this group criticized educational credentialism, the university admission policies, and, in particular, uniformity in education.[2]

After releasing his own plan to reform education shortly before the December 1983 general election, in March 198, the re-elected Nakāsone proposed to the Japanese Diet the establishment of an Ad Hoc Council on Educational Reform. The council would be under Nakāsone's direct control by reporting to the Prime Minister's office and not to Mombushō. The establishment of any kind of formal body with the authority to bypass Mombusho had not occurred in Japan since the Occupation. Most Japanese observers viewed such a move as the most serious attempt in forty years to reform education in Japan.

---

[1] Leonard J. Schoppa, Education Reform in Japan: A Case of Immobilist Politics (New York: Routledge, 1991), 171-210.

[2] Japanese Education Today, 64.

The Diet established the council in August 1984 after much debate. Appointees to the 25-member council included public and private university presidents, top business leaders, former government officials, and a few educators. The Ad Hoc Council, whose name was changed in 1986 to that of National Council on Educational Reform (NCER), was given a three-year mandate to engage in a comprehensive study of education and present recommendations for reform.

Prime Minister Nakāsone was correct in assuming that not only members of a few study groups, but large numbers of the public as well, were concerned about "exam hell," the rigid centralized control exercised by Mombushō, and too much emphasis upon the school one attended rather than what he or she learned. However, even though several opinion polls documented this public discontent, other evidence indicated the term "mixed feelings," to be a more accurate description of prevailing public attitudes toward the educational system.

For example, many Japanese believed that the examination ordeal was both a good builder and test of a young person's character. It is a larger culturally based Japanese belief that life is difficult and requires all people to work long and hard. The same parents who complain about the hardship their children encounter in the examination process may also regard the examination wars as good preparation for life, since students learn about its true difficulty through undergoing this ordeal.

With some exceptions, Mombushō officials were no burning proponents of reform of a system which they primarily designed and orchestrated. The Japan Teachers' Union (JTU), while long an opponent of entrance examinations and educational credentialism, deeply distrusted the Nakāsone government and its motives for attempting to reform education. The political left has dominated the JTU since the union's inception and the teacher organization regards the LDP as a tool of Japanese big business.

Great ambiguity about reform existed even among leaders of other government agencies, politicians, university presidents, and top management in Japanese corporations. For example, while many corporate leaders strongly supported greater flexibility in Japanese education so that the system would produce more creative, innovative, and internationally minded employees than in the past, other business representatives did not share this viewpoint. Some corporate managers were quite happy with the high general educational levels of employees and felt it was unwise to tamper with success. A number of executives, particularly those in large companies, supported the sorting function of the educational system since the competitive nature of entrance examinations for elite universities and the subsequent recruiting process meant they were assured a constant supply of "the best and brightest" Japanese young people.

Many Japanese public and private sector elites were also quite critical of schools and universities for not teaching students to be more assertive as individuals and more international in orientation. However, while many business executives and other elites were quite happy with these notions in the abstract, they were uncomfortable at the prospect of actually interacting on a regular basis with Japanese employees who were at ease around foreigners and who were of independent mind.

The internationalists were also confronted by educational reformers who desired that the Japanese system become more conservative. Several of the reform council shared a strong belief that the rise in school violence and other deviant behavior among Japanese students had occurred because contemporary young people were not taught appropriate traditional Japanese values.

Nakāsone was an articulate proponent of the conservative view. Even though he attracted public attention by arguing that Japanese young people could make their country stronger by becoming more internationally minded, Nakāsone also contended that before Japan could act with confidence internationally, more citizens needed to develop a true respect for their own cultural roots.

Nakāsone bemoaned the lack of attention to indigenous values in postwar Japanese education. He felt that filial piety, good morals, and patriotism should again be taught in Japanese schools to restore a sense of traditional "Japaneseness" among the nation's youth. This kind of talk, to many teacher union activists and university professors, was dangerous nationalistic posturing that aroused memories of the militaristic 1930s and 1940s.

The National Council on Educational Reform issued four major reports during its three-year life. The reports included a number of findings and several rather modest recommendations. A summary of council recommendations is provided below.

Major Areas Addressed by the National Council on Educational Reform

1. <u>Lifelong Education</u>. The council affirmed the need to broaden education to include more opportunities for citizens to learn throughout life while de-accentuating educational credentials. A specific recommendation adopted by the Mombushō that emerged from concern over this issue was the expansion and name change of the Ministry of Education's Social Education Bureau to the Bureau of Lifelong Education.

2. <u>Diversification and Reform of Higher Education</u>. The Council recommended reform of higher educational institution selection processes, curriculum flexibility, and research policies. Although some higher education reform is beginning, no changes in university admission policies substantive enough to lessen the examination pressures and educational credentialism now present in Japanese society seem to have resulted from the council's efforts. This is largely because powerful interests, including the universities and even part of the corporate sector, were against significant change and thwarted attempts.

3. <u>Elementary and Secondary School Reform</u>. Although a number of reforms were recommended, including changing the school calendar, changing the textbook selection process, reform of the teacher education process, and the establishment of special six-year secondary schools, no major changes resulted from the recommendations. Again, a number of interests, including Mombushō in the cases of six-year schools, the school calendar, and textbook selection, opposed fundamental changes.[3]

4. <u>Internationalization of Japanese Education</u>. Recommendations in this area were quite broad and included reforming Japanese elementary, secondary, and higher education so as to develop an increased international perspective among Japanese; improvement of foreign language instruction and of Japanese language instruction to foreigners in Japan; improvement in both the education of Japanese youth living abroad and in the treatment they received in schools upon returning home. However, the basic ambiguity of many Japanese regarding the possible trade-off between becoming more internationalized but, perhaps, less "Japanese" was reflected in the recognizance in the final council report of the need for internationalism to be built on a foundation of a renewed understanding on the part of youth of what it means to be Japanese. Although there is movement in a number of the areas that were mentioned in the council reports, no major public policy was implemented directly as a result of the reports.

5. <u>Decentralization of the Educational System and Promotion of Individuality</u>. In addition to the credentialism and examination entrance process, the issue of making the Japanese educational system less

---

[3] One curricular change resulting from the commission report is the requirement that the Japanese flag and national anthem be used in school opening and graduation ceremonies. This is a quite controversial mandate and, as of the publication of this book, many schools seemed to be ignoring this curricular change.

centralized and more responsive to the needs of individual students was a major concern of the council. The 1987 final report included the statement that in education, "The emphasis should be placed on diversity rather than uniformity, on flexibility rather than rigidity, on decentralization rather than centralization, and on freedom and self-determination rather than uniform control."[4] Although general recommendations were made in this area, no specific public policy has been implemented at the time of this book's publication that achieved the recommendations of the council. Interest group opposition, both on the part of the Mombushō and the Japanese Teachers' Union was effective in stopping substantive deregulation and decentralization of the schools.[5]

Many educational and political analysts and the general public believe that the National Council on Educational Reform was a failure. Only a few concrete recommendations actually emerged from the process and no recommendations were implemented that effectively addressed problems such as "exam hell," and overcentralization in the Japanese educational system. Moreover, some observers of the 1980s reform efforts argue that lack of action on the really controversial issues was because the National Council exhibited a persistent tendency to avoid areas of conflict.

There is little question that Japanese ambiguity about how much to reform the system; opposition or, at the very least, reluctance on the part of the Ministry of Education to change what many of its employees consider to be an effective system; vested interests such as juku with a stake in the status quo; and the failure of the Nakāsone government to politically outlive the National Council on Educational Reform were all obstacles to significant reform.

Even though the results of the recent reform movement failed to meet public expectations, tremendous publicity surrounding the entire process served to create a greater awareness by many Japanese that there is still a great need to make the educational system more flexible and responsive to students and a

---

[4] Hans Weiler and Miyako Eriko, "Reform and Non-Reform in Education: The Political Costs and Benefits of Reform Policies in France and Japan" (Annual Meeting of the American Educational Research Association, San Francisco, March 27-31, 1989), 35. Available through the U.S. Department of Education Office of Educational Research and Improvement, Washington, D.C., ED309543.

[5] Most of the summation and the preceding description of the politics of recent educational reform attempts are excerpted from Shoppa, Education Reform in Japan, 211-250; and from the Fourth and Final Report of the National Council on Educational Reform (Tōkyō: Ministry of Education, Science, and Culture, 1987).

changing society and economy. Perhaps the National Council's major contribution to educational reform was to keep momentum alive through broadening the dialogue.[6]

In addition to the new attention in Japan to lifelong education that was discussed in the last chapter, significant changes in the internationalization of Japanese education and in higher education reform are now already beginning to occur. It is to these dynamic aspects of Japan's educational system that we now turn.

The Internationalization of Japanese Precollegiate Education

The recent reform effort continued to keep the Japanese public aware of international education issues. Also, despite a strong sense by many Japanese that traditional values are most important, Japan's new economic power, foreign pressure, interest in Japan by citizens of other countries, and interest by Japanese youth in international experiences are resulting in educational change.

The growth of Japanese economic power has meant many Japanese and their families now live on average six months to two years in foreign countries. One of the most publicized issues within Japan is the educational fate of children who travel with their parents to overseas business postings.

By 1988 over 44,000 Japanese children in grades one through nine were living and studying in foreign countries. During the 1980s the number of these students returning each year to Japanese schools grew dramatically. In the late 1960s only about 2000 Japanese children returned annually to elementary and secondary schools after living abroad. By 1987 the number of annual returnees had risen to over 10,500. Many Japanese educators and parents, as well as government and private sector organizations, now grapple with the twin problems of educating Japanese youth while they are overseas and easing the often major adjustment problems these youngsters experience when they return to Japan.[7]

---

[6] The argument that the National Council on Educational Reform actually achieved more than many observers give them credit for is articulated in the article by Ichikawa Shōgo, "An Investigation into Educational Reform in Japan," Japan Quarterly xxxviii, no. 3 (July-September 1991): 350-354.

[7] Education in Japan 1989: A Graphic Presentation, 124-125; and Merry White, The Japanese Overseas: Can They Go Home Again? (New York: The Free Press, 1988), 26.

The major academic problem families with children face when the father is given a foreign assignment by his company directly relate to high school and university entrance examinations. Since much of the content of these examinations is directly from the national Mombushō curriculum, even if a Japanese youngster attends a high quality foreign school, he or she is not likely to do well enough upon entrance examinations for prestigious or even middle-level educational institutions without substantial supplementary instruction.

Many families who have been assigned to a foreign country choose to either have the mother and children remain in Japan or leave the children with relatives so as to avoid taking students out of the Japanese "educational loop." The older a student is the greater the likelihood he or she will be left in Japan when a parent or parents go to another country. By the mid 1980s, while 87 percent of elementary children went with their parents to another country, only 72 percent of junior high students accompanied their families abroad. Just 51 percent of upper secondary students traveled abroad for the foreign posting. Because many parents still have higher educational expectations for sons than daughters, male children and young people are more likely than females to remain in Japan when a family goes abroad.[8]

Both Japanese communities abroad and the Japanese government attempt to keep young people competitive for future entrance examinations upon returning home. As of 1988, of the 44,000 Japanese elementary students living abroad over 18,000 or 40 percent attended special supplemental "Saturday schools" in addition to foreign schools.[9] These schools, which can be found in virtually every urban area in countries that have sizable Japanese populations, meet each Saturday for a half or full day. Teachers are usually members of the local Japanese community. However, in the larger Saturday schools, Mombushō will pay the salaries of a principal and perhaps a head teacher who are professional educators.

Japanese language and mathematics are the two subjects that receive the most attention in Saturday schools because of their importance in Japanese

[8] White, The Japanese Overseas: Can They Go Home Again?, 37.

[9] Education in Japan 1989: A Graphic Presentation, 125.

entrance examinations. The Mombushō also provides curriculum materials for students in Saturday schools.

There are also full-time Japanese schools that employ the Mombushō curriculum in a number of foreign countries where Japanese reside. Most of these institutions are elementary schools, but several countries, including Germany, Great Britain, and the United States have Mombushō-accredited high schools. By 1988 over 17,000 or 39 percent of Japanese children abroad attended full-time Japanese schools in the host countries. The remainder of Japanese students abroad attended local schools of the host country.[10]

The much publicized adjustment problems of returnee children are in part because the Japanese educational system, like the larger culture, tends to overstress group conformity at the expense of individuality. During much of the past two decades, the Japanese media used such descriptors as "international masterless samurai," "wounded children," "half-Japanese," and "foreign Japanese" for children who had been overseas.[11]

Teachers of these children report such behaviors as serious problems with the Japanese language, depression and moodiness, excessive demonstration of individualistic and "selfish" behaviors, reluctance to eat standard Japanese food, and discomfort with the typical school work loads and teaching styles found in Japanese classrooms. For older students, particularly those who were not enrollees in Japanese schools while abroad, there is the added tension created by feelings of inadequacy about running the "examination race."

The Ministry of Education, particularly in the Tōkyō area where a disproportionately high number of returnee children live, has designated several public schools as sites for special programs for returnee reorientation. A few private schools, such as the International Christian University Attached High School, have designed comprehensive programs especially to attract returnees. Some universities, including several of Japan's leading public and private institutions, make special provisions to use additional criteria than just entrance examination scores when considering a returnee's application.

---

[10] Ibid., 125. The private Japanese school, Mēji Gakuen, opened the first Japanese high school in the U.S. in 1989. By 1991 the school had an enrollment of 110 students. At the time of this book's publication, Keiō University has also opened a Japanese high school in New York City.

[11] White, The Japanese Overseas: Can They Go Home Again?, 27.

Although the educational system is attempting to respond to the plight of returnees, many Japanese feel not enough has been done yet to meet the needs of this group of young people. During the education debates of the 1980s, some reformers demanded that Japanese look upon young people who spent time in other countries not as problems but, particularly because of their foreign language skills, as national treasures. Significant progress by the majority of Japanese in moving toward the latter mind set still remains a future hope.

The entire question of foreign language proficiency in Japan is viewed by many political leaders, educators, and the public as another problem in the internationalization process that needs to be better addressed. Traditionally, spoken English has been given short shrift in Japanese schools and university English instruction to such an extent that most Japanese and many Japanese teachers of English speak only a few words or sentences of the language. In order to improve English language instruction, the Mombushō initiated programs in 1979 and in 1988 where small numbers of Japanese teachers of English spend either sixty days or six months at government expense in English-speaking countries to improve their language skills.

The Japan Exchange Teaching (JET) Program is an even more extensive effort to improve English instruction than the Japanese teacher study tours. JET is a national government initiative in which Mombushō, along with the Ministries of Foreign and Home Affairs, cooperate to bring foreign young people to Japan to serve as assistant English teachers.

In the JET Program, young college graduates from such countries as Australia, Canada, the U.K., and the U.S. are employed as assistant English teachers in the public schools or as coordinators for international relations within local government offices. JET fellows participate in the program for one year and then have the option of working in JET for a second year. Although there were government programs in the 1970s to bring Americans and British English teachers to Japan, JET is a major initiative. By the 1991-1992 school year, a total of 2,874 young people from English-speaking countries worked in JET. In that year all but 175 of the JET fellows served as assistant English teachers.

Although the JET Program has grown steadily, it receives mixed reactions from foreign participants and Japanese. JET teachers complain that assignments are too vague, they are not given appropriate orientation, and that the examination

216

driven nature of high school education means they lack enough class time to actually improve the teaching and learning of conversational English. Japanese, in turn, complain that some JET participants are unmotivated and ignorant of Japanese culture. Still, there are many JET success stories in individual Japanese schools and communities.[12]

Internationalization of Education: Colleges and Universities

Throughout the 1980s Japan's economic progress also had other effects upon internationalization. Foreign governments pressured Japan during economic negotiations to develop a more international perspective and use its great economic resources to aid international relations. Outside pressure, as well as the efforts of internationally minded Japanese government bureaucrats and private-sector employees, resulted in substantial new receptivity by universities toward foreign students who wish to enroll. In 1982 there were only about 8,100 foreign students in Japan. Seven years later, in 1989, the number had more than tripled to a total of 31,251.

In 1985 the Japanese government announced a goal of hosting 100,000 foreign students by the year 2000.   Although the national government started scholarships for foreign students in 1954, funds for the national program for foreign students and for regional government and private-sector scholarships have been dramatically increased in recent years. The Peoples' Republic of China sends the most university students to Japan, followed by South Korea, Taiwan, Malaysia, and the United States.

It is quite likely that increased levels of informal individual and group interactions now occurring between Japanese university students and their foreign classmates will serve to broaden the international horizons of young Japanese.[13]

---

[12] Description of the JET Program taken from Education in Japan 1989: A Graphic Presentation, 126-127; and "JET Flourishes by Sending Teaching Assistants to Japan," Japan Now (Washington, D.C.: Embassy of Japan, August 1991): 1; and from question and answer sesssion at a meeting of Japanese and Americans interested in international exchange sponsored by the University of Tennessee at Chattanooga Japan Project and the Japan Center for International Exchange on September 17, 1990 in Chattanooga, Tennessee.

[13] Information on recent increases in foreign students in Japan from Yamāmōto Kīyoshi, "Foreign Students in Japan," Occasional Paper No. 03/90, ED327443 (National Institute for Educational Research: Hiroshima University, June 1990); and Glen Shive, "Survey of Events 1990, East Asia," Comparative Education Review 35, no. 2 (May 1991): 387-388.

As relations between Japan and the United States have broadened and deepened, in addition to a large number of exchange programs, several U.S. branch campuses designed for both American and Japanese students have opened in Japan. The older institutions of this type were branch campuses of such American universities as the University of Maryland and were established to offer courses for U.S. servicemen and other Americans in Japan.

The newer branch campuses opening in recent years are, for the most part, intended for Japanese students. Although Temple University opened a branch for Japanese students back in 1982 and now has two branch campuses, it was a suggestion in a joint 1986 communiqué issued by President Ronald Reagan and Prime Minister Nakāsone Yasūhiro calling for more such campuses that gave significant publicity to such an idea. About the same time, a group of Diet and U.S. Congressional representatives formed the USA-Japan Committee for Promoting Trade Expansion, which also began to actively attempt to match Japanese locales with American campuses.[14] These developments resulted in significant exploration by American universities as to the possibility of opening branch campuses in Japan and similar queries by Japanese universities about the possibility of establishing programs in the U.S. In both cases exploration led to the establishment of programs or institutions. As of March 1991 seventeen American universities and colleges had established branch campuses in Japan that offered programs leading to bachelor's degrees, another five had set up language schools, and three other institutions offered post-graduate programs.[15]

By 1990 at least fifty Japanese junior and senior colleges had established various programs in the United States. Despite exceptions such as the merger of Salem College of West Virginia with one of Tēikyō University's American programs that created the U.S-based Salem-Tēikyō University, a smaller number of Japanese programs in the U.S. are four-year degree programs than their U.S. equivalents in Japan. The Japanese programs in the U.S. tend to be one-semester or one-year exchange programs with Japanese students then returning to their home campuses to complete degrees. A second major difference in the Japanese

[14] Jon Choy, "Education Reform in Japan: Will The Third Time Be The Charm?", JEI Report, no. 45A (Washington, D.C.: Japan Economic Institute, November 30, 1990), 10-11.

[15] Drew Poulin, "U.S. Colleges Have Large Lessons to Learn in Japan," The Japan Times, weekly international ed. 31, no. 4, October 21-27, 1991, 14-15.

and American institutions who have begun programs is that both public and private American colleges are launching ventures while thus far the large majority of Japanese colleges that have established American programs are private.[16]

There are no typical curricular models for these international campuses. However, in one program of studies used by several American university branches whose enrollees are Japanese, students study for two years at the branch campus in Japan and then have the option to transfer to the main campus in the United States to complete the bachelor's degree.

These international higher education ventures to date both offer promising opportunities and present problems. A major problem is that the American branch campuses in Japan fail to qualify as universities under Ministry of Education guidelines. Rather, they are classified as miscellaneous institutions. If a Japanese enrolled at a branch campus in Japan wishes a university degree recognized by the Ministry of Education, he or she must transfer to the main campus in the United States, since Mombushō does recognize degrees from foreign universities. Other problems of the ventures include recruiting U.S. faculty to live in Japan, language, money, and concerns about the quality of both instruction and students in these programs.

The competitiveness of Japanese graduates of American branch campuses in the labor market of their own country is yet another problem. While future developments could very well change present mind sets, it is very questionable at best that major Japanese employers, with their long-time habit of recruiting graduates of a few elite universities will, in the immediate future, consider the first graduates of these joint ventures and foreign branches as prime candidates for positions. Yet the branch campuses and other experiments in the internationalization of higher education are daring ones indeed for Japan.[17]

While most Japanese college and university students studying in other countries are either in graduate schools are on short, semester-length or less exchange programs, if all Japanese post-secondary students who engage in some

16 Gail S. Chambers and William K. Cummings, Profiting From Education: Japan-United States International Educational Ventures in The 1980s, (New York: Institute of International Education, 1990), Appendix I, 144-160. Note that the number in the text for Japanese institutions is an estimate, as the variety and short duration of many Japanese programs in the U.S. make formulation of precise totals very difficult.

17 Choy, "Education Reform in Japan: Will the Third Time Be The Charm?", 10-11.

form of study in foreign countries are taken into account, their growth has been dramatic since 1980. In that year there were only 14,000 Japanese studying in foreign universities, while by 1990 the number increased six-fold to 84,000 students. These numbers alone represent a significant internationalization of Japanese higher education over a relatively short period of time.[18]

Structural University Reform?

While Japanese universities have made much progress in internationalization, they are still regarded as mediocre by world standards. The educational reform movement of the 1980s seems to have at least indirectly begun what could prove to eventually become fundamental changes in the structure of Japanese universities.[19]

One National Council on Educational Reform criticism of the university system was that it suffered from too much regulation and centralization. This led to much conformity on campuses. In 1991 Mombushō, the very ministry responsible for what many believe to be the stifling regulation of universities, extensively revised its "University Establishment Standards," the basic document through which the ministry exercised rigid control over higher education.

Under the old system Mombushō had the power to mandate, in both public and private universities, how many students could attend a particular class, the time of day or evening a university could hold classes, and even the dimensions of campus buildings. Mombushō also mandated that each university require "general education" for all first- and second-year students. The thirty-six credit general education courses accounted for more than one-fifth of the undergraduate curriculum and included subjects in the humanities, social sciences, foreign languages, natural sciences, and physical education.

The new standards essentially leave the above decisions up to the individual university. However, if an institution wishes to eliminate mandatory

---

[18] Shive, "Survey of Events 1990: East Asia," 388. Most Japanese college and university students who study in a foreign country do so in the United States or somewhere in Western Europe.

[19] See chapter five for an analysis of the problems of Japanese universities.

general education or make other changes in course requirements, it will still need Mombushō's approval before the changes can take effect.

The new standards also include a liberalization of ministry regulations on the organization of universities and more university flexibility in determining how many faculty may be hired and what constitutes appropriate faculty job assignments. How much actual change will occur in higher education because of Mombushō deregulations is difficult to predict. Japanese university presidents have a tradition of deferring to faculty governance and, in general, Japanese academicians are conservative about institutional change. Currently, many professors benefit from a system that is hierarchical and often discouraging of innovative work or interdisciplinary efforts by junior instructors.

However, there are already a few colleges and universities, including Kyōto University, one of Japan's most prestigious institutions of higher learning, experimenting with such curricular innovations as interdisciplinary programs. If the new Mombushō standards result in true deregulation, they could bring about significant structural university reform. Even the entrance examination system, the aspect of Japanese higher education that has changed the least throughout time, could eventually be profoundly affected if enough universities change their structure, hiring policies, and curriculum.[20]

As the new century draws near, powerful economic and societal forces external to either the universities or Mombushō have tremendous potential to change higher education in Japan. Japan is clearly in transition from a manufacturing-dominated to a services-dominated economy. In 1970 over 50 percent of all Japanese workers were employed in manufacturing, agriculture, mining, or fishing. In the same year under one-half of all workers were employed in services-related fields. By 1989 almost 60 percent of all Japanese workers earned their livings in services provision.[21] Government forecasts indicate that by the year 2000 almost two-thirds of the Japanese work force will be employed in

---

[20] Nana Mizūshima Regur, "Japan's Colleges, Given Go-Ahead for Reform, Face Big Decision," The Chronicle of Higher Education 37, no. 45 (June 24, 1991): A.31.

[21] Anzai Yōichi, ed., Japan 1991: An International Comparison (Tōkyō: Japan Institute for Social and Economic Affairs, n.d.), 21.

services while slightly over one-third of workers will remain in manufacturing, agriculture, mining or fishing.[22]

What remains of the Japanese manufacturing sector is becoming increasingly "high tech," as the production of such products as computers and high-definition television displaces low-value-added industries such as textiles and ship building. Government and private sector policy makers see these changes as important in keeping Japan internationally competitive. However, other modern industrialized countries are working toward the same kinds of economic changes. Although in the future the Japanese are likely to be very competitive in both the provision of services and manufacturing of high technology products, they will face fierce competition from other countries who see similar economic endeavors as highly desirable.

Changes to sophisticated services provision and "high tech" manufacturing are likely to cause restructuring within many Japanese companies. Economic restructuring will most likely result in new demands on higher education by companies and the public sector. The lifetime employment system is likely to remain an important aspect of Japanese business well into the future. However, there are already signs that companies, in the face of increasingly rigorous domestic and international competition, are both rethinking the high costs of a large permanent labor force and experiencing a greater need for the infusion of midcareer employees who possess, rather than company loyalty, highly specialized skills such as software development or knowledge of international finance.

In the future a potential job candidate's university major will probably become more important to employers. The specific university that an individual attends could very well become less of a factor in determining his or her desirability as an employee.

In Japan, reformers have already called for increasing the intellectual quality of the undergraduate experience and for expansion and improvement of existing graduate programs in higher education. If the economic trends described above reshape the organization of Japanese companies, the pressure for significant reform of higher education from government and business will continue.

---

[22] "Changing Structure of Japan's Work Force," News from Japan (Washington, D.C.: Japan-U.S. News and Communications, November 7, 1987).

Throughout the post-World War II years, a major priority of both the ruling Liberal Democratic Party and the Japanese national government bureaucracy has been to assist Japanese business to prosper in order that wealth would be created for the country. Even though Japan's universities are notoriously conservative regarding internal change, they will likely find it quite difficult to resist both the demands of industry and the national government for significant changes in how students are educated.

Social as well as economic trends should also act to stimulate reform of Japanese higher education in the immediate future. As described in chapter five, within Japanese society there are declining numbers of 18-year-olds and an increase in demand for further educational opportunities by people who are past the typical age for university attendance. Universities can avoid declining enrollments by accommodating more foreign and nontraditional students. The recent increases in foreign student enrollment described earlier show no signs of abatement. As of 1990, in an effort to tailor programs for adult learners and other nontraditional students, a number of Japanese universities were sending study teams to the United States to examine continuing education departments.

The Prospects for Other Changes in Japanese Education

Despite public disappointment over the lack of results from the Nakāsone initiative of the 1980s, if substantive internationalization of the entire system and reform of higher education occurs, it will likely have profound domino effects upon other aspects of school and university education in Japan. As described earlier, many Japanese are concerned about too much conformity and centralization in formal educational institutions.

Japanese students who leave the system to live abroad and return, university students who either study abroad or attend foreign branches in Japan, foreign students who attend Japanese universities, and foreign English-speaking university graduates who work in Japanese schools, all constitute an increase in the number of heterogeneous actors within Japanese educational institutions. This in turn increases pressure to change aspects of the educational system that tend to block rather than facilitate accommodation of these new clients.

Reform of the Japanese university has an even more profound possible impact upon other educational institutions and practices. It is certainly difficult to imagine the entrance examination not being an important rite of passage into the Japanese university. Still, the pressure for a higher-quality undergraduate intellectual environment and the increasing heterogeneity of Japanese university students will probably diminish the importance of the examination in the future. Already some prestigious universities are changing entrance examinations in English to include conversational tests and making special exceptions for returnees who have not been through the cramming process but show academic potential.

If university entrance examinations become less important, the potential increases for fundamental changes in the secondary school classroom environment. At the secondary school level the overemphasis upon rote memorization, the great pressure many students feel, and even recent rises in school truancy will probably only change for the better when the examination system loses some of its power over student and teacher behavior. Such changes can probably only occur after universities make fundamental changes in university entrance policy.

While the future prospects for significant upgrading of higher education and for improvement of an already excellent elementary and secondary educational system are by no means guaranteed, a continued emphasis upon lifelong education seems to be a certainty in Japan. Even though changes in permanent employment could weaken the incentive large public and private institutions now have to spend time and resources on the human capital development of their employees, other powerful aspects of Japanese life and culture seem to ensure the nation will have a disproportionately high percentage of lifetime learners relative to many other nations.

The long-time respect for education that permeates Japanese culture is a product of quite-hardy Confucian ideals that still influence Japanese. Despite flaws, the formal elementary and secondary educational system provides most young people with basic skills that enable them to continue to learn in the adult years. Although there is certainly evidence that many Japanese born after 1960 desire a more relaxed life style, the national affinity for hobbies and other forms of active self-development often lends itself to a lifetime of intellectual growth.

Japan's high-quality newspapers, journals of opinion, and public electronic media also provide ample opportunities on a regular basis for the many who desire to broaden and deepen their knowledge of the world.

The unending pursuit of knowledge, coupled with an impressive propensity to put forth great effort are perhaps the major reasons for the great economic success of Japan. For well over a century the Japanese have made education a top national priority. There is absolutely no reason to expect that education will be afforded any less attention as Japan enters the twenty-first century.

Questions for Comparison

1. Many of the leading critics involved in the Japanese educational reform movement of the 1980s argued that too much control by the National Government Ministry of Education, Mombushō, was stifling Japan's educational system. Has this criticism of national government intrusion also been prominent in the recent American educational reform movement?

2. Although the most recent Japanese educational reform movement dates back to the mid-1980s, a national concern about improving American schools goes back to the beginning of the same decade and continues today. What are the reformers' major criticisms of American schools?

3. In your opinion does American education need more internationalization? Why or why not?

4. In Japan, colleges and universities are regarded as institutions that are in great need of reform. Is the same the case with American universities?

5. What types of changes do you think are needed in American educational institutions in order that they may better prepare workers for the future economy?

226

Additional Reading

Works about Japanese educational reform in the 1980s are just beginning to emerge. The most comprehensive book to date available in English is Leonard James Schoppa, Education Reform in Japan: A Case of Immobilist Politics, New York: Routledge, 1991. Merry White, The Japanese Overseas, Can They Go Home Again?, New York: The Free Press, 1988, is a quite readable account of the plights of both young and adult "returnees." Profiting From Education: Japan-United States International Educational Ventures in The 1980s, by Gail Chambers and William Cummings is the best study available on joint Japan-U.S. higher education ventures. The study was published in 1990 by the New York-based Institute of International Education.

Because the American educational reform movement has been occurring since about 1980 and has not yet subsided, there are a number of books available on the subject. Three of the best are Samuel B. Bacharach, Education Reform: Making Sense Of It All, Boston: Allyn and Bacon, 1990; John Goodlad, A Place Called School: Prospects for the Future, New York: McGraw-Hill, 1984; and Theodore Sizer, Horace's Compromise: The Dilemma of the American High School, Boston: Houghton Mifflin Company, 1984.

Japanese Glossary

Amae - Can be translated as "dependency wishes." Amae is a central concept in the work of psychiatrist Doi Tākako who argues that Japanese are taught early to unconditionally take advantage of the help of close others.

Burakumin - The burakumin are Japan's largest minority group. Although they have the same racial, cultural, and national origins as Japanese, burakumin have historically been discriminated against by other Japanese. Prejudice and discrimination against burakumin is thought to have originated because they participated in such occupations as butchery that violated religious teachings.

Bushidō - "Way of the Warrior." The term came into common use during the Tokūgawa years to mean the ethical code of the ruling samurai class. Absolute loyalty and a strong sense of personal honor were important components of bushidō.

Chūgakkō - Lower secondary schools.

Daigaku-Ryō - A Confucian training institution for government administrators established in the 7th century during the reign of Emperor Tenji. By the end of the Heian Period the Daigaku-Ryō had lost its influence.

Doryo - The Japanese term depicting an equal rather than a sempai-kōhai relationship between two males in an organization.

Gakurekishugi - Educational credentialism in Japanese. The term describes the great emphasis many employers and much of the general public place upon what school or university a student attended.

Gakushū juku - Juku that are for elementary and junior high school students.

Gambaru - In Japanese, the word means to persist or hold firm. "Gambatte kudasai" or "please persist" is a constant exhortation heard in Japanese schools.

Han - Small groups of five to six children who work within the kūmi.

Heian Period (794-1185) - This period of Japanese history began when Emperor Kammu established Heiankyō (now Kyōto) as the imperial capital of Japan and ended in 1185 when Mināmoto No Yoritomo's forces defeated those of the Taira family, thus allowing the shōgunate to be established in Kāmākura.

Hoikuen - Nursery schools supervised by Kosēishō, the National Ministry of Health and Welfare.

228

Juku - Private schools which teach subjects for students who are preparing for examinations or attempting to do better in school. Juku also teach nonacademic classes.

Kakushu gakkō - These institutions are private, miscellaneous training schools that offer various programs to high school dropouts and graduates. Kakushu gakkō program length might vary from three months to more than one year.

Kāmākura Period (1185-1333) - This historical period roughly corresponds to the life span of the Kāmākura shōgunate. During this time, considered to be part of Japan's medieval history, the city of Kāmākura was the unofficial capital of the country.

Kana - The Japanese syllabary alphabets. Two sets of kāna are used in the modern Japanese writing system. Hiragana is used for native words and any words of Chinese origin that are not written in kanji (Chinese characters). Katakana is typically used to write foreign words from European languages.

Kanji - These are the Chinese-origin pictographs that form the integral part of the Japanese writing system. Although there are at least 40,000 kanji, educated people, on average, use between 2,000 and 3,000 kanji. Mombushō identifies 1,846 kanji that are essential for basic literacy.

Koto senmon gakkō - Technical colleges usually offering five-year programs that include two or three of the high school years and two years of post-secondary work. Most koto senmon gakkō have engineering and science curricula.

Kūmi - Japanese word for school class. There are stronger groupism connotations within the meaning of kūmi than the English word "class."

Kyōiku - Education.

Mēiji Period (1868-1912) - The period of history that is considered the beginning of modern Japanese history. The years were also the dates of the reign of Emperor Mēiji.

Mombushō - The Japanese National Government Ministry of Education established during the Mēiji Period.

Murōmachi Period (1333-1600) - The Murōmachi years, which began with the fall of the Kāmākura shōgunate, were characterized by great cultural achievement and continual societal strife. Historians debate when the period ends.

Nāra Period (710-794) - The period began when the capital was moved from Fujiwarakyō to Heijōkyō (now the city of Nāra). The Nāra Period was a time of great Chinese influence in Japan.

Nemawashi - The term literally means cutting around the roots of a plant before it is transplanted. Nemawashi has become a famous term in Japanese business decision-making. In that context, nemawashi is the system of careful consultations among a number of employees of an organization before a decision is reached.

Ochikobore - Students in Japanese schools who are achieving several grades below their classmates.

Rōnin - The term meant masterless samurai during the Tokūgawa years. Today rōnin are high school graduates who do not enter their chosen university the first time they try and continue to study for entrance examinations.

Samurai - The literal meaning is "one who serves." Samurai were the warrior elite of modern Japan who became the ruling class of the country from the late 1200s until the Mēiji Restoration of 1868.

Senshū gakkō - Special training schools. The most popular are senmon gakkō, or special (1-2 years) training colleges for high school graduates.

Sempai-kōhai (senior-junior) - These are informal, but important, relationships that are pervasive in a variety of Japanese organizations. The relationship is usually limited to males. Sempai act as the mentors of kōhai while kōhai reciprocate with respect and loyalty.

Sensei - Teacher.

Shākai kyōiku - Social education. In the past this term has been used to describe community education outside of formal educational institutions. One example is the courses offered at citizens' public halls.

Shijuku - Private educational institutions during the Tokūgawa years offering more advanced instruction than terākoya. Pupils came from all parts of Japan and from all social classes.

Shīken jigoku ("examination hell") - The term, which refers to the rigors of Japan's school and university entrance examinations, first came into use early in this century.

Shōgakkō - Elementary schools.

Shōgun - Customarily translated as "barbarian-subduing generalissimo." Shōguns were in effect military dictators who dominated Japanese politics for most of history between 1192 and 1867.

Sūnao - The Japanese word for obedience and compliance. The development of sūnao in children is a major goal of Japanese preschool educators.

Terākoya - These were commoner schools that existed during the Tokūgawa Period. The root word of terākoya, terā, means Buddhist temple. Earlier,

Buddhist priests were dominant in village instruction, but by the mid and latter Tokūgawa years, terākoya were mostly secular.

Tokūgawa Period (1600-1868) - Also called the Edo Period, the Tokūgawa Period was marked by the political domination of the Tokūgawa shōguns. During the period, Japan was at peace, isolated from most of the rest of the world, and developing a quite sophisticated culture and economy.

Yobikō - A special kind of juku where high school graduates and high school students prepare for university entrance examinations.

Yochien - Japanese kindergartens which operate under Mombushō supervision for children between the ages of three and five.

Works Cited

Abdoo, Frank. "Music Education in Japan." Music Educator's Journal 70, no. 6 (February 1984): 52-56.

Anzai Yōichi, ed. Japan 1991: An International Comparison. Tōkyō: Japan Institute for Social and Economic Affairs, 1990.

August, Robert. "Yobikō: Prep Schools for College Entrance in Japan." In Japanese Educational Productivity, eds. Robert Leestma and Herbert J. Walberg, 290. The University of Michigan, 1992.

Altbach, Philip, and Viswanathan Selvarathnam, eds. From Dependence to Autonomy: The Development of Asian Universities. Kluwer Academic Publishers, 1989.

Beauchamp, Edward, and Richard Rubinger. Education in Japan: A Source Book. Garland Publishing Inc., 1989.

Becker, James, and Tokūyāma Māsatō, eds. In Search of Mutual Understanding: Joint Japan-United States Textbook Study Project. National Council for the Social Studies, 1981.

Berman, David. "A Case Study of the High School Extrance Examination in Chiba Prefecture, Japan." Theory and Research in Social Education xviii, no. 4 (Fall 1990): 387-404.

Bronfenbrenner, Martin. "Economic Education in Japan at the University Level." Journal of Economic Education 16, no. 4: 270.

Caudill, William, and Helen Weinstein. "Maternal Care and Infant Behavior in Japan and America." Psychiatry 32, no. 1 (1969): 12-43.

Chambers, Gail S., and William K. Cummings. Profiting From Education: Japan-United States International Educational Ventures in The 1980s. New York: Institute of International Education, 1990.

"Changing Structure of Japan's Work Force." News from Japan. Washington, D.C.: Japan-U.S. News and Communications, November 7, 1987.

Chira, Susan. "In Student's Game Plan, College Can Be a Racquet." Teacher's Manual for Video Letter from Japan II. The College Years. The Asia Society, 1988.

Choy, Jon. "Education Reform in Japan: Will The Third Time Be The Charm?" JEI Report no. 45A. Washington, D.C.: Japan Economic Institute, November 30, 1990), 10-11.

Christopher, Robert C. The Japanese Mind. Fawcett Columbine, 1983.

Clark, Rodney. The Japanese Company. Yale University Press, 1979.

Cole, Robert. Strategies For Learning: Small-Group Activities in American, Japanese, and Swedish Industry. University of California Press, 1989.

Course of Study for Elementary Schools. Tōkyō: Ministry of Education, Science, and Culture, 1983.

Cremin, Lawrence. Preface to American Education: The Colonial Experience 1607-1783. Harper and Row, 1970.

Doi Tākako. The Anatomy of Dependence. Tōkyō: Kōdansha, 1973.

Dore, Ronald P. Education in Tokūgawa Japan. University of California Press, 1965.

_____. Introduction to Education and Examination in Modern Japan, by Amano Ikuō. University of Tōkyō Press, 1990.

Dore, Ronald P. and Sako Māri. How the Japanese Learn to Work. London: Routledge, 1989.

Dorfman, Cynthia Hearn, ed. Japanese Education Today. Washington, D.C.: Government Printing Office, 1987.

Duke, Benjamin. The Japanese School: Lessons for Industrial America. Praeger, 1986.

Education in Japan 1989: A Graphic Presentation. 11th ed. Tōkyō: Ministry of Education, Science, and Culture, 1989.

Ellington, Lucien. Japan: Tradition and Change. Longman, 1990.

Ellington, Lucien, Jack Morgan, Richard Rice, and Anthony Sugilia. The Japanese Economy: Teaching Strategies. Joint Council on Economic Education, 1990.

Evans, Robert. "The Transition from School to Work in the United States." In Educational Policies in Crisis: Japanese and American Perspectives, William K. Cummings, 142. Praeger, 1986.

Fallows, Deborah. "Japanese Women." National Geographic 177, no. 4 (April 1990): 52-53.

Fallows, James. "Gradgrinds Heirs." The Atlantic 259, no. 3 (March 1987): 20.

"Fourth and Final Report of the National Council on Educational Reform." Tōkyō: Ministry of Education, Science, and Culture, 1987.

Fūjita Marĭko. "It's All Mother's Fault: Child Care and the Socialization of Working Mothers in Japan." The Journal of Japanese Studies 15, no. 1 (Winter 1989): 67-92.

Gittelsohn, John. "Japanese Universities Taking a Cue from National Politics, Now Face Their Own Crisis of Complacency, Analysts Say." The Chronicle of Higher Education 36, no. 3 (September 20, 1989): 45.A.

Hawley, Willis D. "The Education of Japanese Teachers: Lessons for the United States." In Fit to Teach: Teacher Education in International Perspective, ed. Edgar B. Gumbert, vol. 8, 33. Georgia State University, 1990.

Hashĭmoto Masānori. The Japanese Labor Market in a Comparative Perspective With the United States: A Transaction-Cost Interpretation. W. E. Upjohn Institute for Employment Research, 1990.

Hendry, Joy. Becoming Japanese: The World of the Pre-School Child. University of Hawaii Press, 1986.

Hess, Robert, et al. "Family Influences of School Readiness and Achievement in Japan and the United States: An Overview of a Longitudinal Study." In Child Development and Education in Japan, eds. Harold Stevenson, Āzuma Hĭroshi, and Hakuta Kēnji, 155-156. W. H. Freeman and Company, 1986.

Hirāmatsu Kazuō. "The Role of Accounting Education and Research in Japanese Corporations." The Sixth Annual Conference on Accounting Education (Kyōto, Japan, October 8, 1987).

Ichĭkawa Shōgo. "An Investigation into Educational Reform in Japan." Japan Quarterly xxxviii, no. 3 (July-September 1991): 350-354.

James, Estelle, and Gail Benjamin. Public Policy and Private Education in Japan. St. Martin's Press Inc., 1988.

Japan's Junior Colleges Being Absorbed by Parent Universities." Teacher's Manual for Video Letter from Japan II. The College Years. The Asia Society, 1988.

"Japan's Schools: Why Can't Little Taro Think?". The Economist, 315, no. 7651 (April 21, 1990): 22.

"JET Flourishes by Sending Teaching Assistants to Japan." Japan Now. Washington, D..C.: Embassy of Japan, August 1991.

Jones, Randall S. "The Economic Implications of Japan's Aging Population." In Japan: Exploring New Paths, ed. John Choy, 80. Washington, D.C.: Japan Economic Institute of America, 1988.

Kasāura Tatsuō. "A Century of School Excursions." Japan Quarterly xxxiv, no. 3 (July-September 1987): 287-290.

Kāya Michiko, ed. The Life of a Junior High School Student. Tōkyō: International Society for Educational Information, 1985.

Kobara Tomōyuki. "The Revision of the Social Studies Curriculum in Japan: A Crisis in Social Studies." The Social Studies Teacher 10, no. 1 (September-October 1988): 10-12.

Kōdansha Encyclopedia of Japan. Tōkyō: Kōdansha, Ltd., 1983.

Krishner, Bernard. Japan As We Lived It: Can East and West Ever Meet?. Tōkyō: Yohan Publications Inc., 1989.

Lebra, Takie Sugiyama. Japanese Women: Constraint and Fulfillment. University of Hawaii Press, 1984.

_____. Patterns of Japanese Behavior. University of Hawaii Press, 1976.

Lewis, Catherine. "Cooperation and Control in Japanese Nursery Schools." Comparative Education Review 28, no 1 (February 1984): 78.

_____. "Children's Social Development in Japan." In Child Development and Education in Japan, eds. Harold Stevenson, Azuma Hiroshi, and Hakuta Kēnji, 196. W. H. Freeman and Company, 1986.

_____. "Japanese First Grade Classrooms: Implications for U.S. Theory and Research." Comparative Education Review 32, no. 2 (May 1988): 170.

McConnell, Campbell R. Economics: Principles, Problems, and Policies. 10th ed. McGraw-Hill, 1987.

Morōoka Kazūfusa. "Continuing Education: The Japanese Approach." Bulletin 28 of the UNESCO Principal Regional Office For Asia and the Pacific. (Bangkok, Thailand: United Nations Institute, September 1987), 58.

Morioka Kiyomi. "Privatization of Family Life in Japan." In Child Development and Education in Japan, eds. Harold Stevenson, Azuma Hiroshi, and Hakuta Kēnji, 63-74. W. H. Freeman and Company, 1986.

Nagāshima Hidēsuke. "Parents Struggle Financially to Assure Children's Future Success." Japan Times, weekly international ed., March 5-11, 1990, 5.

Nakayama Shigēru. "Independence and Choice: Western Impacts on Japanese Higher Education." Higher Education 18, no. 1 (1989): 33.

Nishiō Kanji. "Reshaping Education for Today's Needs." Teacher's Manual for Video Letter from Japan II. Suburban Tōkyō High School Students. The Asia Society, 1988.

Passin, Herbert. "Japan." In Education and Political Development, ed. James S. Coleman, 274. Princeton University Press, 1965.

_____. Society and Education in Japan. Teachers College Press, Columbia Univeristy, and East Asian Institute, Columbia University, 1965.

Philip, Leila. The Road Through Miyama. Random House, 1989.

"Poll Reveals New Attitudes in Japan Toward Work and the Home." News From Japan. Washington, D.C.: Japan-U.S. News and Communications Center, March 14, 1988.

Poulin, Drew. "U.S. Colleges Have Large Lessons to Learn in Japan." The Japan Times, weekly international ed., 31, no. 4, October 21-27, 1991, 14-15.

Pyle, Kenneth. The Making of Modern Japan. Washington, D.C.: Heath, 1978.

Regur, Nana Mizūshima. "Japan's Colleges, Given Go-Ahead for Reform, Face Big Decision." The Chronicle of Higher Education 37, no. 45 (June 24, 1991): A.31.

Reischauer, Edwin. The Japanese Today: Change and Continuity. Belknap Press, 1988.

Rohlen, Thomas. Japan's High Schools. University of California Press, 1983.

"Rōnin Fed Up with Cramming." Japan Times, January 19, 1988, 2.

Rosenbaum, James. "Linkages Between High Schools and Work: Lessons from Japan." Policy Studies Associates, Inc., 1989.

Schoppa, Leonard J. Education Reform in Japan: A Case of Immobilist Politics. New York: Routledge, 1991.

Seiichi Hirāi. "Japanese Education Costs Rising Rapidly." The Japan Times, weekly international ed., March 5-11, 1990, 12.

Shigēkane Yōshiko. "Learning for Joy at a Cultural Center." Japan Quarterly XIII, no 4 (Tokyo: Asahi Shinbun, October-December 1985): 412-417.

Shive, Glen. "Survey of Events 1990, East Asia." Comparative Education Review 35, no. 2 (May 1991): 387-388.

Simons, Carol. "They Get By With a Lot of Help From Their Kyōiku Mamas." Smithsonian 17, no. 12 (March 1987): 44-53.

Singleton, John. Nichū: A Japanese School; Case Studies in Education and Culture. Irvington Publishers, 1982.

Steinhoff, Patricia. "Hijackers, Bombers, and Bank Robbers: Managerial Style in the Japanese Red Army." The Journal of Asian Studies 48, no. 4 (November 1989): 724-740.

Stevenson, Harold. "Learning to Read." In Child Development and Education in Japan, eds. Harold Stevenson, Azuma Hiroshi, and Hakuta Kēnji, 217-235. W. H. Freeman and Company, 1986.

Sugīhara Seishirō. "Educational Expenditure in Japan and the United States." East West Education II (Spring 1990): 32.

Takashi Fukuchi. "The Founding of a University of Senior Citizens." In World Perspective. Case Descriptions on Educational Programs for Adults: Japan, ed. Morōoka Kazūfusa, 126-145. (Battle Creek, MI: Kellog Foundation, August 1989).

Tasker, Peter. The Japanese: A Major Exploration of Modern Japan. E. P. Dutton, 1987.

Thurow, Lester, ed. The Management Challenge: Japanese Views. MIT Press, 1985.

Tobin, Joseph, David Wu, and Dana Davidson. Preschool in Three Cultures. Yale University Press, 1989.

Troost, Kay Michael. Presentation to the National Science Foundation in Washington, D.C. on April 13, 1983.

Victoria, Daizen. "Japanese Corporate Zen." In The Other Japan, ed. Patricia Tsurumi, 131. M. E. Sharpe, Inc., 1988.

Waley, Arthur, trans. The Analects of Confucius. Random House, 1938.

Weiler, Hans, and Miyako Ēriko. "Reform and Non-Reform in Education: The Political Costs and Benefits of Reform Policies in France and Japan." San Francisco, CA: Annual Meeting of the American Educational Research Association, March 27-31, 1989.

White, Merry. "High School Students in Japan." Teacher's Manual for Video Letter from Japan II. Suburban Tōkyō High School Students. The Asia Society, 1988.

_____. The Japanese Educational Challenge: A Commitment to Children. The Free Press, 1987.

_____. The Japanese Overseas: Can They Go Home Again?. New York: The Free Press, 1988.

Whitehill, Arthur. Japanese Management: Tradition and Transition. Routledge, 1991.

Wojtan, Linda, ed. Introduction to Japan: A Workbook. Youth for Understanding, 1986.

Yamāmōto Kīyoshi. "Foreign Students in Japan." Occasional Paper No. 03/90, ED327443. National Institute for Educational Research: Hiroshima University, June 1990.

Yamāmūra Yoshiaki and Kōjima Hidēo. Child Development and Education in Japan, eds. Harold Stevenson, Āzuma Hiroshi, and Hakuta Kēnji. W. H. Freeman and Company, 1986.

Yee, Albert. "Why Asia's Schools Don't Make the Top Ranks." Japan Times, March 16, 1988, 286-287.

Yoshidā Rītsuko. "Harvest of the Standard-Score Greenhouse." Japan Quarterly 38, no. 2 (April-June 1991): 163.

Index

A

academic high schools, 83-85, 97, 98, 102, 109, 111, 114, 116, 158, 171, 199
amae, 37, 38

B

book stores, Japan, 2, 3, 123, 184, 185
burakumin, 7

C

citizens' public halls, 194-201
compulsory education, 17, 24, 27, 55-58, 85, 86, 91, 92, 94-96, 100
Confucianism, 12, 13, 19, 20, 28, 29, 61, 112, 185
cultural centers, 95, 191-194, 196, 201

E

educational finance, 56, 99, 158
educational/business linkages, 171-173, 181
elementary school course of study, 54, 58, 65, 66, 71, 72, 74
elementary school teachers/administrators, 55, 57, 58, 60-65, 69-72, 74, 79, 87, 100
English, 54, 77, 83-85, 89, 90, 93, 96, 98, 101, 104-109, 118, 120, 121, 126, 134-137, 154-156, 160-164, 179, 181, 185, 193, 196, 199, 215, 222, 223, 226
entrance examinations, 24, 54, 64, 90, 92, 95-98, 111, 113, 114, 116, 120, 121, 123-129, 131, 133, 134, 135, 146, 153, 160, 161, 163, 164, 174, 192, 204-210, 213, 214, 220, 222, 223

F

fathers, Japanese, 35, 36, 57, 59, 60, 131, 213
fief schools, 17-20
foreign students in Japan, 136, 151, 162, 210, 216
Fundamental Code of Education, 22

G

gambare, 94, 148
group, the; groupism, 4, 14, 20, 23, 25, 28, 29, 38, 39, 48, 49, 50, 58, 76, 77, 92, 93, 95, 96, 113, 166, 204, 214, 216

H

head teachers, 42, 64, 65, 87, 103, 104, 213
hierarchy, 4, 8-11, 13, 14, 20, 28, 29, 39, 76, 92, 98, 113, 124, 143, 148, 153, 189, 206
hoikuen, 41, 42, 45

I

Imperial Rescript on Education, 23, 28
infants, Japanese, 3, 33, 36-39
internationalization of education, 150, 151, 162, 206, 210, 212, 215, 216, 218, 219, 222, 225

J

Japanese language, 9, 15, 18, 27, 63, 66, 67, 69, 70, 71, 77, 87, 88, 98, 104-107, 120, 126, 135, 136, 210, 213, 214
Japanese students in foreign universities, 151, 177, 210, 218, 219, 222
job rotation, 167, 175-178, 180